Foreword by Dick Iverson

Growing
STRONG
Churches

19 Keys to a Healthy, Growing Church

BILL SCHEIDLER

CITYBIBLE
PUBLISHING
WWW.CITYBIBLEPUBLISHING.COM

PUBLISHED BY CITY BIBLE PUBLISHING
9200 NE Fremont, Portland, Oregon 97220

City Bible Publishing is a ministry of City Bible Church and is dedicated to serving the local church and its leaders through the production and distribution of quality materials. It is our prayer that these materials, proven in the context of the local church, will equip leaders in exalting the Lord and extending His kingdom.

For a free catalog of additional resources from City Bible Publishing, please call 1-800-777-6057 or visit our web site at www.citybiblepublishing.com.

PRAISE FOR *GROWING STRONG CHURCHES*

There is an old saying (that's still very true!) that runs like this: "Methods are many, principles few, methods may vary, principles never do." Bill Scheidler has captured the truth of this in his book, *Growing Strong Churches*. Church leaders in our generation are constantly looking for new methods for church growth. Methods come and go, constantly change, but principles have an eternal quality about them. Wise church leaders will follow the principles that are so clearly laid out in Bill's excellent book.

—KEVIN J CONNER
Waverley Christian Fellowship
Melbourne, Australia

Bill Scheidler has been a key leader who knows how to build healthy churches from the foundation up. He is a uniquely gifted writer that pulls principles and insights from scripture that is easily understood by the reader. This book would be a great tool for any local church leader who is committed to building healthy churches.

—FRANK DAMAZIO
Senior Pastor, City Bible Church
Portland, Oregon

The nineteen keys explained by Bill Scheidler in *Growing Strong Churches* provide excellent resource material. This extremely wise presentation reflects many years of serious thought, hands-on experience, and interaction with church leaders around the world. I admire Bill personally and highly recommend this marvelous source book and church manual for church leaders and workers.

—ERNEST GENTILE
Author of *Worship God!*, *The Glorious Disturbance*,
and *Your Sons and Daughters Shall Prophesy*
San Jose, California

TABLE OF CONTENTS

FOREWORD

You are holding in your hands a book that began in the heart of the Apostolic Leadership Team of Ministers Fellowship International. As we were discussing how we could better help pastors and leaders around the world build strong, healthy, growing churches, we realized that it would be a huge help to be able to put one book in their hands that reflects a summary of the primary keys that we have found that bring life, strength, health, and balance to the local church.

Bill Scheidler was commissioned with the task of writing such a book. *Growing Strong Churches* is the result of that effort.

Bill is one of the finest teachers and theologians that I know. He has worked with me for over 30 years as an elder in the church, a coach to church planters, a church trouble-shooter, an author, and a professor in Portland Bible College. I do not believe that there is anyone better suited to lay out these biblical principles to local church health.

I know that as you follow the principles of this book, which are rooted in the Bible, that you will experience the joy of a healthy, growing church. May God bless you as you read this book and walk in the truths that are unfolded.

—DICK IVERSON
Chairman, Ministers Fellowship International

Chapter One

INTRODUCTION TO CHURCH GROWTH

I n the last number of years there has been quite a strong emphasis among pastors and church leaders on the subject of church growth. Nearly every Christian publication is filled with advertisements promoting conferences, resources, and other materials aimed at equipping pastors for increasing the size of their local churches.

These conferences generate a lot of interest among pastors, because everyone wants to see their church grow. It doesn't matter if you are pastoring a church of fifty or one hundred thousand, you want to go to the next level and continue to grow. If you are pastoring a church of fifty, you would like to reach one hundred. If you are at one hundred fifty, you want to want to break the two hundred barrier. If you are one thousand, you want to see two thousand or five thousand involved in the church.

Every pastor desires growth and influence. This is something that God has put into the heart of a person. It is not a selfish or vain thing for a leader to desire more. In fact, growth and influence are built into God's first great commission that He gave to man. God said to the first man, "Be fruitful and multiply; fill the earth and subdue it; have dominion over...every living thing that moves on the earth" (Gen. 1:28).

God placed Adam and Eve on an earth that was in need of some work. He placed them in a garden and instructed them to dress and keep that garden and to extend the borders of the garden to encompass the rest of the earth. Adam and Eve were not to be satisfied with the comfortable nature of the garden in Eden. They were to work so that all of the earth reflected the order and majesty of that garden. This would require having offspring and bringing them into the work with him.

While humanity's charge related to the natural earth, God gives today's pastors and leaders the charge to extend His spiritual kingdom to the four corners of the earth. God has made it clear that He is not satisfied with a few spiritual offspring. He wants His house to be full (Luke 14:23). He is not willing that any should perish (2 Pet. 3:9). He wants to bring many sons to glory (Heb. 2:10).

God continually uses terminology that would indicate that He is interested in the masses. Jesus instructed His disciples to go into *all the world* (Mark 16:15). He told them to make disciples of *all nations* (Matt. 28:19). He further admonished them to be witnesses in Jerusalem, Judea, Samaria and to the *ends of the earth* (Acts 1:8).

GROWTH IS A NATURAL PART OF LIFE

Growth is a natural part of life. In fact, growth is one of the signs that something is alive. This is true in the natural realm (e.g. a garden), and it is true in the spiritual realm (e.g. a church). If a church is alive, it should be growing. If there is no growth occurring, then there is something wrong.

It is amazing how simple this is. If we had a new baby born to us, we would be concerned if that baby did not grow. In fact, when babies are first born it is not uncommon to weigh them every day to make sure that normal growth is taking place. If the baby doesn't gain weight at the proper pace, there is cause for concern. If the head doesn't grow in proper proportion to the body, there is also cause for concern.

It is rather obvious when we are talking about a natural baby that if there is no growth, something is wrong. But we are often not as concerned when we are talking about a church that is not growing. We seem to be satisfied if the church stays at a comfortable place or at the same level for long periods of time, perhaps even decades.

There are some churches that have hung between one hundred and two hundred members forever. They gain a little only to lose a little. They are up for a while until something happens and then they are down again.

At some point in time we have to realize that there are things that can contribute to growth, and there are things that can hinder growth. We obviously want to practice those things that contribute to growth (e.g. watering, fertilizing, proper pruning, etc.) and we want to avoid those things that can hinder growth.

GROWTH IS MANIFEST IN TWO MAJOR FORMS

Part of our problem is that we often see growth in a single dimension. Yet in reality, growth is manifest in two major forms. If we fail to understand this, we will not see the long-term fruit of sustained church growth. One form of growth is not to be preferred over the other. In fact, both forms of growth are mutually dependent.

The first and most common type of growth is *multiplication or quantitative* growth. This is the growth in numbers. It is the most common growth desired by pastors. At times pastors and leaders will compromise personal convictions to see this kind of growth happen. One of the things that contributes to a pastor's concern in this area is that quantitative growth is the type of growth that is used most often as a means of comparison. It is not uncommon for pastors to ask or be asked at gatherings, "What is the size of your church?"

When this question is asked, the person asking expects the answer to be given in terms of a specific number. Often the pastor feels a sense of pride or shame based on the answer he must give to this question. The temptation exists for pastors to manipulate the number to leave a better impression. I have been to churches where I expected many more people to be in attendance at a Sunday service because of what the pastor had told me on the phone. When I actually attended the services of the church, I realized that the pastor had computed his figure based on weekly attendance (that is, the total attendance at all services held during the week).

Why are we so tempted to play the "numbers game"? Why are we so hesitant at times to "tell it like it is"? Perhaps it is because we see growth as

a one-dimensional issue. We do not realize that numbers alone do not measure the strength of a church. A church can be large in number but weak
when it comes to its level of commitment and its ability to take on challenges that require sacrificial giving of time, talents, and treasures.

The second type of church growth is *edification or qualitative* growth.
This has to do with the quality of a church and indicates a building up of
the church in areas of maturity. Paul indicates that we are to excel in the edi-
fying of the church (1 Cor. 14:12). This type of growth is reflected in the
concepts of maturity, strength, depth, and discipleship. A church body can
actually be relatively small in number and yet be powerful in its ability to
accomplish vision, fulfill purpose, and influence its world.

One form of growth is not to be preferred over the other. When it comes
to natural offspring, we all want our children to grow in size, but we also
want them to grow in maturity. One without the other is abnormal and
problematic. If our child grows in size but remains immature, that child will
never be able to become independent and fulfill the purpose for its life. If
the child grows in mental maturity but does not grow in size, there is also a
limited ability to put into practice all that one knows or desires.

In the church world it is much the same. If a church only focuses on
multiplication, it is easy to make decisions based only on how to increase the
numerical size of the church. At times this thinking may even tempt pastors
and leaders to compromise what they believe to increase the number of
people in the church. In this case you could easily end up with a crowd
(numbers) but not a mighty army of God (strength). In this type of church
the attendance may be strong, but at the same time there may be a low level
of commitment among the membership and a limited ability to fulfill the
vision of the Lord for that congregation.

On the other hand, if we focus on edification or maturity alone, it is
easy to become inward in our emphasis. We can glory in the fact that while
we are small in number, we are powerful in prayer, in our family life, in our
worship, or in our Christian character. Our testimony might be "We are not
large, but we are mighty." We can see ourselves as God's select army that has
paid the price and withdrawn from the world to live a near monastic existence in honor to God.

After a while this kind of church can become withdrawn and lose touch with the real world and with the task of reaching out in evangelism. It is easy for a spiritual pride to develop among such a group where their sense of accomplishment comes from their personal perfection, doctrinal exactness, or being a faithful remnant. This type of church has depth, but no power to influence their world. They are a well-kept secret.

The Church in the New Testament did not see growth as one-dimensional. They believed in evangelism and reaching out to the masses. From the very first day, their numbers grew from 120 to 3,120 as Peter spoke to the masses assembled in Jerusalem on the day of Pentecost (Acts 2:41). Soon after that, several more thousand responded and became part of the church (Acts 4:4). The early believers took the commission of Christ seriously. They believed in multiplication growth.

However, these people were not just a crowd of undisciplined followers. It is clear that the early church also believed in the other parts of the commission of Jesus to see to it that these converts were baptized, discipled, and taught to observe all that Christ had commanded. These converts that were added to the Lord were also added to the church and continued steadfastly in the apostles' doctrine, fellowship, the breaking of bread, and prayers (Acts 2:42).

The early church leaders ministered to the crowds that came in such a way that these people who followed them became true examples of Christian love who were willing to expend their lives and all of their resources for the sake of the Kingdom of God (Acts 2:44-47; 4:32-37; 11:26). The early church leaders believed in edification or qualitative growth.

This is summed up for us in Acts 9:31 where Luke states, "Then the churches throughout all Judea, Galilee, and Samaria had peace and were *edified*. And walking in the fear of the Lord and in the comfort of the Holy Spirit, they were *multiplied*" (emphasis mine).

GROWTH IS NOT A SIMPLE MATTER

In the church, as in natural life, growth is not a simple 1-2-3 process. Some seminars on growth tend to oversimplify the situation when it comes to church growth. This same thing happens so often when people are trying to tell us how to be healthy and stay healthy. Everyone has his or her own theory or "pet" cure for "what ails you." Everyone is looking for that new miracle supplement or wonder drug that will fix it all.

I am sure we have all read articles in magazines or seen TV commercials that promote the latest cure-all. Whether it is as simple as megadoses of vitamin C or something more complex like coffee enemas, there is a desire for a quick remedy that will work in every situation.

Unfortunately, when it comes to our natural health, there are no easy formulas and no automatic progressions. "Eat right, get plenty of rest, and drink lots of water" works most of the time, but sometimes you do all of these things, and there is still a problem. Similarly, there are no simple answers to the church growth issue. Here are six reasons why that is so:

1. Church growth is not a simple matter because all individuals and churches are different.

No two people or churches are exactly alike. This is one of the great mysteries of creation—the infinite variety in nature. Billions of people have lived on the earth, and no two are exactly alike. Hundreds of thousands of churches exist in the world today, and no two of them are exactly alike. There is a great beauty in this, and there is also a great challenge with this.

There are many things that make us different, and that creates for us a unique challenge when it comes to balanced growth. Each church faces a unique challenge that is created by the fact that each has a different make up, a different heritage or background, a different cultural context, and a different purpose and vision. In addition, churches are in different stages of development and have experienced different dealings of God. Just as with children, churches do not always grow at the same rate.

In spite of the differences, there are things that will always be the same. There are principles from God's Word that will work in every generation, every culture, every nation, and in the life of every person. As we seek to build the church, we must focus on the timeless and the eternal and seek to adapt the universal principle to the individual situation.

2. Church growth is not a simple matter because all ministers do not have the same capabilities.

It is clear from Exodus 18:25 that different leaders have differing capacities. Jethro, Moses' father-in-law, spoke of rulers over thousands, hundreds, fifties, and tens. God has given everyone varying levels of grace, faith, and gifting (Rom. 12:1-8). Jesus Himself referred to those that were given one, two, and five talents to invest in the work of the Kingdom (Matt. 25:15).

I believe that God gives varying degrees of talent to meet varying situations in various communities. Every community regardless of how large it is needs a godly expression of the church. But in saying this, it is important to emphasize that it doesn't matter whether we are one-, two- or five-talent ministries, God expects each one to increase. The one-talent ministry is expected to increase in the same proportion that the five-talent ministry increased.

This is where our personal responsibility comes into play. God gives us the gifts that we need to fulfill His will for our lives, but we must sharpen them and work with them in such a way as to maximize their effectiveness.

God increases us as our capacities increase. If we are not doing well with a hundred, He may not give us five hundred. If we are not doing well with five hundred, He may not give us a thousand. God wants all of us to increase in capacity. God won't put more into our hands until we do a good job with what we have.

3. Church growth is not a simple matter because all geographical areas are not the same.

Even though I have never talked to a pastor who didn't believe he was in a "hard place," it can be seen from Scripture that not all places are the same. Paul and the apostles had different results in different places. Jesus told those He sent out two by two that they would encounter different levels of response as they went from village to village.

Some places are more "prepared" such as Samaria when Philip went there to preach the Gospel (Acts 8). Some places are very hard such as Lystra where the people threw stones at Paul as he preached the message (Acts 14:19). Lystra and Athens were tough areas. Corinth responded well numerically, but maturity was a problem. Antioch and Samaria responded very quickly.

There is no question that some places are very hard. Usually, the smaller the community, the more difficult it is to start a church. Usually, the more isolated a community, the more difficult it is to start a church. Nevertheless, God wants churches in all of these communities.

4. Church growth is not a simple matter because all growth depends upon the moving of God's Spirit.

No pastor can save anyone. No leader can heal anyone. No church can bring a city to Christ without the moving of the Holy Spirit. The truth is that God must move if we are going to increase. We may sow and water, but it is God who gives the increase (1 Cor. 3:6).

Some places seem to be under a special cloud of God's presence at various times and seasons. When Philip went to Samaria, he was entering a field that was ripe, and nearly the whole city turned to Christ. Antioch was under a similar cloud, so that in two short years Barnabas and Paul were able to establish a strong pattern work there.

God is still sovereign and still rules in the affairs of men (Ps. 107:31-38). He is the one who opens and closes doors. He is the Lord of the harvest. It is He with whom we are co-laboring.

We see this at various seasons around the world. One recent example has to do with what is happening in South Korea. Dr. Yonggi Cho pastors the largest church in the world in Seoul. Yet Seoul has several churches that are over fifty thousand in size. Certainly Dr. Cho is to be admired, but it must also be acknowledged that God is doing something unique and extraordinary in that nation. Following his methods alone will not produce identical results.

5. Church growth is not a simple matter because there are many essential ingredients to the normal growth process.

Growth is a complicated process because there are many ingredients that contribute to growth in humans and in the church. In the human diet we need a variety of things. You can take any one of those needful things, overemphasize it to the exclusion of other things, and you will have a problem. Protein is good for you, and it is essential if you are going to develop strong muscle tissue. But too much can be harmful.

I knew a man who at the age of forty was experiencing acute liver disease. He was in pain constantly, and the doctors were having a difficult time discovering what was causing his problems. They treated him unsuccessfully for several years and were even discussing a transplant.

Finally on one of his visits to the doctor he was asked some questions that he should have been asked much earlier. The doctors suddenly realized that this man had been taking heavy doses of a protein supplement. As the doctors probed more fully, they discovered that this man had been drinking protein powder for over twenty years. He started in school when he was playing football and doing weight training. But when football and weight training ended, he just kept drinking the powder, thinking that if some is good, more must be better. Little did he know that it was the large, repeated overdose of protein that was killing him. When he stopped taking the extra protein, he began to improve.

Nutrients must be balanced to produce the proper effect. You need many different kinds of vitamins, minerals, and nutrients to sustain life. The same is true in the church. We don't just need one thing; we need many things in balance to be a healthy expression of the church. Sometimes church growth is oversimplified in church-growth conferences. At times there is a focus on one key that has worked for a given church or pastor. The impression given is that if you just take this key, you will get the same results. Pastor after pastor has come home from conferences ready to institute the new "miracle cure" to a dying body only to find another thing that just doesn't work. A single message may bring crowds for a season, but it will probably not bring a balanced maturity to the believers. Eventually the sickness will show up again, and another remedy will have to be sought.

6. Church growth is not a simple matter because some people simply work harder than others.

This is a principle that is often overlooked at pastors' conferences. That is, the harder you work, the more likely you are to prosper. Someone once asked a famous golfer, "Golf involves quite a bit of luck, doesn't it?" To which the golfer replied, "Yes, and the more I practice, the luckier I get!"

The Bible puts it this way, "He who gathers by labor will increase" (Prov. 13:11) or "The soul of the diligent shall be made rich" (Prov. 13:4). The fact is, there is no substitute for hard work. Some churches grow more quickly because the leaders in those churches work harder than leaders who pastor works that don't grow so quickly. Sad to say, there are pastors and church leaders who do not work hard. In a sense they are robbing God by taking money from the tithes but not working hard in return.

GROWTH IS COMPLEX, NOT SIMPLE

As we study the Scriptures, it is important that we discover all of the factors that have a bearing on this thing called church growth. We don't want a church that merely has a lot of people. We want a church that grows in number but also grows in depth and maturity so that it can truly demonstrate the principles of the Kingdom of God and be used by God to touch the nations of the world.

We cannot afford to isolate one verse or set of verses that has a pleasant ring to it. All Scripture is God-breathed, and all Scripture is profitable for the equipping of the Church for growth. There is not one key to growth, but many keys. To neglect any one of them is to weaken the church and make it less likely for the church to become the "glorious church" against which the gates of hell will not prevail.

KEYS TO SUSTAINED CHURCH GROWTH

As pastors and church leaders seek to build the church, they cannot be nearsighted but need to see themselves as those that lay the foundations for many generations to come. Too often it is easy for us to think of decisions in terms that will affect our lives personally. This is one of the problems with a democratic form of government. The people tend to vote according to what is best for them in the immediate sense. Often there is no regard for the effect that these immediate decisions will have on the long-term and what will be the consequences of those decisions for subsequent generations.

As we build the church, we have to be thinking of building a church that stands from generation to generation. When Jesus introduced the concept of the church, He did not see it as a temporary institution that would be "here today and gone tomorrow." The church was designed with eternity in mind.

It is so sad to see a cyclical pattern repeated in much of the church over the centuries. If you look back over the last one hundred years and study the subject of revival, you will see great examples of the moving of God in a generation or in a specific church. God was doing exciting things; people were getting saved, delivered, and healed.

In those revival times when large numbers of people were responding to the Gospel and the moving of the Holy Spirit, large church buildings were constructed to take care of the crowds. In many cases those buildings still exist, but most of the congregatons are no longer growing, and many church buildings are nearly empty. They have become monuments of a past visitation of God. They have become museums where we can conduct tours and talk about what God did in the past.

It is sad, but this cycle is repeated over and over again. It is rare in our day to find a church that is over fifty years old and is still growing, where people are still coming to Christ, and where there is a high level of excitement among the church membership.

For this reason some books will suggest that the best thing to do is to shut that church down and start over. They have suggested this because statistics show that more evangelism and growth takes place in new church plants. In new plants there is a greater excitement and sense of calling than in older, more established works.

This is a sad commentary on the church. There has got to be a better way. I don't think this is what Jesus had in mind when He said, "I will build My church and the gates of Hades shall not prevail against it" (Matt.16:18).

The church that Christ is building is built for success. It is build to endure. It is build to fulfill God's desired purpose right up to the return of the Lord.

Theologically, most of us would agree with this statement. Most of us would, however, suggest that this kind of overcoming really pertains to the universal church or the greater Body of Christ and not to an individual congregation or local church. My contention is that it has to do with both. The local church must be a microcosm of the universal church. The eternal principles that God has given to us must work on the local level where we live. Local churches that are indeed built by Christ have within them the power to sustain positive growth and movement from generation to generation.

So why do we not see this happening today? Why is it that the life span of most churches is so short? Why do we lack the ability to sustain our vision from generation to generation?

It is my contention that we are not able to sustain long-term growth because we are not building for the long term. Our tendency is to build for the immediate.

It is much like the two builders that Jesus used to illustrate two ways of building. One built on the rock; one built on the sand. These builders in Jesus' story were not illustrating the difference between Christians and non-Christians, because both of these builders were in a place of hearing the Word of God. These builders were distinguished by their responses to the Word. The wise builder heard the Word of God and put it into practice. The foolish builder heard the Word of God but did not practice it.

I was in another country sharing in a pastors' conference. I was teaching much of the material that is in this book. I asked the host pastor if what I had been teaching was new material for them. His reply to me was, "We have heard these things before, but we are not practicing them!"

Sad to say, the Word does us no good unless we are willing to put it into practice. We are often like the foolish builder. It is not that we do not know the Word; it's that putting it into practice requires hard work, personal sacrifice, patience, and endurance.

The foolish man cut corners in the building of his house. It may have seemed from casual observation that this man had "beaten the system." His house went up quickly, it didn't cost as much, and he was able to live in it sooner. The wise man took more time, expended much energy in digging out debris, paid the price for a good foundation, and endured comparisons to the foolish builder who lived in his house first.

There is no indication how long these houses stood side by side. It may have been for a rather long time. The foolish man may have been tempted to mock the wise man for his conservative nature, feeling that he was way ahead of the game. The wise man may have been tempted to wonder whether all of his caution, his tedious following of the blueprints, and his extra cost had been worth it.

However, all wondering ceased that fateful day when the rains, winds, and floods came and beat against their houses. No matter how long they had stood side by side up to that point, when the pressure mounted as they had never experience it before, the wise man's house stood, but the foolish man's house fell. It fell quickly, just as it had gone up quickly. It fell greatly. It undoubtedly became a reproach and a negative testimony to many.

If we are going to build churches that last, there can be no short cuts. There can be no divergence from the divine pattern. No matter how difficult it is, no matter how much it costs, we must build according to the principles of the Word of God.

As we build, we must visualize an oak tree as opposed to a mushroom. A mushroom can come up overnight and draw some immediate attention to itself, but it can vanish just as quickly in a puff of smoke. An oak tree grows more slowly but it grows with strength. Eventually its branches stretch out, and it provides shade and covering to much territory. Oak trees can be hundreds of years old and yet still producing many seeds and bringing forth many new offspring.

In this book we want to talk about oak-tree churches. What are the keys to building this type of church? We understand that there may be a cost. We understand that we may have to exercise patience as we give the principles a chance to bring forth. We understand that many of these things will cross our culture. We understand that there will be pressure by people and other church leaders to compromise these keys for the sake of the immediate. But we have to believe that time and long-term fruit will testify to the higher wisdom.

What are the ingredients of such an oak-tree church? How can we build such a sure house? As I indicated before, there is not one key, but many keys. There is not one ingredient, but many ingredients necessary for long-term success. It's like baking a cake. All of the ingredients in the recipe are important if the cake is going to turn out like the author of the recipe intended. To leave one ingredient out is to change the entire outcome. To substitute a similar ingredient for the specified ingredient will have an adverse effect as well.

Let me summarize the keys to church growth that we will be amplifying in the subsequent chapters. These keys will ensure that the church will grow both in number and in substance, in both quantity (multiplication) and quality (edification).

KEY #1: *If a church is to grow and prosper from generation to generation, that church must determine to build in harmony with God's eternal purpose.*

God has a purpose that has been behind every one of His actions throughout history. He only has one plan, and every man, woman, and child has been created to be an active part of that plan. The church is to be God's instrument or vehicle through which that purpose is brought forth.

All of our activity as believers and as churches must be measured against God's eternal purpose. Whether or not what we are doing has any kind of eternal significance is directly related to whether or not what we are doing is in harmony with what God is doing.

However, if we do not understand God's eternal purpose, how can we know if what we are doing makes any sense? The eternal purpose of God represents to us "the will of God." It is that purpose and will of God that ultimately endures forever. If we want our work to endure, if we want it to be composed of gold, silver, and precious stones instead of wood, hay, and stubble, then our work must line up with God's work and God's purpose. In chapter 3 we discuss the eternal purpose of God.

KEY #2: *If a church is to grow and prosper from generation to generation, that church must determine to choose the Word of God over tradition.*

Many people come into the local church with a good deal of personal history. This history can include good or bad experiences with other pastors and churches. This history can include a certain religious tradition, background, or doctrinal belief system. This history can even include cultural practices or a cultural mind-set.

Unfortunately, not all of our traditions are helpful when building the local church. Not all of our traditions are based on the Word of God or are consistent with the principles of the Word of God.

The Bible speaks of two types of traditions. There are good traditions that reinforce and actually help us live the principles of the Word. There are also bad traditions that render the Word of God ineffective. If we are to become all that God wants us to become, we cannot worship the past. We have to be willing to examine our traditions and change them if they are hindering our progress.

This willingness to change applies to culture as well. While we are all interested in preserving cultural expressions, not all cultural expressions are based on divine principles. In some cases our very culture needs to be challenged by the principles of the Word of God. We cannot hang on to things just because that is the way we have always done them. We must allow our minds and our thinking processes to be renewed and ultimately conformed to the mind of Christ and His thinking process. In chapter 4 we will discuss the issue of tradition and how it relates to church-growth patterns.

KEY #3: *If a church is to grow and prosper from generation to generation, that church must determine to be responsive to present truth.*

God's dealings with man have been progressive throughout history. The journey of every person and every church is represented as a path. We are all on spiritual journeys that are being led and directed by God. If we are going to progress to completion, we must maintain responsive hearts to the personal and corporate dealings of God.

No one has attained to perfection. No person or movement has all of the answers. Luther was led by God in his generation, but he did not understand all truth. Calvin, Wesley, Knox, Simmons, Simpson, McPherson are all great names in the history of the church, but all of them only understood in part. No one has it all. Everyone has room to grow.

Things that are alive change. One of the problems with many churches and church movements is that most of them began in an attitude of growth and change, but they didn't maintain an openness to further understanding and insight. God is moving progressively through history. If we are going to stay current with God, we must continually move forward.

I am not talking about change for the sake of change. I am talking about God-directed, biblically-based change that is consistent with the nature and purposes of God. In chapter 5 we will discuss God's dealings with the church throughout history and some of the things that He seems to be saying today. We will talk about God's restoring the church to its former glory and leading the church to its ultimate destiny.

KEY #4: *If a church is to grow and prosper from generation to generation, that church must determine to build according to the divine pattern for the church.*

God has a plan and a pattern for His church. Our success is dependent upon our ability to follow the pattern, not in our creativity to develop our own pattern. While this sounds basic, it is not the common understanding of many. In fact, there are those who would argue that there is no specific pattern for the local church in the New Testament.

There are those who suggest that God has given us great flexibility to develop a plan or methodology and that all that really matters is our heart. God does want our hearts to be in right relationship, and He does want us to be sincere in our devotion to Him. But is that all God is after? The Bible indicates that God is searching for those who will worship Him in spirit and in truth. It is not to be an either/or proposition. We are not to choose between having a spiritual relationship with little emphasis on truth or a truth encounter with little emphasis on relationship. God is interested in both. In chapter 6 we will be discussing the sources from which we can get a pattern and how important it is to seek the Lord according to His pattern.

KEY #5: *If a church is to grow and prosper from generation to generation, that church must determine to build to please God, not man.*

Much of what we hear today in church-growth materials has to do with presenting the church in a way to which people can easily respond. I think it is important to examine our forms, methods, and procedures so that we are not being offensive to mankind over the wrong issues.

However, do we give as much consideration to how God feels about our service? Is it possible to be very pleasing to man but at the same time be offensive to God? How much does God care about how we do things in the church? How much is He concerned about what is preached in His name? Sometimes we can actually be guilty of being more merciful than God Himself is.

The Bible says that the fear of the Lord is the beginning of wisdom. If we are going to represent God to the world, we must not be afraid to truly represent God. We actually must be more concerned about being God pleasers than people pleasers. In chapter 7 we will talk about the importance of not being ashamed of the Gospel, not being ashamed of presenting Christ for who He is, and not being ashamed of biblical guidelines that are clearly taught in the Word of God.

KEY #6: *If the church is to grow and prosper from generation to generation, that church must place a high level of emphasis on the local church as the instrument that God uses to extend His Kingdom on the earth.*

In the New Testament every believer was vitally connected to a specific local church. It is in the local church that people are saved, discipled, and become committed, functioning members. It is through the local church that God's purposes are going to be made a reality in any given community.

Many today focus on the universal church and its worldwide expression. That is an important truth that we all must acknowledge. But how does that concept translate into the believer's daily life? How does the believer walk out the injunctions of Jesus to make disciples of all nations? Where does the believer find discipleship, accountability, equipping, ministry expression, and mission fulfillment? It is in the context of the local church.

Many people have had negative experiences on the local-church level and have decided not to be committed members of any local church, choosing rather to focus on the Kingdom of God and the universal expression of the Body of Christ. Jesus indicated that in the local church we would have to deal with offenses (Matt. 18:15-20). But we must deal with them rather than walk away from them, because God is going to use the local church as His instrument to fulfill His intended purpose. He has no other plan. Rather than write the local church off, we should put our hearts into it to make it the best that it can be. In chapter 8 we will be focusing on the local church and highlighting its place in God's plan of the ages.

KEY #7: *If a church is to grow and prosper from generation to generation, that church must determine to build up the saints on all levels.*

All leaders give lip service to the concepts of the Body of Christ. We all believe that leaders are given to the church by Christ to equip the saints for works of service. We all believe that if the church is going to be successful, every member of the body will have to be discipled, taught, equipped, and released into their respective functions.

But are we actually structured in a way that does this? What do we do with our new converts? How much of an investment are we making in the lives of our children and the youth of the church? Are saints really moving on into greater levels of maturity and getting a personal vision for their lives? What kind of specific training is taking place in the church?

If the work of the church is to extend beyond one generation, each local church must place a high priority on putting a strong vision into all of the generations present in the church today. In chapter 9 we will be looking at what the church is doing with the spiritual babes, the children, the young saints, and the old saints in the house.

KEY #8: *If a church is to grow and prosper from generation to generation, that church must determine to strengthen all of the families of the church.*

The church will be no stronger than the individual families of the church. Today there is an all-out attack on the family. People are coming into the church broken, abused, abandoned, and fragmented. Parents are having trouble with their children. Children are having trouble with their parents. Relationships between husbands and wives reflect an all-time low.

There is no point in working on restoring the church if we are not working just as hard to restore the families represented in the church. The family is still the basic unit of society, and the church must bring solutions to the individual families and indeed to society itself.

Revival and spiritual encounters are not the only answer for the family. Practical tools must be put into the hands of every man, woman, and child if we are going to see a change in the church. Since most people have not had a positive role model, and the models promoted through the entertainment industry are less than biblical in their expression, the church must stand up and equip parents, marriage partners, and young people who still have their future before them. In chapter 10 we will discuss how pastors and church leaders can strengthen the families in their churches.

KEY #9: *If a church is to grow and prosper from generation to generation, that church must determine to develop and release the gifts and ministries of its membership.*

The church must be a place where people can get a vision for their lives and discover the purpose for which they were created. Not only must they receive this vision, but they must also be developed, mentored, and given opportunities for the release of these gifts and ministries.

Part of this process involves making people aware of God's purpose in their lives. Another part is to help define spiritual gifts and biblical ministries so that people can measure themselves accordingly.

The church of today needs the supernatural element embodied in the gifts of the Spirit. The church needs the word of wisdom, the word of knowledge, healing, miracles, prophecy, and the other gifts if it is going to do the works of Christ on the earth. The church needs all of the ministries of Christ functioning in our day if the church is going to complete the ministry of Christ. The church needs apostles, prophets, evangelists, pastors, teachers, showerers of mercy, healers, intercessors, encouragers, and givers. In chapter 11 we will look at the church's role in developing its constituency into full-time ministers of Christ.

KEY #10: *If a church is to grow and prosper from generation to generation, that church must determine to structure itself with a biblical expression of team ministry.*

The New Testament does give us a structure for government in the church. The church is not a one-man operation or dictatorship. It is not a democracy where every member gets an equal vote. It is not to be ruled by committees composed of those willing to serve.

God has a form of government outlined in the New Testament that could best be described as team ministry. The church is not to be led by one person but by a team of called individuals who meet the biblical qualification for leadership. This team is led by a set-man or chief elder who gives vision and momentum to the group.

Church structure is certainly not to be the focus of the church, but if the church is going to have the ability to be led by the Head of the Church, the Lord Jesus Christ, its government must be of such a nature that the will of the Lord may indeed be done. In chapter 12 we will talk about biblical leadership and how important it is to the local church's overall success.

KEY #11: *If a church is to grow and prosper from generation to generation, that church must determine to exercise spiritual discipline relative to its membership.*

Church discipline is almost unheard of in today's church world. Confronting another church member about his or her sinful lifestyle is not only neglected, the very thought of it is despised by most church members.

It is interesting that the only time Jesus talked directly about the local church was in the context of discipline (Matt. 18:15-20). He seemed to indicate that there would be problems in the church, and these problems would not go away by themselves. He actually gave a rather specific procedure in which such confrontation was to take place.

What would happen in the natural family without any discipline? There would be chaos. Selfishness would be the rule of the day. People would function on the basis of feelings rather than principle. There would be a tendency to only do what had to be done to get by. Sounds a little like some churches!

The church is to be more than a loosely-knit group of followers. It is to be a disciplined army on the march against the powers of darkness. Followers are to become disciples. Disciples are to become warriors. Warriors are to become overcomers. In chapter 13 we will look at the need to come up to a stronger level in our expression of the character of Christ to prepare us to be channels of His love and His power.

> **KEY #12:** *If a church is to grow and prosper from generation to generation, that church must determine to promote the biblical concepts of faith and sacrificial giving.*

Someone has said, "vision is spelled m-o-n-e-y." There is a truth to that statement. If the church is going to be all that it is to be, God has got to be able to deal with the "love of money" issue in the hearts of His people. It is going to take a lot of money to fulfill the Great Commission. It takes money to reach out to your own community, not to mention sending people to the nations of the world.

The early church saw money as a tool. It was one of the resources that God had placed in their hands to fulfill their spiritual charge. They were willing to lay these resources at His feet much like the woman with the alabaster box.

In actual fact, tithing is to be only the beginning of our giving. It is God's cure for covetousness and is designed to release us into greater adventures in giving. God wants to bless the people of God with much more than they need, but not for the purpose of building bigger barns or houses or driving more expensive cars.

If the church is going to influence society it must be touched by a spirit of generosity and a spirit of contentment. The wealthiest person in the world today is not the head of some computer company. The wealthiest "person" in the world today is the Body of Christ! In chapter 14 we'll discuss God's financial plan for the church.

KEY #13: *If a church is to grow and prosper from generation to generation, that church must determine to focus on those things that promote the manifest presence of God in its gatherings.*

God's presence is still the key to the church's success. The thing that made Israel distinct among the other nations was the pillar of cloud and the pillar of fire. Israel was a nation that was covered by the manifest presence of God. Just so, the church is to be the place where God's presence is manifest. Jesus indicated His desire to be in the midst of the church (Matt. 18:20).

If the church does not have a supernatural touch upon it created by an awareness of God's presence, it is no different than any other social organization. The church is not like another social organization. It is the Temple of the Living God!

But are there things that we can do that release a sense of God's presence among us in a greater way? Are there things that we can do that will elicit a response from the unlearned or the visitor that says, "God is truly among you" (1 Cor. 14:25)?

God is no respecter of persons. However, He is a respecter of principles. There are principles that God respects or honors. When we cooperate with those principles, we can expect the desired result. When we violate those principles, we can just as surely expect to be disappointed. In chapter 15 we will discuss some key principles that put God in the highest place in our corporate gatherings.

KEY #14: *If a church is to grow and prosper from generation to generation, that church must determine to develop house-to-house ministries.*

There are not many specific methods outlined in the New Testament concerning the program of the church. One exception to this is the apparent universal existence of house-to-house ministry in the New Testament church.

It appears that this house-to-house ministry went well beyond individual fellowship among believers. It seems to have included a certain amount of structure to minister to the needs in the churches and to reach out in evangelism.

There is no question that the fastest growing churches in the world today have some form of cell ministry. Is this just another fad? Or have they tapped into a divine principle or a pattern that should be considered by every church seeking to follow the biblical model? In chapter 16 we will discuss this current phenomenon and how it has a bearing on what God wants to do on the earth today.

KEY #15: *If a church is to grow and prosper from generation to generation, that church must determine to develop a strong corporate prayer life.*

When the Bible speaks of the house of the Lord, it ascribes a name to His house, "a house of prayer for all nations." The church is to be first and foremost a house of prayer. The early church lived and functioned in the atmosphere of prayer, not just personal prayer, but corporate prayer as well.

While personal prayer is vital to the personal life and vitality of the individual believer, corporate prayer is vital to the life and vitality of the congregation. There is no question that the devil does everything that he can to keep believers off of their knees.

Paul makes it clear that prayer is a critical, offensive weapon against the forces of wickedness. Jesus made it clear from His teaching and personal example that no one is strong enough to stand on his own—we all need the strength, direction, and power that come from a life of prayer.

In chapter 17 we will discuss the importance of prayer in the life and ministry of the church. The more committed we are to the principle of prayer, the more effective we will be as channels of God's Spirit to the world.

KEY #16: *If a church is to grow and prosper from generation to generation, that church must determine to make unity a priority.*

Unity is one of the keys to having influence. One of the things that has hindered evangelism and church growth is the lack of harmony in the local church. When people come to a church, they can tell whether or not there is peace in the camp. People are looking for a safe haven, a place of rest. They do not want to be joined to another tense situation. They do not want to be in a place where gossip, personal politics, and relational conflicts exist. The church is to be different. It is to be a place where we treat one another like brothers and sisters, where we live for one another, resolve our differences, and march toward a common goal.

Unity is important in the local congregation, but it is equally important in the greater Body of Christ if we are going to see the nations touched. One of the greatest hindrances to the spread of Christianity is the division within Christianity. One group is at odds with another group, Christians tearing down other Christians. It is rare in a community for pastors to be united in purpose to reach their city together. Pastors are too often busy competing with other pastors for the same few people while the harvest is lost.

God wants to change our concepts in these days. He wants to bring pastors and leaders together for a common harvest. He is giving key leaders a vision of the Body of Christ and the Kingdom of God that will help to unite them and break down long-existing barriers. The prayer of Jesus will be fulfilled prior to the return of the Lord for His completed bride. In chapter 18 we will be looking at unity, diversity, and maintaining a kingdom perspective.

> KEY #17: *If a church is to grow and prosper from generation to generation, that church must understand the principle of servanthood and practice it inside and outside of the church.*

Christ personally demonstrated what it was to be great in the Kingdom of God. He modeled a kind of ministry and lifestyle that was so radical by the world's standards and so powerful by God's standard that it changed the world. Jesus personally demonstrated the power of the Kingdom when He humbled Himself and became a human being and was willing to become the sacrifice for sin. He demonstrated it to His followers at the Last Supper when He took up the towel and washed the feet of His disciples.

The church of Jesus Christ must have this same spirit upon it. If the church is going to touch the world, it will touch it with the love and spirit of service that Christ had. Love is an irresistible force. Love will gain the church favor with God and man. In chapter 19 we will look at this spirit of servanthood and how it grows the church spiritually and numerically.

> **KEY #18:** *If a church is to grow and prosper from generation to generation, that church must determine to take Christ's commissions seriously.*

Christ gave a commission to His disciples during the forty days that He spent with them prior to His ascension into heaven. They were not to begin implementing that commission until the Holy Spirit came upon them, which happened on the Day of Pentecost. That commission was not just for those early disciples. That commission belongs to us as well.

Christ's commission was a multifaceted commission. It involved being witnesses and preaching the Gospel in all the world. It involved making disciples of all nations and nationalities. It involved pastoring the harvested and teaching them to live a separated life. It involved releasing people into the nations.

If the church of today is going to fulfill this commission, we must reach out to the lost. We cannot be satisfied with church growth that is dependent upon Christian people moving from one congregation to another. Many churches today revel in the fact that they have become large, and yet statistics show that in the United States the total number of Christians has not changed significantly.

If the church of today is going to fulfill this commission, we are going to have to get serious about church planting and world missions. We are going to have to preach the vision, raise the money, equip our people, and send the laborers into the harvest. The harvest is still ripe. The laborers are still few. In chapter 20 we will discuss the call upon the church to be God's instrument to extend the Kingdom of God.

KEY #19: *If a church is to grow and prosper from generation to generation, that church must determine to maintain a first-love experience among its membership.*

Jesus came to the church of Ephesus in the book of Revelation with words of commendation and words of challenge. He commended them for their love for the Word and their pure doctrine that had exposed heresy and false apostolic ministries. He commended them for their tireless activity when it came to a zeal for good works. But He also challenged them concerning their personal relationship to Him.

It is so easy to become church experts and doctrinal bookworms that we can miss the Lord of the Church or the Man of the Book. We can lose sight of what it is all about. God created man for relationship. He wants us more than anything else.

As we seek to honor Him in building a church that is technically correct in every way, we must remember not to lose Him in the busyness of it all. Mary and Joseph lost track of Jesus in the midst of religious activity. When they discovered their loss, they had to go back and find out where they left Him.

Jesus must stay central in all that we do. It is still all about Him. In chapter 21 we will challenge pastors and leaders to keep Christ and the Cross central in all of the preaching, activity, and administration of the affairs of the church.

Chapter Three

GOD'S ETERNAL PURPOSE

KEY #1—*If a church is to grow and prosper from generation to generation, that church must determine to build in harmony with God's eternal purpose.*

God has a purpose that has been behind every action throughout history. All of the work of the Father in creation plus all of the work of the Son in redemption plus all of the work of the Holy Spirit in sanctification has been aimed at the fulfillment of this purpose. Every single thought and action taken by God in His dealings with mankind, His dealings with nations, His dealings with individuals, and His dealings with churches has been totally consistent with that plan and purpose.

Because of this, all of our activity as believers and as churches must be measured against God's eternal purpose as well. Whether or not what we are doing has any kind of eternal significance is directly related to whether or not what we are doing is in harmony with what God is doing.

However, if we do not understand God's eternal purpose, how can we know if what we are doing makes any sense? The eternal purpose of God represents to us "the will of God." It is that purpose and will that ultimately endures forever. If we want our work to endure, if we want it to be composed of gold, silver, and precious stones instead of wood, hay, and stubble, then our work must line up with God's work and God's purpose.

GOD HAS ONLY ONE PURPOSE

One of the most important things for us to see is that God has but *one eternal purpose* that He is working toward. God is not double-minded, uncertain, or unstable. On the contrary, God is very methodical, determined, and definite in everything that He does.

God is not like we are when it comes to projects and purposes. God is not one to begin several projects and leave them all incomplete. God has always completed everything that He has attempted. We often fail to complete our purposes because we are caught by surprise. We often fail to estimate the time or the cost of the project. We are very fickle and often lose interest in a project before we ever complete it.

God is not like that. God is not double-minded. He has but one will, one plan, one law, and one goal (Mal. 3:6). If God were limited by the human faculties of reason and sense perception, He would be more like us in terms of accomplishment. But since God has infinite faculties (i.e., omniscience, omnipotence, omnipresence, immutability, omnisapience), He is able like no one else to declare the end from the beginning and see His plan come to fruition.

Unforeseen snags cannot surprise God. He cannot over or underestimate what is required to complete a project. God does not change His dealings with man based on the emotion of the moment, but He continually works all things after the counsel of His own will.

Sometimes, sad to say, we picture God much like the gods of the Greek pantheon, playing a little heavenly chess game with people's lives, changing His approaches to fit His moods and tampering with lives just for the sport of it. We need to clear our thinking. Our God is not motivated by changing whims. He is not motivated by a sense of adventure. God is motivated by a pure heart of love, and that heart of love has devised an eternal plan that will glorify Him and bless others for eternity.

A HEAVENLY PERSPECTIVE

One thing that has hindered us from knowing God's eternal purpose is our limited perspective and frame of reference. We tend to look at God's plan in terms of what we have seen happen in our lifetime rather than what has happened for all time. We tend to look at God's plan by looking at one specific work of God, rather than looking at the workings of God from the beginning to the end.

A good way to visualize our problem is by comparing the total plan of God to a parade. There are many elements that go into a parade, but none is complete without the other. If we were observing a parade through a knothole in a fence, because of our limited perspective, we might totally misunderstand the nature of a parade.

At one moment when we looked, we might see a clown. From this we might be tempted to draw a conclusion that a parade is like *a circus.* If we looked for another moment in time and saw a horse with a rider, we might be tempted to conclude that a parade is like *a rodeo.*

But a parade is not a circus or a rodeo. The only way you will be able to really understand a parade is to gain a better perspective. You will have to get above the fence and see the end from the beginning. In doing so, you will see where the clowns fit in, where the horses fit in, and how all the elements fit together.

Too often when seeking to understand the purposes of God, we have looked at God's dealings with the Jewish nation and made that the whole. Or we have looked at God's dealings with the church and have made that the whole. Or we have looked at God's desire to destroy the works of darkness and have made that the whole. Or we have looked at God's desire to make us worshipers and have made that the whole. Or we have looked at God's desire for good pleasure and have made that the whole.

But the thing God wants us to do is to come up and sit with Him in heavenly places where we can get a true perspective of God's eternal purpose. When we do this, we will see that each aspect or portion of truth has a place and fits beautifully into the whole. There is a place for the Jewish nation; there is a place for the church; there is a place for character development and worship. They are all important. There is no contradiction. They all relate to the whole.

Everything God has done has been essential for the ultimate realization of His divine purpose. When finally we see that one purpose, all of God's dealings with humanity comes into proper perspective, and we can clearly see how we as individuals fit into that plan of God that He has had from before the foundation of the world.

DETERMINED BY GOD

As we seek to discover the eternal purpose of God, the first thing we need to realize is that the eternal purpose of God was determined by God Himself in the council of the Godhead. John tells us that "There are three that bear witness in heaven, the Father, the Word, and the Holy Spirit, and these three are one" (1 John 5:7).

Because of this fact, God Himself is able to establish His Word and confirm His Word "by the mouth of two or three witnesses" (2 Cor. 13:1). This is exactly what God did in eternity past. God established the purpose in Himself according to His good pleasure (Eph. 1:9). He did not consult man or angels because they were not yet created, and they were all to be a part of that plan.

ESTABLISHED BEFORE TIME BEGAN

The eternal purpose of God was settled by God, before the foundation of the world (Eph. 1:4). Our place in that overall scheme was also determined before the world began (2 Tim. 1:9, Titus 1:2).

God did not haphazardly begin His creative works. Before God did anything, He had a plan. He had a blueprint. He had a goal in mind to which all of His creative energy, redemptive energy, and sanctifying energy would move.

All of God's actions are calculated carefully. All of God's doings are in perfect harmony. All is related to the one goal, the one purpose for the universe, the earth, the angels, and man. All relate to the mystery of His will.

HIDDEN IN AGES PAST

Even though God has always had but one purpose in his dealings with man, that purpose was not fully understood by man in the Old Testament age (Eph. 3:5). In fact, when the prophets prophesied of the things that would come, they only wondered—they did not understand (Matt. 13:17). God was reserving the full revelation of this mystery for another time.

The only comfort that God gave to the prophets was the consolation of knowing that what they were seeing and speaking was for a later time (1 Pet.

1:10-12). The patriarchs and the prophets were living in days of shadow and form when the revelation of the mystery of God's will was kept secret. It would not be until the sending of the Holy Spirit in the New Covenant that these secrets would be opened up and revealed. The irony is that it was going to be through the very Scriptures penned by these men in ages past that this mystery was going to be made known (Rom. 16:25-26).

MADE MANIFEST IN THE PRESENT AGE

Paul, more than anyone else in the New Testament age, seems to be the one to whom God brought this understanding. While others were wrestling over many peripheral areas because of their limited perspective, Paul's eyes seemed to have been opened as to the magnitude of God's plan. He is able to say that God gave him knowledge of the mystery by a special revelation.

> *For this reason I, Paul, the prisoner of Jesus Christ for you Gentiles—*
> *if indeed you have heard of the dispensation of the grace of God which*
> *was given me for you, how that by revelation He made know to me*
> *the mystery (as I wrote before in a few words, by which, when you*
> *read, you may understand my knowledge in the mystery of Christ),*
> *which in other ages was not made known to the sons of men, as it has*
> *now been revealed by the Spirit to His holy apostles and prophets.*
> Ephesians 3:1-5

We are continually reminded by Paul that this hidden purpose is now made manifest (Rom. 16:25-26; Col. 1:26). There was a change in dispensations in which it suited God's purpose to open our understanding in this area. We are no longer in the age of shadows; we are living in the light of the Holy Spirit who is ready to illuminate our understanding. We are not living in the age of the prophets when they desired to know but could not know. We are living in a day when God has a desire to reveal these things to us.

UNFOLDED LITTLE BY LITTLE

Because the full understanding of God's purpose was reserved for a certain age, nowhere in the Scriptures does God tell us in outline form the beginning from the end. God has given some tremendous, divine clues through-out His Word that when pieced together make up a magnificent whole. (Note to reader: It should be remembered that if we come to a correct understanding of the whole, all the pieces should fit. If at anytime in our interpretation we have to strain or stretch any verses, we must challenge our understanding of the whole.)

GOD'S PURPOSE BEGINS WITH GOD HIMSELF

In attempting to unravel some of the divine mystery of God's purpose we must of necessity begin with God Himself, because when the purposes of God were established, no one was there but God. In the beginning God dwelt alone (Gen. 1:1). Before there ever was an angel, a star, a galaxy, or a person, God's purpose was established. God did not do anything without purpose, but all His ways were known to Him from the beginning (Acts 15:18). It follows then that if we are going to understand God's purpose, we must look for clues in the biblical revelation of the nature of God.

But how can we know the nature of God? Man cannot know God's nature unless God first reveals Himself to man. God's ways are past finding out unless He chooses to reveal them to us. The beautiful thing about our God is that He has chosen not to remain a mystery but has a desire to make Himself and His nature known to His creation.

The Scriptures of the Old and New Testaments are a testimony to this desire of God. God has broken into history and moved by His Spirit on the hearts of man to bring to us a Word that is breathed by the very mouth of God. In this Word, God has given man an opportunity to know Him in His nature and purposes. Apart from this Word we can only know God's power and being, but through this Word He has given us a true picture of His nature.

What kind of God do we serve? What kind of God rules the universe? What are His character qualities? What is His attitude toward His creatures? What limits has He chosen within which to operate and function? All of these and other questions can only be answered by God Himself.

God has given us the answers to these questions, but they must be searched out in the Word. God did not give us *summa theologica* on the nature of God. Yet these answers are available to the humble seeker of God's truth. God generally hides Himself from the halfhearted. But if we are diligent, there is no reason why we cannot discover an answer to all of these questions in God's Word.

GOD IS THE SAME, YESTERDAY, TODAY, FOREVER

One of the most important revelations as to the nature of God that is foundational to our study of the plans and purposes of God prior to the foundation of the world is that of the immutability of God. God has told us that He does not change. God will change His mind (humanly speaking) in relation to judgment on His people when they change their mind, but He never changes in His essential character, His being, and His nature (Mal. 3:6; James 1:17; Heb. 6:18).

The implications of this are very important to us because it means that if God is indeed unchanging in His character, nature, and being, then He is the same today in those qualities as He was two thousand years ago. It means that He is the same now as He was two million years ago. It means that He is the same as He was when in eternity past He was dwelling alone. He is the same today as He was before there ever was an angel, a star, a galaxy, or a person.

If God is eternal now, He was eternal then (Ps. 90:2). If God is omnipotent now, He was omnipotent then (Rev. 19:6). If God is omniscient or all-knowing now, He was omniscient then (Rom. 11:33).

The same is true in regard to God's moral attributes. Even though God's moral attributes require an object on which they may be expressed, yet we still have to believe that they are descriptive of the very heart or essence of God. Therefore, if God is holy now, He was holy then (Isa. 6:3). If God is just now, He was just then (Ps. 145:17). If God is love now, He was love then (1 John 4:8, 16).

GOD IS A FATHER

One of the most central and basic revelations of the nature of God that Jesus Christ emphasized in His life and ministry was the concept of the fatherhood of God. Of all the tremendous revelations of grace and truth that come by the Son of God, this manifestation of the Father is by far the most significant.

In the Gospel of John this is made very clear when John says, "No one has ever seen God; but God's son, He who is nearest to the Father's heart, has made Him known" (John 1:18, NEB, See also Matt. 11:27 and Luke 10:22).

The important thing for us to see is that if God is a Father now and has the heart of a Father now, then He had a heart of a Father from the foundation of the world. In the Old Testament age, God was as much a Father as in the New Testament age. This truth, however, is not explicitly outlined in the Old Testament. In spite of that, every so often God gave them a clear word that He was a Father to His people (See: Exod. 4:22-23; Deut. 32:6,11; 2 Sam. 7:14-15; Ps. 2:7, 68:5, 89:26, 103:13; Prov. 3:11-12; Isa. 63:16, 64:7-8; Jer.3:4,19; 31:9; Mal. 1:6, 2:10).

THE HEART OF A FATHER

The coming of Jesus, however, initiates a new age, the age of grace and truth, and the age of fulfillment. Into this age comes Jesus with a powerful revelation of God as our Heavenly Father, having the heart and passions of a father. It is in this central revelation of God as a father having the heart of a father that we find a tremendous clue to the establishment of the purpose of God from the foundation of the world.

When God was dwelling alone in eternity past, He had the heart of a father. It is only through our fatherhood that we can fully understand some of the feelings that are present in the heart of a father. Our own fatherhood reveals to us some of the things that a father desires more than anything else.

God had the heart of a father and also, therefore, the desires of a father. Those desires are expressed in five key ways:

1. A Desire for Reproduction of Self/Image and Likeness

There is a desire in the heart of every father to have offspring that reflect the image of the father or that bear the family resemblance. God, too, is interested in an offspring that would be a true reflection of Him. He is interested in reproducing His character and image in His creation.

2. A Desire for Multiplicity of Seed/Fruitfulness

One of the greatest promises to the fathers of the Bible is that of multiplicity of seed. Even though children are now, in our day, looked at by many as a curse, God originally gave them to man as the highest of blessings. The great promise that Abraham treasured above all was his fatherhood of many nations. As a father, God shares in this desire. Having only one Son did not fully satisfy the heart of God. God has a desire for many sons and daughters.

3. A Desire for Reproduction of Ministry/Partnership

In the heart of every father is the desire to mentor and develop ministry in his offspring so that they might share in the ministry of the father. This desire is reflected in the Eastern custom of the training of sons in the vocation of the father. Jesus was trained under the hands of Joseph to follow him in his occupation. The Father God desires to bring His offspring into partnership with Him in His occupation, that of ruling the universe.

4. A Desire for Communion/Relationship

In the heart of every father is the desire for appreciation to be expressed from his children and for there to be a high level of communication between him and his children. There is a desire for the cultivation of a deep personal relationship where the offspring are not just sons and daughters but friends. God has this desire in relation to those whom He fathers. This is not to be a relationship based on coercion, but a relationship built on love and the expression of free will.

5. A Desire to Provide a Bride for His Son

In the Old Testament the father had the right to arrange the marriage of his son (Genesis 24). God, too, would arrange a divine marriage for His Son by providing a worthy bride for Him.

GOD'S PURPOSE WILL SATISFY HIS HEART

When God began His creative work, all of this was in His heart. He began by creating an order of beings that would be servants to His higher order. He began by creating the angelic hosts, after which He created the universe of worlds. These angelic hosts were to be the ministering spirits of the Kingdom of God. They did not satisfy the heart of the Father, but they were to be ministers to those who would.

The angels had a divine order to them much like a well-organized army. They are even referred to as the heavenly host or heavenly armies. The main function of this creation was to worship God and do His bidding.

One of the highest beings in this created order was Lucifer, the light bearer. He was entrusted with a spectacular ministry as the covering cherub in relation to the very throne of God. He was a superbly created being who had access to God's very presence. His primary ministry seems to have been in relation to music and worship. Most likely he was the worship leader of the universe whose job it was to direct all of the heavenly worship to God Himself.

How long this ministry continued we do not know, but the day came when Lucifer, who was a channel of worship to God, began to look at himself and to notice what a beautiful creation he really was. As he did, he began to desire some of the worship that rightfully only belonged to God. He desired to be exalted above all the other creatures of God and coveted perhaps even the place that God had prepared for a future creation.

When this iniquity was found in Lucifer, he led a rebellion in heaven that involved a third of the angels, and another kingdom was established opposed to the Kingdom of God. When Satan fell, every angel's loyalty was tested. Most of the angelic host remained loyal to God and are presently fulfilling His intended purpose.

When Satan fell, God did not destroy Him, because just as God had used him as a vessel of honor, so He was going to use him as a vessel of dishonor to assist in fulfilling His purpose. He was going to use him in a negative way to help mature the offspring that He would produce.

God did, however, remove Satan from his place of ministry in the heavenly hosts. He did prepare a place of final judgment for Satan and his angels, but He reserved his ultimate judgment until a later time when he would no longer be useful to the fulfillment of God's original purpose. In fact, God was going to give the privilege of dealing with Satan to the new creation that he would bring forth.

When Satan fell, he not only took many angels down with him but he also marred the worlds that God had created. Genesis 1:2 describes the wasted condition to which a good earth had fallen.

God began the restoration of all that he had made to prepare the earth for the coming of his greatest creation—man. All that God did in Genesis 1 was to prepare for man. Man was going to be the creature that would satisfy the Father's heart. God revealed His heart in Genesis 1-2 when He declared His purpose. Notice how the language of this chapter shows the heart of the Father.

"Let Us make man in Our image" (Gen. 1:26).

This corresponds to the Father's desire for the reproduction of Himself. Man's character is to conform to God's character. He is to be fashioned in the likeness of God.

"Be fruitful and multiply" (Gen. 1:28).

This reflects God's desire for multiplicity of seed. Adam and his wife, Eve, were to replenish or fill up the earth with offspring all reflecting the same image and likeness.

"Have dominion" (Gen. 1:28).

This dominion over the earth was to be preparatory for dominion over greater things. God had a desire for man to rule with him, but He was to prepare us by giving us degrees of responsibility. The divine principle is that we must be faithful in small things before we can be entrusted with greater things.

"The sound of the LORD God walking in the garden in the cool of the day" (Gen. 3:8).

This was not a strange occurrence on the day of the fall; it was a common occurrence for God to fellowship with His creation. The man and woman were created for His good pleasure.

"It is not good that man should be alone" (Gen. 2:18).

It is the normal thing for a man to have a bride. So it is with God's Son. Even as God built a woman for Adam, He had a desire to build a many-membered bride for His Son (Matt. 16:18).

"And subdue it" (Gen. 1:28).

Man had the responsibility of subduing the earth. The implication here is that man had an enemy to face. There is the implication that some being would come with whom Adam and Eve must contend. That being was Satan himself. Yet when God's plan was finished, man would have the privilege of subduing even Satan (Romans 16:20). When God placed man and woman in the garden, it was their responsibility to subdue the earth. By Adam and Eve's faithfulness in tilling and dressing the garden, the whole earth would become a Garden of Eden.

MAN'S STRUGGLE AGAINST SATAN

When God created man, Satan viewed him as a threat to him and his ultimate victory. Satan's primary purpose was no longer bringing glory and service to God, but trying to frustrate the purposes of God and win humans over to his kingdom. In order for him to frustrate the purpose of God, he had to try to corrupt God's creation, which was destined to fulfill God's purpose. This is when we find Satan introduced in Genesis 3.

Satan was successful in seducing the woman and man, but he was not successful in frustrating God's purpose. Satan caused Adam and Eve to fall from the image of God, to forfeit the dominion, and to corrupt his way, yet God made a provision for man in the "Seed of the woman" (Gen. 3:15). It would be through this Seed that the ultimate purpose of God would be realized—that purpose being *to have a many-membered "person" in the image of God with whom He might establish relationship and who would qualify for rulership and dominion and for the honor of being eternally linked with the only-begotten Son as one flesh.*

In one respect the purpose of God would be greater in that God would do the greatest miracle of the ages before the face of Satan who chose to exalt himself. He would take a weak, death-doomed creation, and through the humility and sacrifice of His Son and man's faith and reliance on God, He would make them into all that God desired from the beginning. He would demonstrate to Satan what true wisdom really is.

SIN DID NOT SURPRISE GOD

We can ask ourselves, "did the fall of man catch God by surprise? Did He suddenly have to alter His purpose?" The obvious answer is, "NO!" To even imply that a finite being can frustrate or surprise an infinite being is to thoroughly misunderstand the greatness and the omniscience of our God.

As created beings, we could never catch God by surprise. God in His omniscience has absolute foreknowledge. When He created Satan, He knew he would fall. When He created man, He knew he would fall. "Why did He go ahead and create us if He knew that we would fall?" Because He also knew what He would do in regard to our fall. He also knew that through the Incarnation man could ultimately come to full stature. He was able to look beyond the fall of man to the finished product that was set before Him, and He felt it was worth the price.

Jesus had this same attitude when it came to His death on the cross. Because of the joy that was set before Him, because of the glory that would follow, He endured the cross and despised the shame. God, therefore, was willing to pay the price, because in His infinite foreknowledge He knew that the final product of the creation/redemption process would satisfy His father's heart.

In Genesis 3:15 God comes to the man and comforts him with the hope of a redeemer who would make the realization of God's purpose possible. Six facts about this salvation of man are upheld by this passage:

1. Salvation is initiated and worked by God. Apart from this man has no hope.
2. God's plan of salvation will destroy Satan, the enemy. Satan's head (i.e. the seat of his authority) is to be crushed.
3. God's plan includes all of mankind, all of the offspring of Adam and Eve, not merely one nation or individual.

4. God's plan will be realized through the work of a mediator that is born of a woman.

5. God's plan involves the suffering of the Redeemer, His heel is to be bruised.

6. God's salvation will be experienced as a part of history even as the fall of man is part of history.

All of the pre-Incarnation history is seen as an expectant preparation for the coming of the Redeemer. From Genesis 3:15 on, the primary thrust of the recorded Word is the preparation and realization of the Seed of the woman who would make it possible for man to be restored to God's intended plan and go on to fulfill His intended purpose. From this point on we can see God's concern over all the aspects of His purpose in preparing a people to fulfill that purpose.

God's concern is that His people experience all aspects of the birthright and blessing (involving rulership, priesthood, fruitfulness, character,, and victory over enemies) that relate to this one central purpose. All of the covenants that God made with people deal with nothing but different aspects of this one purpose.

The whole Bible is a revelation of the unfolding drama of this one central purpose of God. The plan is initiated in the first chapters of Genesis, and it is achieved in the closing pages of the book of Revelation.

GOD WILL NEVER BE FRUSTRATED

Man is fickle, and more often than not when he begins something, he gets discouraged in the middle, and the project ends up in a pile in the corner of the attic or basement. Man is impatient, and when he sees that a desired project may take some tedious hours of work, he is liable to abandon the project. Man is easily frustrated in his tasks because oftentimes he does not realize the difficulty of a task until he is in the middle of it. When he eventually realizes some of the frustration involved, he is prone to abandon the project and try something else. Man is affected by moods and whims, emotions and changing desires.

God is totally opposite to man in this regard. God, who knows the end from the beginning, takes all things into account before He ever begins anything. He is not like the man building a tower who failed to count the cost at the outset. God knew what the cost would be. He knew that His plan would cost Him the Incarnation and the Crucifixion, and yet He was willing to pay the price. God knew all of the things that Satan would do to frustrate His purpose, but He deemed it worthwhile to go ahead.

Now that God has begun, He is totally consumed with the realization of His original goal. Being omniscient, there was absolutely nothing that He did not foresee and for which he did not allow. Being omnipotent, there is absolutely nothing that will stand in the way of God's achieving His goal. When God sets a goal or establishes a purpose, the thing is as good as done.

Scripture is very clear on this point. Notice the confidence that Isaiah expresses in the purposes of God.

> *The LORD of hosts has sworn, saying, "Surely, as I have thought, so it shall come to pass, and as I have purposed, so it shall stand: That I will break the Assyrian in My land, and on My mountains tread him under foot. Then his yoke shall be removed from them, and his burden removed from their shoulders. This is the purpose that is purposed against the whole earth, and this is the hand that is stretched out over all the nations. For the LORD of hosts has purposed, and who will annul it? His hand is stretched out, and who will turn it back?"*
> Isaiah 14:24-27

The obvious response to these questions is "No One!" Once God has determined or purposed something, no one can annul it. Once God has begun to work, no one will be able to turn His hand back. No one! This includes man, angels, and even Satan himself! God will use any tool or vessel necessary to accomplish His goal.

THE CYCLE OF THE RAINS

God likens this whole principle in His character and nature to the cycle of the rains. He compares the cycle of the rain and snow to the cycle of His Word.

Just as the rain and snow that fall from the heavens do not return to heaven until they first accomplish their intended purpose (i.e. watering the ground, producing fruit), so it is with the Word that goes forth from God's mouth—it always accomplishes the purpose for which it was sent. It always brings forth the intended fruit of the earth (James 5:7) before it returns to Him again.

> *"For my thoughts are not your thoughts, nor are your ways my ways," says the LORD. "For as the heavens are higher than the earth, so are My ways higher than your ways, and My thoughts than your thoughts. For as the rain comes down, and the snow from heaven, and do not return there, but water the earth, and make it bring forth and bud, that it may give seed to the sower and bread to the eater, so shall My word be that goes forth from My mouth; it shall not return to Me void, but it shall accomplish what I please, and it shall prosper in the thing for which I sent it."* Isaiah 55:8-11

God's Word has gone out, and just as sure as it has gone forth it will accomplish all that He desires it to accomplish. He will fulfill His purpose.

HIS PURPOSE IS BEING ACCOMPLISHED IN THE NEW TESTAMENT CHURCH

While God has been working toward this one central purpose since the beginning of time, it is going to be through the church that this ultimate purpose is going to be realized.

> *To me, who am less than the least of all the saints, this grace was given, that I should preach among the Gentiles the unsearchable riches of Christ, and to make all people see what is the fellowship of the mystery, which from the beginning of the ages has been hidden in God who created all things through Jesus Christ: to the intent that now the manifold wisdom of God might be made known by the church to the principalities and powers in heavenly places, according to the eternal purpose which He accomplished in Christ Jesus our Lord.*
> Ephesians 3:8-11

It is in *the church* where all of God's intended purposes will come to realization. *The church* is God's final instrument that He is using to bring about everything He intended. He is going to use *the church* and His operation through *the church* to bring us to completion, maturity, perfection, and to the lost image (Eph. 4:12-16, Col. 3:10, Rom. 8:28-30). He is going to use *the church* to meet His desire for a bride for His Son (2 Cor. 6:14, Eph. 5:32). He is going to use *the church* to deal finally with Satan (Matt. 16:18-19, Rom. 16:20). He is going to use *the church* to rule and reign with Him for eternity (Rev. 20:6). He is going to use *the church* to bring back mankind into the right relationship to God in fellowship and priestly function (1 Pet. 2:5-9, 1 John 1:3). He is going to use *His church* to fulfill His desire for multiplicity of seed and sinless offspring (Rev. 12). When we realize this, it makes the process of God's dealings in our lives so precious and exciting. He is preparing us by His Spirit for eternity.

PROGRESSIVELY UNFOLDED THROUGHOUT HISTORY

An obvious question that must be answered then is "What is the relationship of the Jewish nation to this eternal purpose?" The Jewish people were used by God under the Mosaic Covenant as His instrument to preserve the Seed of the Woman until Christ came. God used many instruments in the Old Testament Age. He used the patriarchs prior to the founding of the nation of Israel, He used Israel, and He even used the Gentile nations at times to preserve the Seed. God has always been concerned with the same final product. He has moved through stages in the realization of the purpose. Israel was a part of the process but not the end in itself.

When God began in Genesis in the process of redemption the most important part of His plan was the bringing forth of the Seed and the preparation of the world for that coming Seed, the Messiah. The promises made in Genesis were for the whole world, not one nation. The promises were all in Adam.

From the beginning Satan's chief desire was to frustrate and bring to naught the purposes of God especially since God pronounced his doom in declaring that his head (the seat of authority) was going to be crushed (Gen. 3:15). From the birth of the first man-child, Cain, Satan has been seeking to devour, pervert, and destroy man, so that he could in some way keep the Seed of the Woman from begin manifested.

Satan came against the first child, Cain, won him over, and used him to kill the second son, Abel. Satan thought he had destroyed God's plan, but God brought in a substitute seed, "Seth". Satan's main preoccupation was to corrupt the race of men so that this deliverer would never come. As the world was filled with people, Satan was quite successful in perverting the whole race of man (Gen. 6) except for one godly man and his family. To preserve the seed from corruption, God destroyed the wicked world of man and saved the righteous man Noah and his family to begin anew on a cleansed earth.

Soon after Noah's new beginning, Satan was able to fill the heart of Ham in an attempt to pervert the seedline again. As time progressed, the world again fell deeper into sin. One sin led to another sin, and soon idolatry and false religion spread, culminating in the Tower of Babel. God again responded by intervening and destroying the attempts of the enemy. Continually, man's inability to keep himself pure was exposed by the devices of his greatest and most powerful enemy, Satan.

In order to preserve man from Satan and preserve the seedline to Messiah, God called a man named Abraham. He called him out of idolatry and separated him from the world of his day. He prepared him as the father of a nation, a nation that He would use as His vessel to bring forth the Messiah.

To save the nation by a virgin-born mediator, God called one nation and separated them from the other nations. He chose them by His sovereign grace and made them a special and peculiar people. He built a hedge of protection around them which was to be a schoolmaster or guardian for them, to make sure that they got where they were supposed to go. He hedged them in with the law that they might be able to keep themselves pure until the Messiah would come who would be the light of the world.

While Israel was under the law, God made them a showcase of divine principle and government, and the stranger nations were invited to come and join themselves to the true God. Israel was the "church in the wilderness" (Acts 7:38). They were to be the nation of priests that mediated God's principles to the world and were instrumental in preparing the world for the coming Seed.

In many respects Israel as a nation failed to understand and fulfill its ministry to the world. But the law did not fail. The law did preserve a seed-line from Abraham, through David, and up to Mary, from whom the Messiah would come. And from that line, Jesus the Christ was born. He was born as the "Consolation of *Israel*", but He was also the "light of the *world*" (Luke 2:25, 29-30; John 9:5).

With the coming of Christ, the seed or purpose for the hedge was no longer there, so the hedge or guardian was removed. Christ came, and in place of a natural nation, He established a spiritual nation, the church that until His second coming will be the instrument through which God will carry out His purpose.

God's desire was that all of natural Israel would become part of spiritual Israel, the church (Gal. 6:16). Many of them did (Acts 6:7), but most in Israel had been so caught up with the schoolmaster they missed the One to whom it pointed.

We have to see that in all of God's dealings with man His desire has been not for the one nation or one race only, but it involved the bringing together of all nations into one body—the Body of Christ!

God's purpose involved the nation of Israel but not Israel alone. God's purpose was not merely to bless the nations though their connection with the chosen nation, Israel, because that was not something that was hid in ages past (Gen. 12:3). That was something that was taken for granted in the Old Testament age (Gen. 22;18; 26:4; Deut. 23:8, Ps. 18:49).

Paul, however, was able to say that whatever this purpose was, it is something that is now revealed. *God's purpose was to raise up one many-membered body out of all nations, Jew and Gentile, that would fulfill the demands of the Father's heart.*

In the New Covenant something takes place between Jew and Gentile that is exciting in Paul's mind. He uses some significant terminology to describe the new relationship of the Jew and Gentile in the new covenant, including the following:

1. One Body (I Cor.12:13, Eph. 2:16; 4:4).
2. Abraham's Seed (Gal.3:27-29).

3. Children of Promise (Gal. 4:28).

4. Fellow Heirs (Eph. 3:6).

5. The New Man (Col. 3:10-11).

Paul unfolds this purpose in detail in Ephesians 2:11-22. An outline of this passage reveals the following truths:

Paul Describes the Former Condition of the Gentiles

- Gentile in the flesh
- Uncircumcision
- Without Christ
- Aliens from the commonwealth of Israel
- Strangers from the covenants of promise
- Having no hope
- Without God in the world
- Far off
- Enmity from God and man

Paul Describes the Present Condition of the Gentiles

But Now…

- In Christ Jesus
- Made nigh by the blood of Christ
- At peace with God and man
- Made one with the Jew
- Middle wall of partition broken down
- Enmity abolished
- One new man
- Both reconciled to God in one body
- Preaching of peace to those who were far
- Both have access to the Father

Paul Describes the New Relationships That Results:

- No more strangers and foreigners
- Fellow citizens with the saints

- Of the household of God
- Jew and Gentile joined together

There is now no distinction in Christ between the Jew and Gentile. When Christ came, all those Jews who did not believe were cut off the tree of faith, while all those Gentiles that believed were grafted into the tree of faith. The visible expression of that tree is the church, the one new man, the household of faith and the temple of God.

Hence, in order for the eternal purposes of God to be realized, it necessitated the "mysterious" coming together of both Jew and Gentile into one. Both the believing Jew and the believing Gentile are perfectly joined together into one new man (Eph. 2:21).

Now any unbelieving Jew who turns to Christ becomes part of the church. Now any unbelieving Gentile who turns to Christ becomes part of the church. Once in the church they become "perfectly joined together." To maintain any national, racial, or natural distinction in the one new man is to divide the Body of Christ, for in Christ there is neither Jew nor Gentile, bond or free.

THE CHURCH IS IN THE CENTER OF GOD'S ETERNAL PURPOSE

What makes all of this so exciting is that understanding God's eternal purpose changes our whole perspective on what God is doing in the church. The church is not an accident. It is not a second thought on the part of God. It is not a parenthetical invention to kill some time while God's perfect plan unfolds. It is not a substitute for something else that is more important. It is not a "fill in."

The church is at the very center of God's will, and it is the very instrument that God will use to accomplish His eternal purpose. When we realize this, we know that we are not just "killing time," but that God is presently moving in our hearts to conform us to His image and to bring forth His glorious purposes within us. Hallelujah!

LOCAL CHURCHES MUST BUILD
ACCORDING TO GOD'S PURPOSE

That is why it is so critical for us to analyze what we are doing in the church. In our activities and programs, are we functioning in total harmony with God's eternal purpose? If we are, we can expect God to bless them with His anointing. If we are doing our own thing, we cannot expect that same blessing.

As we make plans in the church, we must continually ask, "Is this in harmony with the purpose of God?" "Are we doing what God is doing?" "Does this hinder or further the work of God on the earth today?"

Even the activities within our programs themselves can be measured against God's purpose. Our children's and youth ministries must be measured by the product that they are attempting to create. Our programs are not to be merely for the purpose of providing "babysitting" or "social function;" they are designed to develop the character of our children, to inspire them to sharpen their skills and abilities so that they personally can become instruments of God to extend His Kingdom and His purpose to their world. Our programs are preparing a generation to be used of the Lord to crush the serpent's head.

When we build this way, we are flowing with God. We are co-laborers together with Him, and we can expect His blessing on all that we do.

Chapter Four

THE WORD
AND TRADITION

*KEY #2—If a church is to grow and prosper from
generation to generation, that church must determine
to choose the Word of God over tradition.*

Many people come into the local church with a good deal of personal history. This history can include good or bad experiences with other pastors and churches. This history can include a certain religious tradition, background, or doctrinal belief system. This history can even include cultural practices or a cultural mind-set.

Unfortunately, not all of our traditions are helpful when building the local church. Not all of our traditions are based on the Word of God or are consistent with the principles of the Word of God.

Decades ago I worked with a pastor in the Lutheran Church for a season. He was a wonderful man of God who loved the Word, preached it with authority, and ministered it faithfully as a pastor for nearly thirty years. In fact, he was the one who told me that I needed to have more Scripture in my messages.

During my time working with him, we got into a small disagreement over the subject of the baptism of the Holy Spirit and speaking with other tongues. Knowing that he was a man of the Word, I challenged him to do a Bible study with me on the subject and see what Scripture actually said in this regard. He agreed, and we spent a day together looking at the various verses.

At the end of the day, I could tell from his comments that he was actually seeing something for the very first time. I thought this would mean a big change for him and was starting to get a little excited. However, we finally ended our discussion with his statement, "Are you suggesting that I should get up in front of my people and tell them that for thirty years I have been misleading them regarding this area? I can't do that."

I couldn't believe what I was hearing. He loved the Word. He now saw something in the Word for the first time. But because it was not in keeping with his tradition, training, or past experience, he could not embrace it. In addition, his personal pride would not let him get up and say, "I didn't have full understanding when I preached on this area before, but now I understand in a new way."

The Bible speaks of two types of traditions. There are good traditions that reinforce the principles of the Word and actually help us to live them (Luke 4:16). There are also bad traditions that render the Word of God ineffective (Matt. 15:6; Col. 2:8). "Old" is not always bad, and "new" is not always good or improved.

THERE ARE GOOD TRADITIONS

Paul indicated to the church at Thessalonica that there were some things that he had established while he was with them that were good and that would be helpful to them if they were going to be all that God wanted them to be. He encouraged them to hang on to these things because they brought life and were consistent with the overall purposes of God.

He told them to "stand fast" in the traditions in which they were taught (2 Thess. 2:15). The word for "stand fast" in the Greek here is *steeko*. It means "to stand fast, persevere, persist." In fact, Paul encouraged them to take special note of those who did not cooperate with those traditions (2 Thess. 3:6).

In our church over the years we have had a tradition that has reinforced the Word and purposes of God. It is something that we have practiced for years, but it is not something that is commanded by God. It is not a sacrament in the sense of water baptism or the Lord's Table, but it has been helpful to reinforce certain biblical principles.

We have had the practice of dedicating babies. When parents have a child, we encourage them to bring that child before the church and present him or her to the Lord in an atmosphere of worship, exhortation, and prayer. This is something that was commonly done in the Old Testament, but it is not something that is commanded in the New Testament. It is a tradition. We are not better because we do it. Nor are we worse off if we do not do it. Children who are not presented in such a way are not living under a cloud of disobedience. It is a tradition.

However, we think that it is a good tradition. It is a good tradition because it helps us to continually reinforce certain biblical principles that need to be reaffirmed regularly. It affirms the sanctity of life and that all life comes from God. It affirms the fact that children are a stewardship from God and that all parents will give an answer to Him for how they treat them. It affirms the responsibility of parents in bringing their children to Christ. It affirms the connection of the natural family and the spiritual family (the church) in the childrearing process.

Up to this point this tradition has been good for the church, and it has served the purposes of God. However, this tradition could become negative. If we started to preach that the child must be dedicated to be saved; if we preached that parents who did not do this were irresponsible; or if we begin to equate the dedication of children to infant baptism or christening, then we could be stepping over the line.

As much as we enjoy doing dedications, we can never put this practice on the same level with other admonitions of Scripture. It is a tradition, and we fully recognize that fact. If at any time it begins to conflict with or hinder what God wants to do, we must be willing to let it go.

TRADITIONS CAN BE BAD

It is tragically possible for something to start out good and end up bad. In Israel's history we have an example of this. When they were in the wilderness, God used a brazen serpent that was lifted up on a pole to bring life, health, and deliverance to His people after being bitten by vipers (Num. 21:8-9). After that incident was over, the children of Israel kept this object to remind them of God's deliverance and faithfulness to them. So far, so good.

However, as time when by, this object, which had been so mightily used of the Lord, became a snare to them and an object of idolatry (2 Kgs. 18:4-5). During a time of revival in Israel, Hezekiah had to break this idolatrous image into pieces. The people now needed deliverance from the thing that had been used to bring them deliverance in the past.

Sometimes things that begin well can become a snare or something that actually hinders us from moving forward. Sometimes we need to quit doing some things that we have always done to make room for what God wants to do. Sometimes we cannot take hold of our present until we let go of something from our past. If we are to become all that God wants us to become, we cannot worship the past. We have to be willing to examine our traditions and change them if they are hindering our progress.

I was in a developing country a few years ago for an extended period of time. While I was there, I observed a tradition among several of the churches. Most of these churches were in the practice of celebrating Communion on the first Sunday of the month. On this particular Sunday I also noticed that most of the women in the congregation wore white dresses for their Communion celebration. This had now become a tradition in these churches.

I am sure that when the first woman decided to wear a white dress for Communion Sunday, her heart was in the right place. I am also sure that the others who followed her example were just as sincere. But, unfortunately, as time went on and others followed suit, it became a real block and source of stumbling to many.

What had begun as a nice gesture of honor and reverence to the Lord had now become something that was detracting from the meaning of the Communion Table and was now dividing the Body of Christ. What happened eventually (because this was a poor country) is that women who were too poor to buy a white dress either stayed home on Communion Sunday or came but felt unclean and embarrassed.

This tradition was now making the Word of God of no effect. The Communion Table was despised instead of anticipated, people felt dirty instead of cleansed, condemned instead of forgiven, and separated rather than united. The purposes of God in the Table of the Lord were totally negated.

TRADITIONS TAKE MANY FORMS

Traditions come in many forms. In some cases we are dealing with our religious tradition. This has to do with our personal experience in a local church, a church group, or a religious denomination. All of us come from somewhere. All of us have done things or been taught things in a certain way. All of us tend to like the way we do things because we tend to be comfortable with that which is familiar.

It doesn't matter if we are talking about the length of the service, the way we sing certain songs, the architecture of the church building, the form of government in the church, or anything else. If we have done something a certain way over a long period of time, that must be the way it is to be done.

Pastors coming to new churches face this mentality all the time. The pastor wants to change something. It might be something as insignificant as the location of a table or another piece of furniture. He will find resistance from someone, "Pastor, you have to understand, we have always had that table in that spot." Or "Pastor, that table was donated by my great grandmother, and it must stay there."

After a while the pastor realizes there are no such things as "insignificant" changes. Many a pastor has heard his ideas shot down with the little seven-word phrase "We never did it that way before." That phrase is often treated like the trump card when all reason fails.

I remember when we were attempting to revise our church constitution to more accurately reflect the biblical model of eldership that we had come to embrace. There were a handful of individuals that resisted any changes. Even after we went through the Scriptures on the subject in an effort to lead them to see that the changes we were advocating were indeed the biblical form, it was not enough. To them, doing it the way they had always done it was more important than the Word of God.

The Pharisees of Jesus' day had many religious traditions. Many of these traditions were probably rooted in something that at the time of their inception made perfect sense. But as times changed, the traditions remained the same or lost meaning and became a hindrance rather than a help to their receiving their Messiah.

When Jesus came on the scene, He came into a setting that was steeped in tradition. His message challenged many of these traditions and forced many to decide between what He was saying and their traditions. Unfortunately, in many cases the people preferred their traditions.

TRADITION AND CULTURE

Traditions, however, are not only religious in nature. Traditions can be personal, they can be familial, or they can be cultural. We all have personal things in our lives with which we are comfortable that at times come into conflict with the Word of God. God's Word indicates, for instance, that we should "say" our prayers. For some that is uncomfortable. They would prefer to pray silently. The fact that "silent" prayer is not really found in the Bible has no bearing on the discussion. The whole issue becomes one of personal preference.

This applies to culture as well. While we are all interested in preserving cultural expressions, not all cultural expressions are based on divine principles. In some cases our very culture needs to be challenged by the principles of the Word of God. We cannot hang on to things just because that is the way we have always done them. We must allow our minds and our thinking processes to be renewed and ultimately conformed to the mind of Christ and His thinking process.

Sometimes missionaries have been criticized for trying to westernize African or South American cultures. With so much emphasis on the historical preservation of native cultures, some feel that it is terrible to tamper with these issues. I agree that we do not want to change culture for the sake of change. Nor do we want to ever promote the idea that one culture is superior to another. On the other hand, we do need to see our cultures redeemed. They still need to submit to the Word of God.

My contention is that there is a culture of the Bible that is universal. That is, whenever an individual or national culture comes into sharp contrast with a principle or precept in the Word of God, the culture itself will have to give way. Some things within the culture have no conflict with biblical culture.

Often there is a cultural way of dress that is very unique and beautiful. No one wants to see that change. However, if the cultural dress is no dress at all, that culture will have to give way to the clear biblical guidelines regarding modesty and nakedness.

Cultural dancing can present the same challenge. Some cultural dances may be totally harmless and community orientated by their very nature. Other cultural dancing may be inseparably tied to idolatrous rituals that evoke and seek supernatural encounters with a pantheon of demonic spirits.

I once heard of an African tribe who had turned to the Lord as an entire village. When they would receive tourists from the Western world, they would be asked by the visitors to perform some of their cultural dances. The missionaries would invariably encourage the native peoples to cooperate with the request. After a while one of the key leaders of the village confronted the missionary and asked, "Why do you have us perform these dances for visiting tourists? Don't you realize these dances were part of our pagan religious practices? Don't you realize that these dances were designed to open us up to the control of demonic spirits? Don't you realize what a spiritual battle we face every time we do this?"

Needless to say, that was the end of that. Now I'm sure that these dances were lovely and colorful. But they were part of a tradition that needed to die.

God does not take something away from us unless He intends to replace it with something better. However, if we are to receive the "better," we must hold loosely that to which we are clinging. The Word of God must be the screen through which all of our practices in the church are filtered.

God promises to confirm His Word with signs following. We cannot expect God to bless our word and our traditions especially when they do not harmonize with His Word. Traditions are bad if they are dead, finished, fulfilled, only man-made, or if they try to supersede or contest the Word of God.

If we are to grow and prosper as local churches or as a church movement, we can have no "sacred cows." We must be willing to constantly evaluate everything. Is it still producing life? Or has it become a source of idolatry?

Chapter Five

RESPONDING TO TRUTH

KEY #3—*If a church is to grow and prosper*
from generation to generation, that church must
determine to be responsive to present truth.

God's dealings with man have been progressive throughout history. The journey of every person and every church is represented as a path. We are all on spiritual journeys that are being led and directed by God. If we are going to progress to completion, we must maintain responsive hearts to the personal and corporate dealings of God.

God's plan is progressive. What God began in Adam, He continued through Abraham and Israel. He will end up completing His plan in and through the church. Each generation must build on the past and be responsive to the present dealings of God in their generation. God is speaking to the church today; it is our responsibility to hear His voice and be established in present truth.

THERE IS SUCH A THING
AS A "NOW" WORD

There is such a thing as "present truth." Notice what Peter writes to the church in his day,

Therefore I will not be negligent to remind you always of these things,
*though you know them, and are established in **present truth**. Yes, It*

*think it is right, as long as I am in this tent, to stir you up by remind-
ing you, knowing that shortly, I must put off my tent, just as our Lord
Jesus Christ showed me. Moreover I will be careful to ensure that you
always have a reminder of these things after my decease.*
2 Peter 1:12-15

God has a "now" word or "present truth" for each generation (Heb. 1:1-
2). Just like the prophets of old saw a vision and heard a word from the Lord
for their generation, God has a word and a vision for our generation. There is
something that God wants to say to every one of us as individuals, as local
churches and as the universal church worldwide. Just like the prophets of old,
we need to seek the Lord for that which is our responsibility in our generation.

*Of this salvation the prophets have inquired and searched diligently,
who prophesied of the grace that would come to you, searching what, or
what manner of time, the Spirit of Christ who was in them was indicating when He testified beforehand the suffering of Christ and the
glories that would follow. To them it was revealed that, not to themselves, but to us they were ministering the things which now have been
reported to you through those who have preached the gospel to you by the
Holy Spirit sent from heaven—things which angels desire to look into.*
1 Peter 1:10-12

NOT A "NEW" WORD

This word that God is speaking today is not a "new" word. God is not
speaking "new" things outside of His Word, the Bible. He does, however,
bring new illumination to the words that He has given when the time is
right. Even Paul refers to things that were kept secret that were later
revealed to him by the very words and prophecies of those who had gone
before (Eph. 3:1-7).

When God gives us such a word, it is meant to be an area of focus. In
Matthew 16:18, Christ said that He would build the church, which is
likened to a temple or a spiritual house. In the building of a house there is

a time or a season to focus on different aspects of the house. There is a time for every purpose under heaven (Eccles. 3:1).

A WORD FOR TODAY

God has **a word for today** (Heb. 3:1-7, 13, 15; 4:1, 7). As God progresses with us through history in the process of bringing forth His purpose, He has a task for every generation. Just as He had a "today" word for Israel. He has a "today" word for us in the twenty-first century. It is a word that reflects what God is saying to the church today, in the present tense.

God's method of teaching or building is line upon line, precept upon precept (Isa. 28:10). What God is doing today is based on what He has done in all of the preceding generations. Each generation of faithful believers has moved us that much closer to the fulfillment of God's eternal purpose. We are standing on the shoulders of those who have gone before. We must hear God's voice today.

A WORD FOR EVERY BELIEVER

This principle applies to us as individual believers, as local assemblies, and as the Body of Christ worldwide. God has a "today" word for every believer. Every believer in Christ is on the path of the just that shines more and more unto the perfect day (Prov. 4:18). Every believer moves from faith to faith, from grace to grace, and from glory to glory (2 Pet. 3:18; 2 Cor. 3:18).

Our lives as individual believers must be characterized by a personal responsiveness to the voice of the Holy Spirit if we are to fulfill our personal destinies. Fulfilling our personal destinies is a life-long journey that requires a life of obedience and personal surrender to God.

Paul serves as a great example to us of someone who at the later stages of his life was still pressing toward the mark of the high calling in Christ Jesus (Phil 3:13-14).

Many believers begin their walk with the Lord with this kind of openness and surrender to the Lord. Many people begin with a genuine sensitivity to the voice of the Holy Spirit because they do not want to miss anything God has for them. However, after some time, it is easy for people to become somewhat hardened and to lose that original responsiveness to and excitement for fresh direction from the Lord. It is easy for them to plateau in their walk with the Lord and cease growing.

The Christian's life should be one of continual growth in the Lord. We are to grow up into Him in all things (Eph. 4:15). That is a process that takes our whole life (2 Cor. 10:15). When we cease to progress forward, we jeopardize our ability to fulfill our destiny and achieve the goal that God designed for us in His great purpose.

One way to measure whether or not you are still on the path of the just is in your ability to answer the question, "What is God saying to you today?" Not "What has God said to you in the past?"

Every believer should be having a "now" encounter with the Holy Spirit. Every believer should have a fresh testimony. Every believer should know what God is trying to work in him or her at any given point in time.

It is sad when a Christian has to reach back five, ten, or twenty years to share a testimony. It is sad when you ask for testimonies of God's dealing in the last three months, and no one can get up to share.

Biblical concepts that describe the walk of the believer are included in words like "change, growth, progress, transformation, advancement, development, maturation, and increase." All of these words and concepts are to be very much the experience of the believer throughout his or her entire walk with the Lord.

The walk with God is a progressive walk, on and on, deeper and deeper, more and more, right up until we meet the Lord whether through the grave or the Second Coming. Paul said, "I am convinced and sure of this very thing, that He who began a good work in you will continue until the day of Jesus Christ—right up to the time of His return—developing that good work and perfecting and bringing it to full completion in you" (Phil. 1:6, AMP).

Nowhere are we instructed to become faint, to relax in our efforts, to settle down, to level off, or to taper off as the years go by. On the contrary, we are to:

- Stir ourselves up
- Press toward the mark
- Take the Kingdom by force

- Possess our inheritance
- Lay hold of the will of God
- Fight the good fight

Most of us start with this understanding. Many of us begin our Christian walk with great zeal, with dedication, with goals, dreams, and spiritual aspirations, with great vitality, with sensitivity to the Spirit, with a sincere desire to please God, and with a desire to make our lives count.

Unfortunately, many Christians get derailed at some point. They slow down, they camp, they become stubborn, and they no longer continue on the path of the just. They can become lukewarm.

God wants us to keep ourselves stirred. He wants us to get back to that first-love experience so that we can experience all that God has for us as individual Christians.

A WORD FOR EVERY LOCAL CHURCH

In the same way that God works with individuals, He works with local churches and church movements. Most churches and church movements began with a responsiveness to the leading of the Holy Spirit in a direct way. God was speaking to the leadership regarding building and planting. Those leaders stepped out in faith and responded to the fresh word of the Lord.

There was a time when Martin Luther stepped out on the word of the Lord and responded to what the Holy Spirit was saying to him. God was opening his understanding to a "present truth" that was burning in his spirit. As a result of his faith, we are walking in the light of that truth today.

God is committed to leading us into His eternal purpose. He is committed to leading our local churches into His purpose. He is committed to seeing the worldwide Body of Christ fulfill destiny.

Because God has a "now" word for believers, churches, and the Body of Christ, at any point in time we should be able to ask a believer, "What is God doing in your life right now?" We should be able to ask an individual local assembly, "What is God saying to your local assembly of believers in this present season?" We should be able to answer the question, "What is God saying or emphasizing across the world today in the Body of Christ?"

A DAY OF VISITATION

In so many ways God is continually speaking. And He will continue to speak until all of His purpose is accomplished. For us it means having an ear to hear what the Spirit is saying (Rev. 2:7, 11, 17, 29; 3:6, 13, 22).

You see, it is possible to miss one's **day of visitation**. Jesus wept over Jerusalem because they did not respond to the moving of the Holy Spirit in their day.

> *Now as He drew near, He saw the city and wept over it, saying, "If you had known, even you, especially in this **your day**, the things that make for your peace! But now they are hidden from your eyes. For the days will come upon you when your enemies will build an embankment around you, surround you and close you in on every side, and level you, and your children within you, to the ground; and they will not leave in you one stone upon another, **because you did not know the time of your visitation.**"*   Luke 19:41-44 (emphasis mine)

When God is visiting the individual, a church, or the church with **a "now" word**, it is important to catch the wave of the Spirit, because in that season of visitation, there is a special grace available to walk through that door. Israel persecuted the word of deliverance through Moses and missed the door when the grace was there (Num. 14). They paid for it dearly. The Jewish people in the first century, by and large, rejected Jesus who represented the present-day moving or visitation of God.

Throughout history we find that many fresh moves of the Spirit have been persecuted by the very people who should have been the most ready to receive them, that is, those who experienced the last move of God. The Lutherans persecuted the Anabaptists, the Methodists persecuted the Pentecostals,, and the Pentecostals persecuted the Charismatics.

A "PROCEEDING" WORD

God has a word that is proceeding out of His mouth. Jesus said, "Man shall not live by bread alone, but by every word that proceeds from the mouth of

God" (Matt. 4:4). In other words, responding to the "now" word of God is the thing that keeps believers alive.

What causes a believer to get sick, dry up, and become unproductive?

What causes a church to do the same? What causes a denomination or organization to become static and formalized?

We lose our life, vitality, strength, vision, and purpose when we cease to be responsive to the "now" word of God.

God wants us to be open and receptive to His voice, to respond with our hearts and to be established in "present truth". The word "established" means "to set fast, to confirm, to be solid or stable". To be solid and stable, we must be established in truth.

BUILDING ON THE PAST

To be established in the present truth we must be **reminded of the past** and be **responsive to the present** dealings of God (See 2 Pet. 1:12-15). This involves two things. First of all we must build on the past. When responding to what God is saying today in terms of present truth, we do not want to forsake the old landmarks. In fact what God is saying today is to be consistant with and built upon that which has gone before (Prov. 23:10). Solomon wisely said, *"Do not remove the ancient landmark which your fathers have set"* (Prov. 22:28).

In his second epistle, Peter tells us that he wants to make sure that we are reminded of the past (2 Pet. 1:12-13, 15). Notice his words to the people of God (bold emphasis mine):

> "I will not be negligent **to remind** you always of these things, **though you know them**, and are established in the present truth."   (vs. 12)

> "Yes, I think it is right, as long as I am in this tent, to stir you up **by reminding you**."   (vs. 13)

> "Moreover I will be careful to ensure that you always have **a reminder of these things** after my decease."   (vs. 15)

We do not want to slip or drift away from the things that we have heard (2 Tim. 2:14). We do not want to become vulnerable to being blown off course by the various winds (Eph. 4:14). As the writer to the Hebrews declares, "Therefore we must give the more earnest heed [all the more careful attention] to the things we have heard, lest we drift away" (Heb. 2:1).

RESPONDING TO THE PRESENT

While it is critical that we build on the foundations laid by those who have gone before, it is just as critical that we be responsive to the present dealing of God. At the same time that we are building on the past, we must be open to what God is saying **today**. We must never close the door to further truth and further light.

So many verses indicate that the walk with the Lord is progressively unfolding before us. Scripture indicates that the path of the just grows brighter and brighter (Prov. 4:18); we are to be changed from glory to glory (2 Cor. 3:18); we are to grow up into Him in all things (Eph. 4:15); we are to be transformed by the renewing of our minds (Rom. 12:1-2); we are to increase more and more (1 Thess. 4:10); we are to grow in grace and in the knowledge of Him (2 Peter 3:18); and our faith is to continue to grow (2 Cor. 10:15).

It is clear from these verses that the walk with God is a progressive walk, on and on, deeper and deeper, more and more, right up until we meet the Lord whether through the grave or the Second Coming.

TIMES OF REFRESHING

Often as God is moving us from one level to another level, we experience times of refreshing from the Lord that facilitate our being able to respond in this season. Just as God moves with us as individuals, so there are special times of refreshing in God's dealings with His people, the church. Peter alludes to this in his message in Acts 3:19-21 where he tells the people:

Repent therefore and be converted, that your sins may be blotted out,
*so that **times of refreshing** may come from the presence of the Lord,*
and that He may send Jesus Christ, who was preached to you before,

*whom heaven must receive until **the times of restoration** of all things, which God has spoken by the mouth of all His holy prophets since the world began.*

These times and seasons of refreshing are consistent with God's overall plan for His people. These times are designated in the Scriptures in several ways including, times of refreshing (Acts 3:19), times of restoration (Acts 3:21), set times (Ps. 102:13), fullness of times (Gal. 4:4), times and seasons (1 Thess. 5:1), day of visitation (1 Pet. 2:2), appointed time (Acts 17:26), time of reformation (Heb. 9:10), time of visitation (Luke 19:44), and time of the latter rain (Zech. 10:1).

DISCERNING THE TIMES

As the people of God, it is important that we discern these times. Jesus criticized the Pharisees and religious leaders of His day because they could read natural signs in the heavens, but they could not recognize the spiritual signs of the times.

*Then He also said to the multitudes, "When you see a cloud rising out of the west, immediately you say, 'A shower is coming'; and so it is. And when you see the south wind blow, you say, 'There will be hot weather'; and there is. Hypocrites! You can discern the face of the sky and of the earth, but how is it you do not **discern this time**?"* (Luke 12:54-56)

*Hypocrites! You know how to discern the face of the sky, but you cannot discern **the signs of the times**.* (Matthew 16:3)

The Pharisees and religious leaders of the day could discern changes in the natural weather, but they could not discern spiritual climate changes.

We must ask God for the spirit of the children of Issachar *"who had understanding of the times, to know what Israel ought to do"* (1 Chron. 12:32). God's Word is given to us to motivate us to do something. There must be a response to every word from God.

UNDERSTANDING GOD'S PURPOSE

When God moves among His people, it is always with a sense of purpose. Understanding the times and seasons of the Lord means discerning God's purpose in those times. What is He trying to accomplish in me? What is He trying to accomplish in the church? What is He saying to this generation of people?

God's special times and seasons usually include **four main ingredients** (See Acts 3:19-21). It should be noted that these ingredients will be present whether it is a believer who is in God's special time in his or her personal life with the Lord, whether it is a local church that is experiencing a special time of visitation in its journey with the Lord, or whether it is the entire church worldwide that is experiencing a fresh moving of the Holy Spirit.

1. **Repentance**—Whenever God moves in a fresh way, our first response must be repentance. This involves a repentance from drifting away from God's way, from a lack of responsiveness to the Spirit, from doing our own thing in our own way, and from neglecting the now word of God.

2. **Conversion**—Repentance leads to conversion. This involves a turning around or changing what we are presently doing or the direction we are presently going. It involves adopting a new lifestyle, methodology, or emphasis according to what the Lord is indicating.

3. **Healing**—Conversion leads to healing. This involves receiving forgiveness, deliverance, and a special experience of the grace of God.

4. **Refreshing**—Finally God brings us into a season of refreshing so that we can enjoy the blessings of obedience. God blows fresh air on His people as they respond to His moving. Thayer defines the refreshing as "A cooling off or refreshing, recovery of breath, a refreshing of one's spirit, a revival."

Notice how the various translations refer to this experience:

"That the times of refreshing, or recovering from the effects of the heat, of reviving with fresh air…"   (AMP)

"Repent in order that [not when] times of refreshing may come."
                                                                (Barnes)

Such times of refreshing will prepare the way for the restoration of the church and the return of Christ ("whom heaven must receive until the times of restoration of all things" Acts 3:21).

To understand, evaluate, and enter into present truth, we must have certain basic understandings. We must understand the unity of God's eternal purpose, the unity of the Scriptures, the relationship of natural Israel to the church, God's method of revelation and restoration, and the historic cycle of decline, restoration, and revival.

1. The Unity of God's Eternal Purpose

Charles Finney once said, *"Revival is finding out which way God is going and going with Him."* God has only ever had one eternal purpose (Gen. 1:26-28; Eph. 1:3-14). This purpose springs from God's father's heart. It was declared in the first two chapters of the Bible, and it will be fulfilled as indicated by the last two chapters of the Bible (See chapter 3 on God's eternal purpose). It involves bringing forth a many-membered "person" in His image (character) who is reproducing after his kind (fruitfulness), who is growing into maturity, who is reciprocating the love of God (worship, fellowship, and relationship), who is capable of ruling and reigning with Christ (function and partnership), and who will one day qualify as a bride for the Son (union).

All of God's dealings with man in both the Old and New Testaments have been a progressive unfolding of that one purpose, God working all things after the counsel of His will (Eph. 1:3-14). God's vision is that the whole earth come into harmony with His declared purpose (Gen. 12:1-3; Exod. 19:5-6; John 3:16; Matt. 28:19-20; Rev. 7:9-10; 5:9-10).

God didn't have one plan under the Old Covenant and another plan under the New Covenant. God has but one Kingdom. Throughout history

He has used different instruments or vehicles through which to extend His Kingdom (e.g. the patriarchs (Gen. 12:1-3), Israel (Exod. 19:5-6), Christ (John 3:16), the church (Matt. 28:19-20). *The instrument God uses may change, but the purpose remains the same.*

2. The Unity of the Scriptures

Second, if we are going to understand, evaluate, and enter into present truth, we must acknowledge the unity of the Scriptures. The Old and New Testaments are **one book with one message** (1 Cor. 10:6, 11). Someone said it this way: "The New is in the Old contained, and the Old is in the New explained" or "The New is in the Old concealed, and the Old is in the New revealed".

The Bible is one book. When Paul wrote to Timothy, he indicated that all Scripture is profitable and able to assist us in fulfilling our destiny (1 Tim. 3:15-17). The only Scripture that Paul had was the Old Testament. Paul lets us know that the Scriptures of the Old Testament were "written for our learning" (Rom. 15:4).

3. The Natural and the Spiritual

Third, if we are going to understand, evaluate, and enter into present truth, we must understand the principle of the **natural preceding and fore-shadowing the spiritual** (1 Cor. 15:46; Rom. 1:20). The Old Covenant represents to us the natural covenant that pointed beyond itself to the spiritual or the new (see diagram).

OLD COVENANT	NEW COVENANT
Natural	Spiritual
Flesh	Spirit
Shadow	Image
Figures	True
Visible	Invisible

When we understand this, it helps us to understand so many of the pairs of things in the Bible (natural and spiritual). There is the natural birth that points us to our spiritual or new birth in Christ (John 3:5). There is natural, national Israel in the Old Testament that foreshadows the spiritual Israel of God in the New Testament, the church (Gal. 6:16, Rom. 9:6). There is the natural Jerusalem or city of God that points us to the heavenly Jerusalem and eternal city (Gal. 4:24-26). There was the natural temple in the Old Testament that foreshadowed the true, spiritual temple of the New Testament (1 Pet. 2:5). There were natural priests and animal sacrifices under the old administration that point to a spiritual priesthood and sacrifices in the new administration (1 Pet. 2:5).

In all of these areas God demonstrated the natural, which led to and was fulfilled in the spiritual. It should be noted that the Cross is the great dividing line between the natural and the spiritual, the shadow and the reality. The book of Hebrews demonstrates the relationship of the Old to the New Covenant by bringing us to better sacrifices, better promises, and better things in general.

God always moves from the lesser to the greater, from the inferior to the superior. The blood of Christ is better than the blood of goats.

4. The Relationship of Israel to the Church

Fourth, in order to understand, evaluate, and enter into present truth, we must understand the relationship of Israel to the church. God has only ever had but one church. This church consists of all those who by faith have believed the Word of God and have walked in faith by obeying that Word. This church consists of all those who were "called out" by God and separated unto His purpose and glory. This church is mystically united through all ages, cultures, nations, and denominations (Matt. 8:11). This church consists of God's chosen people, holy nation, priesthood, and peculiar people (Exod.19:1-6; 1 Pet.2:4-9).

True membership in God's church has always been on the basis of faith and not works (John 8:30-47; Jer. 9:23-25; Rom. 2:25-29; 9:6-8; Gal. 6:16). In order for one to be a child of Abraham in both the Old and New Testaments, one had to possess the faith and obedience of Abraham (John 8:30-47). In both the Old and New Testaments, God is not merely interested in an external sign, but He is interested in the true spiritual circumcision of the heart (Jer. 9:23-26).

God makes it very clear that the inward is always more important than the outward. A true Jew is one whose heart is separated to God (Rom. 2:25-29). A natural connection to Abraham does not make you God's child, but it is a response of faith and a walk of obedience that places you in the family line (Rom. 9:6-8). The "Israel of God" consists of those who walk by faith; it has nothing to do with your natural heritage (Gal. 6:16).

The Scriptures show a unique relationship of the people of God in the Old Testament to the people of God in the New Testament. Notice the similarity of the experiences of Israel (natural) and the church (spiritual). Remember the principle, "first the natural then the spiritual" (1 Cor. 15:46).

- Both were objects of grace (Deut. 6:6-10; Eph. 2:3-9).
- Both were called out of bondage (Exod. 3:7-10; Eph. 2:1-3).
- Both experienced the feast of Passover (Exod. 12; 1 Cor. 5:7).
- Both were separated by water and cloud (1 Cor. 10:1-11).
- Both were to be distinct from other nations (Lev. 20:26; 2 Cor. 6:14-18).

This relationship is further seen in the similarity of titles that are applied to Israel in the Old Testament and the church in the New Testament (see chart).

TERM USED	OLD TESTAMENT	NEW TESTAMENT
A Chosen People	Deut. 10:15	1 Pet. 2:9
A Holy Nation	Ex. 19:6	1 Peter 2:9
People of God	Ps. 100:3	II Cor. 6:16
A Priesthood	Ex. 19:6	1 Pet. 2:9
God's Treasure	Ex. 19:5	Matt. 13:44
Bride or Wife	Is. 54:6; 62:5	II Cor. 11:2-3
God's Vineyard	Is. 5:7	Matt. 20:1; Jn. 15:5
Israel	Is. 44:6	Gal. 6:16
God's Flock	Jer. 23:3	1 Pet. 5:2
A House	Ezek. 18:31	1 Tim. 3:15
A Light	Is. 60:1,3	Matt. 5:14
God's Witness	Is. 43:10	Acts 1:8
A Church	Acts 7:38	Gal. 1:13

Understanding this relationship of Israel to the church is important for three reasons. First of all, if we do not understand this relationship, we will not see the church throughout the entire Bible. God has had His church in every generation. It has consisted of all those who have been called out by God, who have responded in faith, and have separated themselves unto the purposes of God. His church began with the heroes of faith in the patriarchal period including Adam and Eve, Abel, Enoch, Noah, Shem, and Abraham. It continued with the seed of Abraham, Isaac, Jacob, Joseph, Moses, Samuel, and David. It further extends to the seed of David right up to the coming of Christ.

The Old Testament saints looked forward to and had faith in the Christ who was coming. The New Testament saints look back to and exercise faith concerning what Christ did for us on Calvary. Both Old Testament and New Testament saints anxiously await the Second Coming where old and new will be raised together and, for eternity, to enjoy the blessings of salvation.

"Many will come from east and west, and sit down with Abraham, Isaac, and Jacob in the kingdom of heaven."   Matthew 8:11

Second of all, if we do not understand this relationship, we will not see or understand the Old Testament prophecies concerning the church. There are two principal covenants that come into play in this discussion—the old (Moses, the mediator) and the new (Christ, the mediator). The old represented the natural, tangible, seen, visible, which was only a shadow pointing to the new, which is the spiritual, invisible, genuine, and reality.

Natural Israel points to spiritual Israel in the church. The natural priesthood pointed to a spiritual priesthood, the church (1 Pet. 2:5-9). Natural animal sacrifices pointed to spiritual sacrifices (Heb. 9:10-15; 13:15). The natural temple pointed to a spiritual temple (Eph. 2:19-21). The natural kingdom pointed to the spiritual kingdom (Rom. 14:17). Natural Jerusalem gives place to spiritual Jerusalem, a heavenly city (Heb. 12:18-24).

Jesus became the transition point in history when all that is natural gave place to the spiritual. To go back to the natural after experiencing the spiritual is to reject the truth.

If we are going to find the church in the Old Testament, it will be as we understand this—that prophecies concerning the establishing of Zion and rebuilding of the tabernacle of David apply to the church and not a national system, a natural temple or animal sacrifice (Isa. 2:1-4; 4:2-6; 62).

If we do not understand this, we will put all of our energies into building the natural (that which is passing away) and neglect the spiritual or the real. Jesus is building a church. That needs to be our focus too!

5. God's Method of Revelation and Restoration

Fifth, if we are to understand, evaluate, and enter into present truth, we must understand God's method of revelation and restoration (Isa. 28:9-10). God's method of revelation and restoration, whether He is dealing with the believer, an individual church, or the Body of Christ, is always the same. God knows what we can handle and knows that we can only receive a little at a time. Isaiah indicates to us God's method of teaching. It is little by little, line upon line, and precept upon precept. Thankfully we can hasten our movement in God by quickly responding to each thing that God brings to us.

6. The Historical Cycle of Decline and Restoration

Sixth, if we are to understand, evaluate, and enter into present truth, we must understand the historical cycle of decline and restoration or revival. The history of God's people in both the Old and New Testaments has been one of decline and restoration. It appears that there can be no status quo in the purposes of God. We are either reaching forward or we are falling back. As those who want to experience all that God has for us, we must posture ourselves to receive what God is saying today!

When you read and study the Old Testament, at any point in the history of God's covenant people they are either moving away from God or moving back to God. This cycle is best illustrated in the book of Judges where there are at least seven cycles in the period of the Judges alone. The cycle looks something like this: God delivers His people, they come to a place of peace, they soon begin to follow after other gods, God sends judgment upon them, they cry out to the Lord, God delivers His people.

The same type of situation has occurred in church history although it has happened over the course of nearly two thousand years.

The Early Church

The early church began with great strength. It started in a real supernatural way. There were signs, wonders, and mighty deeds as part of the normal experience of the church (Mark 16:15-20; Acts 6:8). They experienced a dramatic power over nature (Acts 8:39), evil spirits (Acts 8:7), sickness and disease (Acts 9:33), death (Acts 9:40), and spiritual darkness (Acts 2:41).

In addition there was a quality of Christian life and practice that was reflected by a love for the truth (Acts 2:42; 17:11; 20:27) and a vital Christian character and lifestyle (Acts 4:34-37; 5:41; 9:13-18; 18:24-28).

As a result there was a dramatic wave of evangelism that affected the world of that day (Acts 4:4; 17:6; 19:20).

The Church in Decline

As centuries passed, the church experienced a gradual decline and loss of experiential truth (See *Present Day Truth,* by Dick Iverson for further details). The later books of the New Testament allude to some of the seeds of this decline where we see references to a loss or weakening of several things including first-love relationship (Rev. 2:1-7), love for the truth (2 Tim. 4:3-5), a servant spirit (3 John 9), a separation from the world (2 Tim. 4:10), and a responsiveness to those in authority (2 Tim. 1:15).

As time went on, we see historical evidences of decline and a loss of "book of Acts experiences" in the life of the church. Things that were once a vital part of the church and Christian experience began to fade from the experience of the average believer. Ministries that were prominent in the book of Acts seem to have atrophied over time (e.g. apostles, prophets).

One could make a list of things that were very common in the book of Acts' expression of the church that by the fifth or sixth century were completely lacking in the organized church. That list would include things like prophecy, the gifts of the Spirit, speaking with other tongues, local church autonomy, believer's baptism by immersion, and the priesthood of all believers.

7. God's Desire, Promise, and Plan to Restore His Church

Seventh, if we are to understand, evaluate, and enter into present truth, we must understand God's desire, promise, and plan to restore His church. The Old Testament word for "restoration" means to return or give back something that was stolen or lost (Joel 2:25). The New Testament word for "restoration" means to set something back again to its former state (Acts 3:21).

Restoration, as it pertains to the church, involves the working of the Holy Spirit to bring the church back to its former state of glory and power and to restore the individual believer to the image of God.

God's heart in this is seen in the prophecies concerning restoration found in the Old Testament, the biblical principles concerning the restoration of that which was lost or stolen, types and shadows of restoration in the Old Testament, and God's dealings in the church world since the days of the Reformation.

God declares His desire in Joel to restore all that the worm had eaten (Joel 2:25). There was a time when the church was a luscious tree with beautiful branches and leaves bearing delicious fruit. Through time this tree withered, and the fruit faded. God's plan is to restore His church to a thing of beauty. The church will arise and put on her beautiful garments once again and become a light to the nations.

God's principles of restoration give us great encouragement concerning this process. Under God's plan, criminals who stole things did not just work off their crime or spend time in jail. They had to restore what was lost. Restoration had to be made for any loss of inheritance (Lev. 25:8-14). True restoration of that which was stolen involved a return of what was lost in greater measure (Exod. 22:1-9). God's desire is not merely to see that which was lost restored, but God wants to see that which is lost restored and the ultimate purpose fulfilled.

God's plan for the restoration of the church is further seen in biblical types of restoration. Samson is a type of the church. Here is a man who began well with many exploits, fell through a spirit of pride into a state of decline and bondage, lost his strength and power over the enemy, but was finally restored to the place where he was able to be used of the Lord to bring a judgment upon the enemy in his last days (Jdg.16:19-30).

God's plan for restoration is also seen in God's work in the church since the Reformation. Since Reformation days, God has been moving on the hearts of men and women of God who were willing to lay down their reputations and even their lives to have a more biblical experience.

Martin Luther and others in his generation were touched by God and given new insight and understanding concerning justification by faith. This was not a new revelation because justification by faith was clearly taught in the Scriptures and experienced by the early church. But it was a fresh illumination to the hearts and minds of believers in Luther's day.

Since the Reformation, truth after truth has been restored in a similar way to the experience of the church. The early Baptists were used to restore the truth of water baptism by immersion. Other subsequent groups fostered the restoration of the priesthood of all believers, sanctification, divine healing, the baptism of the Holy Spirit, the laying on of hands, prophecy, and the gifts of the Spirit. In more recent days we have seen a restoration of truth concerning the five ascension-gift ministries, praise and worship, and biblical church government.

God is getting His church ready for the harvest at the end of the age when the church is to rise and shine and become a mighty threshing instrument in the earth to bring forth the waited harvest.

God is moving in our day to add finishing touches to what he began in the days of restoration.

8. God Is Still Speaking

Eighth, if we are going to understand, evaluate, and enter into present truth, we must understand that God is still speaking and restoring the church today. This process of restoration is going to continue right up to the return of the Lord. Peter said that everything must be restored that has been prophesied (Acts 3:19-21). One of the ways we know that Jesus is not coming back for His church tonight is that there is more work yet to be done. Christ will return when the eternal purpose is complete and not before.

If the church is going to grow and prosper into the generations of the future, it must stay current with the "now" words of God. The church must stay up to date as the pillar of God's presence moves through history.

Some of the "now" words and concepts that God seems to be emphasizing in more recent history include (but are not limited to):

Cell Groups or House-to-House Ministry

Over the last twenty-five years, God has been unfolding a biblical model of using the homes of believers to be centers of light to neighborhoods and centers of evangelism and church growth. While small-group ministry has taken on many different forms, it is clear that God is leading the church into developing a safety net for the harvest. This does not in any way take away from the corporate gathering of the church, but it accomplishes things that cannot be accomplished in the larger gathering.

Church Structure and Government

At the same time that God has been speaking about cell ministry, He has turned the focus of the church to the issue of structure and government. He has been shedding the light of His Word on the biblical concept of elders and team ministry. If the church is going to be able to accomplish its God-ordained purpose, it must be structured in such a way that Jesus can truly be the head of the church.

Apostles and Prophets

While teaching on the five ascension-gift ministries has been around for a long time, it seems that God is highlighting the ministry of apostles and prophets in these days. These ministries, along with pastors, teachers, and evangelists, must be fully functioning in the last days if the church is going to be all that God designed for it to be. These are not superfluous ministries, but they are essential to the church's coming to the measure of the stature of the fullness of Christ (Eph. 4:13).

Prayer and Intercession

While prayer and intercession have always been part of the believer's spiritual weaponry, there seems to be a renewed focus today on becoming experts at war with all of the instruments of war. Believers and churches are becoming extremely prayer conscious as they come to a renewed awareness that God works in tandem with the prayers of His people. Churches are beginning to live up to their name, and they are becoming "houses of prayer for all nations."

Covenant Relationship

One thing that God seems to be making us aware of in these days is that we not only need Him, but we desperately need each other as we face the challenges in front of the modern church. Church leaders who have gloried in their independence are realizing that it is not good to be alone. If we are going to see the purposes of God established in the church, we must be willing to become accountable to one another. This in no way is meant to minimize the importance of local church autonomy, but there is coming a greater recognition of our interdependence in the Body of Christ.

Church Unity

For the last five hundred years the history of the church has been marked by splintering and division. In fact, when I used to teach church history, I would refer to this period as the "splintered church." It is during this period that most of the denominations of Christianity began, to the point that there are literally thousands of Christian denominations in the world today. Something is beginning to change. We are living in a day where God is blurring the lines between this group and that group. In fact, some groups are actually merging. One of the great hindrances to the spread of the Gospel has been the division among Christians. While I do not believe that God is going to restore a physical denomination, He is breaking down the walls that divide us, and we are realizing that our local church will not succeed unless all of the churches in our area succeed.

City Reaching

God is bringing pastors and leaders together in their cities. They are taking their places as the elders in the gates of the city. They are gathering for prayer, relationship building, and developing strategy to reach their cities. They are beginning to realize that if the nations are going to be touched, it begins with their own love for their cities and their working together with other pastors and leaders to see the city reached for Jesus. There is faith in people's hearts that whole cities can again turn to the Lord.

Evangelism and Harvest

Much of what we see happening is in harmony with Jesus' declaration that the harvest is at the end of the age. If we are living in the time of the end, then the Gospel needs to go forth as never before. Our cities must be touched. Our nation must be touched. All the nations of the world must be touched.

SUMMARY

If a church is to grow and prosper from generation to generation, that church must determine to be responsive to present truth. This means staying open to change (change inspired by the Spirit and in harmony with the Word of God). We must never get the idea that we have arrived and need nothing more (Rev. 3:17). This is what the Laodicean church felt. They cooled off and ceased to grow. We must never get so rigid that we feel we have no need of adjustments or enlargements. It is the wineskin that refuses to stretch that will be rent by the new wine. Certainly all new wine must be based on clear Scripture, but we must be open to what God is saying or emphasizing in the church today.

Chapter Six

THE DIVINE PATTERN

KEY #4—*If a church is to grow and prosper from generation to generation, that church must determine to build according to the divine pattern for the church (Heb. 8:5).*

J esus only referred to the church in specific terms on two occasions, and yet in those two places He implied a great deal about what the nature of the church was to be. In Matthew 16:15-19 we find these words:

He said to them, "But who do you say that I am?" And Simon Peter answered and said, "You art the Christ, the Son of the living God." Jesus answered and said to him, "Blessed are you, Simon Bar-Jonah; for flesh and blood has not revealed this to you, but My Father who is in heaven. And I also say to you that you are Peter, and on this rock I will build My church, and the gates of Hades shall not prevail against it."

In Matthew 18:15-20 Jesus said:

Moreover if your brother sins against you, go and tell him his fault between you and him alone. If he hears you, you have gained your brother. But if he will not hear you, take with you one or two more, that "by the mouth of two or three witnesses every word may be established." And if he refuses to hear them, tell it to the church. But if he refuses even to hear the church, let him be to you like a heathen and a tax collector. Assuredly, I say to you, whatever you bind on earth will be bound in heaven, and whatever you loose on earth will be loosed in heaven. Again I say to you that if two of you agree on earth concerning anything that they ask, it will be done for them of My Father in heaven. For where two or three are gathered together in My name, I am there in the midst of them.

Out of these two portions of Scripture many things concerning the nature of the church can be gleaned, all of which are later confirmed in the Epistles of the New Testament. The main truths that Jesus implies concerning the church that He proposed to build are that (1) He Himself is the architect of the church, (2) Jesus Christ is the builder of the church, (3) Jesus Christ is the owner of the church, (4) Jesus Christ commissioned the church, (5) the church is a living and spiritual organization, (6) the church will be holy unto the Lord, (7) the church will be a unified church, (8) the church will be a victorious church, and that (9) the church has a local expression.

For our purposes in this chapter we want to look particularly at Christ's relationship to the church as the architect, builder, and owner of the church.

We all have a desire for a church that overcomes the forces of darkness. We all have a desire to see the church live up to the expectations that Christ enumerated in His words about the church. God's desires are exactly the same as our desires. He wants what we want. Beyond that, He knows exactly what it will take for us to achieve that goal.

God desires every local church to grow, prosper, and be blessed. Why does it appear that some churches are experiencing God's apparent blessing and others are not? Does He play favorites? Is He a "respecter of persons"?

NO! God does not play favorites. He is not a respecter of persons. However, He is a respecter of principles. That is, if we function according to certain divine principles, we will receive God's favor and blessing to a greater extent than we would if we ignored these same principles.

This does not merely apply to the local church. It applies to many different realms including our families, our marriages, our finances, our businesses, and our personal relationships. When we build these areas according to God's pattern, we can expect God's favor in them.

The church is Christ's institution—it is His house. The idea came from God, He designed it, He bought the materials for it with the precious blood of Christ, and beyond that, He intends to live in it. The church is the house of God in the fullest sense.

JESUS IS THE ARCHITECT OF THE CHURCH

Jesus affirms the fact that the church originated in the heart of God. The church is not something that people conceived; it is something that God established in His own mind before there ever was a person on earth (Eph. 1:9; 3:10-11). People are always seeking credit for that which God produces. We can have confidence that the church is a "better idea" simply because it has its origin in the mind of God.

Being the architect, God has the plan, pattern or blueprint for the church. God did not conceive a beautiful idea and then turn it over to the ingenuity of man to come up with a plan to make it work (Heb. 8:5). He didn't do this with the ark of Noah. He didn't do this with the tabernacle of Moses. He didn't do this with the temple of Solomon. And He has no intention of doing this with the church.

As men and women, we must be willing to concede that if God has an idea or a goal, He also has a pattern, a blueprint, or a design by which He will ensure that His idea or goal will be reached. If the Lord is going to build a church, it is basic that He as a wise master builder will construct it according to the divine blueprint or design.

Being the architect, God only has one pattern for the church. We know that God has firmly established a pattern for all things in the heavenly realm (Heb. 9:23). There is one blueprint, and all of the laborers must build according to the same blueprint. As laborers together with God, we need to make sure that the pattern and the blueprint that we are following are truly the pattern and blueprint of God's making.

A PATTERN FROM THE WORLD SYSTEM

There are several sources from which we could get a pattern for the church. First of all, we could get our pattern from *the world system.* Israel had a basic weakness in that at times in their history they looked to back to Egypt or the world system for a pattern. They looked to all the other nations that were not established under the government of God, and they desired to pattern themselves after them. They rejected God's pattern of theocracy for the world's plan of monarchy. They paid dearly for their mistake.

The world's ways will not produce heavenly results. This is a challenge for the people of God today. Are we seeking methods of building God's house that are successful business practices in this world but are not sanctified by God? Do we look at those who have had successful business endeavors and, in an attempt to be successful in man's eyes, copy their ways? Have we been willing to use only God-ordained means to achieve God-ordained results? The pattern of the world can never bring forth life, and even as with Saul, it is doomed to end in tragic failure.

The church of Jesus Christ is more than a business. It is a faith-based institution where we must at times walk in faith and obedience rather than natural wisdom and sound judgment. I am not saying that we cannot learn a lot from the business world about order, financial accountability, and the like. In fact, many churches could do a lot more to pay attention to sound business practices in the function of the church. But the point here is that the church is not just to be built in the light of sound business practice. When it comes right down to it, we must build God's house God's way.

A PATTERN FROM RELIGIOUS TRADITIONS

Secondly, we could get our pattern from *the religious traditions of the past.* Traditions in themselves are not bad. There are good traditions to which we are to hold fast (2 Thess. 2:15; 3:6), but there are also bad traditions. Traditions are bad if they keep us from obeying the Word of God.

Many people in the church today are clinging to traditions because they are comfortable with the familiar. Change is always difficult. Just because certain church groups have done things for many years, it does not put those things on the same level as the Word of God. We may be used to doing something a certain way. We may have done it that way all of our lives. But it is possible that the practice in question is not firmly rooted in the Word of God.

What happens when the Word of God says something but our traditions say something else? Someone has once said that the last words of any dying church are, "We never did it that way before." When the church becomes so crystallized that it can no longer respond to the direction of the Head, it is a dying, paralyzed church.

A PATTERN FROM OUR OWN REGENERATE MIND

Thirdly, our pattern could come from *the mind of regenerate man.* Sometimes we actually believe that just because we have been born again, every thought, idea, or program that comes into our sanctified minds must be from God. We feel that if we were in a posture of prayer when the idea came, that is a sure sign that it came from God. Somehow we feel that our own flesh is on hold while we are praying, and the devil leaves us completely alone.

As a result Christians can feel that as long as they are sincere and are really seeking the Lord with an honest heart, they cannot go wrong. This is a form of deception that Satan would have us buy in to, because he knows that if he can divert the church from God's pattern, the church will lose its effectiveness in the battle against him.

Sincerity is no substitute for obedience to the God-ordained pattern, and it will never produce the same results. A nurse can be absolutely sincere in ministering a certain toxic drug, but the effect is going to be bad no matter how sincere she is.

A PATTERN FROM GOD

Our pattern has to come from *God.* God is a God of order, and He has a plan and pattern for everything He does. Right from the very first chapter of the Bible we are impressed with the fact that God never does anything haphazardly. He doesn't leave anything to chance. He had an order in creation, He had a pattern for the first man (Gen. 1:26), and He had an exacting pattern for worship (Lev.). Even in the children of Israel's conquest of the Promised Land, God had an order.

Over and over we are made to realize that God is very detailed and exact about how He wants things done. He knows that "there are many plans in a man's heart, nevertheless the LORD's counsel—that will stand" (Prov. 19:21).

Many churches have good intentions, but they are not experiencing the blessing of God in these days. Why is one church seemingly blessed while another is not experiencing blessing? Doesn't the Bible teach that God is no respecter of persons? Does God have His favorites?

It is true that God is not a respecter of persons. He doesn't play favorites. He treats all of His children the same. However, in spite of the fact that God is not a respecter of persons, He is a respecter of principles. God has certain spiritual laws or principles that He has established relative to the building of His house.

If we are gong to be successful in these days, we are going to have to be like David. We must be willing to stop what we are doing, find out what we are doing wrong, and seek the Lord after the due order (1 Chron. 15:13).

David had good intentions when he was set in as king. He had a love for the presence of God, and he wanted the presence of God to be restored to the nation. But the way he went about it ended up producing death instead of life.

David could have plowed forward in stubborn self-will. But he was wiser than that. Instead, he stopped what he was doing and searched the Scriptures to discover the biblical pattern. When he discovered the "due order," it was his responsibility to follow it. This is what God wants of us in relation to the church. You see, God has a pattern for the church.

God not only has a pattern for the church, He has had a pattern for every structure that He ever commanded to be built. He had a pattern for the ark of Noah (Gen. 6:14-15). When the ark was to be prepared, God left nothing to the mind of man. God was the only one who knew all that had to go into the ark. He was the only one capable of providing the pattern.

In addition, God provided the pattern for the tabernacle of Moses (Exod. 25:9, 40; Num. 8:4), the temple of Solomon (1 Chron. 28:11-19), Ezekiel's temple (Ezek. 43:10-11), and the eternal city of God (Rev. 21:15). If God was so concerned about these structures, which in many cases are but a shadow of the church, would He be any less concerned about the pattern for the church, the true temple of the living God (1 Cor. 3:10)?

THE PATTERN MAKES A WAY FOR THE GLORY

When God builds a dwelling place, everything in that structure has to measure up to the pattern if we expect Him to fill that structure with His glory. The glory of God can only fill that which is built according to the pattern.

All of the biblical structures we have mentioned were to be places where God's glory dwelt. God's glory would never have filled the tabernacle of Moses if Moses had tampered with the divine pattern (Exod. 40:33-34). God's glory never would have flooded the sanctuary in the temple of Solomon had not Solomon been exacting about strict adherence to the divine blueprint (2 Chron. 5:1-14). So also, the church will never be filled with all the fullness of God, unless we are doing what we can to adhere to the pattern of God (Eph. 3:17-21).

THE PATTERN CANNOT BE VIOLATED

This truth is declared throughout the entire Bible. The pattern of God cannot be violated if we are to experience the blessing of God.

Cain tried to offer God his own ideas about worship, the end result of which was banishment from the presence of God (Gen. 4:1-8). Nadab and Abihu tried to offer strange fire on the altar of incense, and they found out that God is concerned over the pattern (Lev. 10). Uzziah thought he could approach God his own way, and he died a leper as a result (2 Chron. 26:16-20).

If any church is to maintain the presence of the Lord, it must determine that it will accept the pattern of the Word as its pattern. God only promises to bless and fill that which is made according to the pattern (Mark 16:20).

As the people of God we need to be honest with ourselves. Do we believe what we believe because the Word says it, or because it causes no problems? God wants us to step out in faith. He is not interested in our excuses for not following His pattern.

THE PATTERN IS NEVER OUT OF DATE

Some would suggest that the biblical model was fine for the first century, but we are living in the twenty-first century, and we need something more relevant to our times. The truth of the matter is that the plan and pattern of God is never out of date. The style of church architecture may change throughout the centuries, but God's plan for the church has not changed.

God's plan is as applicable today as it was in the church of the first century. Man cannot improve upon God's plan. The foundation and basic structure of every local church should be the same worldwide, even as the framework for every human being is the same. There will be differences of personality and expression, but God has one basic pattern for all churches everywhere in the world!

WHAT DOES THE WORD SAY?

This principle of building according to the pattern of God can be applied to so many areas of practice in the church. We are constantly having to make a choice between man's way, our way, and God's way. This is true in our personal lives in issues related to marriage, family, finances, and business. But it is especially true in the church.

There are so many decisions that must be made about so many different things. There are so many opinions about even some of the simplest issues of our personal lives and our church life. There are so many voices clamoring for our attention and urging us to keep up to date. So many seminars, so many church growth conferences, so many strategies—how do we decide?

We decide like David decided. All of the books, seminars, and opinions are good, but what does the Word say? What does the Word say about family? What does the Word say about money? What does the Word say about my work life? When David was not finding success, he went to the Word and found out he was doing a good thing the wrong way.

This principle applies to so many areas of church life. What does the Word say about our praise and worship? Man's wisdom might suggest one thing. Man's wisdom might suggest we be silent or reverent. Man might suggest that we do nothing that would offend. Man always looks on the outward appearance and therefore evaluates things on the basis of how it looks to the natural man.

Our tradition might suggest something else. There are many religious traditions when it comes to the worship experience. Whatever you have personally experienced in the past can be your preference. I was raised in a traditional church that was characterized by silence, decorum, and a very rigid order of worship where only one person functioned in the service.

Religious ceremonies have a lot of meaning to them, and after a while we can think that the way we do things is the only way to do things. But have we ever examined them against the Scriptures? Is God as pleased with our worship as we are? Are we practicing what the Word teaches regarding worship?

The same can be said of so many other things that pertain to the way in which the church functions. God wants us to walk in obedience to His Word so that we can fulfill our destiny to become a glorious church that experiences the ultimate victory over the wicked one.

Chapter Seven

PLEASING GOD

Key #5—If a church is to grow and prosper from generation to generation, that church must determine to build to please God not man.

Much of what is being taught in church-growth conferences today has to do with being sensitive to where our culture is and making sure that the church is relevant to our culture and our times. This is the challenge of every generation. How can we take the timeless truths of the Word of God and use them to reach our culture in our generation?

The challenge involves how to be culturally relevant yet at the same time maintain a pure Gospel and promote a truly biblical experience. The word *relevant* means "fitting" or "suiting given requirements." Its synonyms include "applicable" and "pertinent."

Ken Malmin, the dean of Portland Bible College, stated the problem this way: "Since the church has been commissioned by Christ to extend His Kingdom throughout the earth, we are continually in need of evaluating our progress. Part of this evaluation has to focus on the world we are trying to reach. Do we understand where people are? Are we aware of the forces shaping their lives? Are we hindering our mission by being out of date? Are we preaching to kinds of people that do not exist anymore? Are we aiming our influence at a society that has moved out of our sights? Or have we, in our attempts to be relevant, compromised some of the very distinctives we should be confronting the world with?"

SEEKER-SENSITIVE CHURCHES

Several of the current church-growth movements are attempting to deal with this issue of relevance. One prominent movement has been called by some the **seeker-sensitive movement**. It has been labeled "seeker sensitive" because it seeks to adjust some of the more traditional styles, methods, programs of the church, and most particularly the church service itself to make them more relevant or at least more palatable to those unfamiliar with Christianity and its sometimes esoteric "lingo." The thinking is that if we soften those things that seem harsh and confrontational to the average member of society, many people will feel more at ease in a Christian service and will be more open to the Gospel particularly if it is presented in a nonconfrontational way.

Some general characteristics of such seeker-sensitive churches would include a more subdued worship expression, a removal of anything from the service that would require explanation (prophecy, tongues, etc.), shorter services (seventy-five minutes or less), more contemporary music, variety of presentation, shorter sermons, and the elimination of direct altar calls that might unduly embarrass those in attendance.

The idea is to remove any barrier to new people's (particularly non-Christians) coming to and feeling comfortable in the main worship service of the church.

FELT-NEED CHURCHES

Another current expression in the Body of Christ that is dealing with the relevancy issue is the **felt-need movement**. The felt-need movement seeks to analyze where the people are at, in an effort to determine what are their most pressing needs. With that in mind, they seek to structure the programs of the church to minister to those particular needs. This is sometimes referred to as the "audience driven" approach.

Some of the characteristics of a felt-need church would be similar to the seeker-sensitive movement with more of an emphasis on various types of support groups (e.g. victim and abuse groups). The messages in these churches would tend to focus on God's love and His healing grace that is offered to all.

THE MANAGERIAL/MARKETING CHURCHES

Yet another modern attempt at relevance has to do with what might be called the **managerial/marketing movement** in the church. While this is quite different from the seeker-sensitive and felt-need movement, this movement (if it can indeed be called a movement) is characterized by its attempt to utilize modern technologies and modern marketing strategies to grow the church. At times the church has been accused of living in the Dark Ages when it comes to utilizing all that is currently available to it for the purposes of spreading the Gospel.

The idea is to take and use the concepts that have proven effective in the current business world and apply them to the various ministries and programs of the church. This movement would be comfortable using telemarketing strategies, media blitzes (including mass mailings, advertising, and billboards), user-friendly concepts, and any other means to reach the populace.

Often they target a special audience or people group, and they tailor their marketing techniques toward that specific group.

On the Positive Side

The issue of relevance has a *positive* and a *negative* side. On the *positive* side, relevancy means that the church must be willing to change its forms and programs to face the demands of the culture in which it finds itself.

This means utilizing *modern technologies* to fulfill the great commission. This means taking advantage of *management techniques* that are in essence an extension of the biblical principle of stewardship to become more efficient in what we do with the resources that we have. This means addressing the *issues* that are truly facing the people to whom we minister to help them become ambassadors in their day to their generation. This means being willing to evaluate our *styles and methods* of doing things to be sure that we are not offensive to the very people that we are trying to reach.

On the Negative Side

On the *negative* side, however, relevance must never be exalted above truth, and it should never lead us to compromise *the eternal principles of God's Word* to which all people must adapt themselves.

This means that while modern technologies should be utilized, they must not be abused and become substitutes for *personal pastoral ministry.* This means that while we employ managerial methods that will help us to be better stewards of our resources, we must not reduce the church to the level of a human business institution without *reliance on the supernatural.*

This means that while the church and its leaders must be in touch with the needs of the people and concerned about meeting those needs, they must not forget their central need for *a personal relationship with God* and the purpose for which all healing is to take place, and that is to become a disciplined army of God, advancing with the sword of the Spirit to reclaim territory lost to the devil and fulfill God's eternal purpose.

This means that while the church should not be living in the Dark Ages in its "look" and approach to society, lines must be drawn when *the Bible clearly addresses issues* of morality, separation from worldliness, and our position in this world as strangers and pilgrims.

RELEVANCY IN BALANCE

As difficult as it is, we must keep things in *balance.* There is a biblical tension that every church and church leader must find a way to handle. There are at least seven issues that the leaders of today's church must face.

1. The issue of INFLUENCE

Where does faith cease to *influence* culture and the culture begin to *influence* the church (John 17:6-19)? As you study the history of the church in society, a case could be made for the fact that the world exerts more influence on the church than the church does on the world. This has not always been the case. The church of Jesus Christ is to be a prophetic people used of the Lord to lead society. It is to provide a godly vision and, if need be, confront society when it goes astray.

Many church movements in our day are gradually lowering the bar of what it means to be a Christian. Instead of standing up and holding up a standard for society to reach toward, many are redefining historical positions on things such as homosexuality, marriage, and non-Christian religions. The real question is, "Who is leading and who is following?" The church is to be the head and not the tail.

2. The issue of BECOMING ALL THINGS

Where does "*becoming all things*" to culture end and the church's responsibility to provoke people to "*become all things*" in Christ begin (Eph. 4:15; 2 Cor. 12:19)? Sometimes in order to be a friend to those in the world system, the church seems willing to settle for less than the mark of the high calling in Christ Jesus.

At times we want so much to be accepted by the world that we are reluctant to use terms that will alienate the non-Christian. We avoid biblical words such as sin, repentance, adultery, greed, and idolatry. We don't like confronting people with issues like discipleship, lordship, and obedience. Then we wonder why people do not change. We wonder why people fail to go on to a life of separation and holiness to the Lord.

3. The issue of NATURAL ABILITIES

Where does utilizing our *natural abilities* and strengths (i.e. the arm of the flesh) begin to supplant or become an acceptable substitute for true visitation and revival (i.e. the arm of the Spirit—see 1 Cor. 2:1-5)? It is so easy today to produce the sound of revival. It is so easy with modern instruments and synthesizers to produce the sound of worship. It is so easy with our knowledge of video production, drama, choreography, and instrumentation to put together a service that is very pleasing to the eyes of humankind.

It is so easy at times that our instruments can actually worship for us. We can lose the spontaneity of the Spirit-directed service where you don't always know in advance what is going to take place. We have song lists, we have worship rehearsals, and we have everything timed and programmed to the minute. Can the Holy Spirit get in? Where is the prophecy, the exhortation, and the song of the Lord that the early church experienced?

Back in the late sixties during the days of the charismatic renewal I was still in the Lutheran Church. One of the pastors in the Lutheran Church had experienced the baptism of the Spirit, and one of his desires was to free up the liturgy of the church service to include some Holy Spirit activity.

The way in which he accomplished it was to rewrite the order of service and put this adjusted order in the church bulletin. If you looked at the program in the bulletin, you would see at two or three places in the program a line of asterisks across the page. At the end of the program it noted regarding the asterisks that at these times the Holy Spirit was free to move in the service.

I think of that incident with fondness. Here was a pastor struggling with how to give the Holy Spirit liberty in the service and yet at the same time preserve a certain decency and order. We might look at his approach as humorous, yet I wonder if the Holy Spirit can find a place in our charismatic liturgies.

The danger here is that we can become so clever in all of our techniques that we almost eliminate our need for God. Once we take our need for God and dependency on God out of the mix, "God experiences" soon give way to external conformity. When this happens, we lose the power to transmit our faith to the next generation. Our faith has become a formula instead of an experience with God!

4.   The issue of a COMFORTABLE EXPERIENCE

Where does our attempt to make people *comfortable* leave off and our need to challenge our people to become *living sacrifices* and spend themselves and their resources on Christ and His Kingdom begin (Rom. 12:1-2)?

Jesus didn't always try to make people comfortable. He called one woman who was asking for his help a "dog" (Mark 7:27-28). He told one man that if he wanted to have eternal life he would have to sell all that he had and give it to the poor (Mark 10:21). He told another man to leave his father and "let the dead bury the dead" (Matt. 8:22).

Jesus did not try to make people comfortable in their sinful condition. He did confront them at times, He called them up to a higher realm, and He challenged them to repent, take up their cross, and give up all to follow Him.

5. The issue of METHODOLOGY/THEOLOGY

When do techniques, style, and *methodology* replace or minimize truth and *theology* (1 Tim. 3:15)? The Bible teaches that the Word of God is quick and powerful to bring deliverance to our lives. It teaches that the Gospel is the power of God unto salvation. It teaches that God has chosen the foolishness of preaching to save individuals.

Too often pastors and leaders in the church of today have become pollsters and methodologists. We tend to criticize this type of leadership in the political realm, but pastors can easily become guilty of preaching what is popular, what is entertaining, and what the people will enjoy. We take a poll to find what the people want, and then we give them what they want.

Many Christians in the church world of today are biblically illiterate. They do not know the Bible. They do not know the books of the Bible. They do not know anything about the nature of God, man, sin, redemption, and the other principle doctrines of the Bible. They may not even need to bring a Bible to our services, because they will not have to open it.

The admonition of Paul to Timothy is still valid for church leaders of our day.

"Be diligent to present yourself approved to God, a worker who does not need to be ashamed, rightly dividing the word of truth" (2 Tim. 2:15). He further reminds Timothy that "all Scripture is given by inspiration of God, and is profitable for doctrine, for reproof, for correction, for instruction in righteousness, that the man of God may be complete, thoroughly equipped for every good work" (2 Tim. 3:16-17).

6. The issue of NUMERICAL GROWTH

When does a desire for *numerical growth* compromise the necessity of *spiritual growth* (Acts 9:31)? We've already discussed this in the first chapter of this book. So often we can change or soften the Word of God for the sake of getting more people into our churches. The question is, "Are we short-changing those people by not giving them all of the equipment they need to be the best kind of Christian that they can be?"

If our goal is only numbers, we will be tempted to make many compromises to achieve that goal. But if our goal is balanced, we can not only build an expression of the church that is appealing to the lost, but one that also has the favor of God and is growing to a place of spiritual maturity (Acts 2:47).

7. The issue of HISTORICAL CONNECTION

Where does our desire for *cultural relevance* end and our responsibility to those who have died in *the faith* begin (Prov. 22:28; 23:10; Jude 3)? While we must be relevant and have a voice to this present generation, we cannot totally divorce ourselves from the church of the past or we may forsake the ancient landmarks that are to be part of our modern heritage.

If we cannot link ourselves back to the New Testament believers, we could easily culturalize all of our theology and end up with no connection to "the faith...once delivered" (Jude 3).

Paul often mentions the subject of faith, but he also talks about "the faith." He encourages us to be obedient to "the faith" (Rom. 1:5), to stand steadfast in "the faith" (1 Cor. 16:13), to examine ourselves to see if we are indeed in "the faith" (2 Cor. 13:5), and to continue and be established in "the faith" (Col. 1:23; 2:7). We are to keep "the faith" (2 Tim. 4:7) as a stewardship that has been entrusted to us.

Paul also seems to indicate that we can depart from or err from "the faith" (1 Tim. 4:1; 6:10, 21). He refers to those who have denied "the faith" (1 Tim. 5:8). In Paul's mind there existed this body of knowledge and experience that had been handed to him. He was not only to keep it, but he was to faithfully transmit it to the next generation.

Those who have died in "the faith" have handed the baton to the church of the twenty-first century. We have a responsibility to them to faithfully transmit the words of life. It is critical that, while we are speaking in relevant terms to this present generation and culture, the message the martyrs bled for is not lost in the transition.

PLEASING GOD

As we seek to build the church in these days, we need to be most concerned that what we are doing pleases God. Does our message please the Lord? Does our worship touch His heart? Do our programs reflect His agenda for the church? Is the church functioning according to the pattern found in His Word?

If what we are doing pleases God, it will reach man who is made in the image of God. Somehow Jesus was able to live as a God pleaser and experience favor with both God and man. As we focus our attention on pleasing God, we will also find favor and influence in our society.

If a church is to grow and prosper from generation to generation, that church must determine to build to please God not man. This means that we must determine never to accommodate Bible truth just to please men. This means we don't water down the requirements for salvation (Acts 2:38-39). This means we don't hesitate to preach the lordship of Christ. This means that as leaders we don't hide the Cross in our preaching and teaching (Matt. 19:21-22). This also means we do not apologize for the God-ordained forms of worship when they are in keeping with the God-prescribed order.

Pastor Dick Iverson, who led a great church in Portland, Oregon, into many of the principles found in this book in the late sixties and early seventies, shares of a time when he was challenged concerning the loud expressions of Davidic worship in the church. People told him, "If you people wouldn't make so much noise when you worship, people would feel more comfortable in the services." His reply to them was, "If we cease to worship in a way that pleases the Lord, the presence of God that they so enjoy will not be experienced in the services. Obedience to the God-ordained principles of worship is the basis for the awesome experience of God's presence."

BELIEVERS' GATHERINGS

One of the great insights that became so freeing in this area is the revelation that the gathering together of the saints is for the strengthening of the sheep (Heb. 12:25). Too often we feel that the purpose of the service is for evangelism. No! Evangelism is what is supposed to be taking place in the market place throughout the week in the lives of our people. The corporate gathering is for the equipping, encouragement and feeding of the sheep.

Pastors should not feel that they have to aim their services primarily at the unbelievers. If we truly magnify the Lord and build up the church, people will still get saved in that context. The church should be involved in the teaching and establishing of the believers (Matt. 28:19-20). When you produce healthy sheep, they will bring forth the lambs (Gen. 1:11). Most of the services of the church should be believer oriented or the lambs will stay lambs.

This does not mean that we are not sensitive to the unbeliever or the newcomer in our midst. We need to do everything we can to make sure that we are not driving people away or hindering their coming to Jesus by our lack of practical sensitivities. We need to make sure we have good ushers, clear signs, ample parking, and friendly greeters. We need to be people sensitive because people are those to whom we are called.

However, at the same time, the church is first and foremost the house of God, the family of God, the bride of Christ, and its highest call is to please God.

Chapter Eight

THE LOCAL CHURCH

Key #6—If the church is to grow and prosper from generation to generation, that church must place a high level of emphasis on the local church as the instrument that God uses to extend His Kingdom on the earth.

In the New Testament every believer was vitally connected to a specific local church. Those that were added to the Lord were added to the body of believers call the church (Acts 2:41, 47; 5:14). It is in the local church that the people who are coming to the Lord are discipled and become committed, functioning members. It is through the local church that God's purposes are going to be made a reality in any given community.

Many today focus on the universal church and its worldwide expression. That is an important truth that we all must acknowledge. But how does that concept translate into the believer's daily life? How does the believer walk out the injunctions of Jesus to make disciples of all nations? Where does the believer find discipleship, accountability, equipping, ministry expression, and mission fulfillment? It is in the context of the local church not the universal or invisible church.

Many people have had negative experiences on the local-church level and have decided not to be committed members of any local church, choosing rather to focus on the Kingdom of God and the universal expression of the Body of Christ. Jesus indicated that in the local church we would have to deal with offenses (Matt. 18:15-20). But we must deal with them rather than walk away from them, because God is going to use the local church as His instrument to fulfill His intended purpose. He has no other plan. Rather than write the local church off, we should put our hearts into it to make it the best that it can be.

THE WORD *CHURCH* DEFINED

In order for us to understand the true importance of the church we have to understand the meaning and usage of the word *church*. The word *church* comes from the Greek word *ekkesia*. This word in its simplest definition means "the called out ones."

In the secular Greek society the word was used commonly and referred to an assembly of free citizens who were called out from their homes and/or places of business to assemble together to give consideration to matters of public interest.

The word is used this way a couple of times in the New Testament. When Paul and his company had stirred up the local god-makers in Ephesus, the citizens of Ephesus had such an assembly in an attempt to deal with the problem. This assembly is referred to by the word usually translated "church" (Acts 19:32, 29, 41).

THE CHURCH IN THE OLD TESTAMENT

When Jesus referred to a church or assembly, He was not introducing a totally new concept. God had His "called out ones" in the Old Testament as well. In fact Stephen referred to the children of Israel as the "church in the wilderness" (Acts 7:38).

In the Old Testament, Israel was the called-out company of the Lord and is often referred to as the "*Kahal Jehovah*" (i.e. the called and assembled people of God). Whenever the Israelites were summoned from their dwelling and gathered unto the Lord, they were referred to as "the called out ones," the congregation or the assembly (Num. 10:7; 20:10; 1 Kings. 8:14; 1 Chron. 29:20; Ps. 40:9; 107:32; 149:1). It is interesting that when the Septuagint translates the Hebrew term "*Kahal*," it uses the term "*ekklesia*".

Israel's twelve tribes encamped around the tabernacle's four sides according to a careful plan. When the trumpet was blown, they assembled before the door of the tabernacle as the people of God, as the "called out ones," to receive God's instructions, commands, or blessings.

THE CHURCH IN THE NEW TESTAMENT

In the New Testament the word *ekklesia* is used 114 times, and 110 times it definitely refers to the "called out ones" of Jesus Christ. Jesus Himself introduces this usage when He refers to "(His) church" (Matt. 16:18). The personal pronoun "My" differentiates this company from all other groups of people.

This church to which Jesus refers is not just any gathering or assembly; it is "His" gathering and "His" assembly. It includes those who have been called out from their place of habitation in this world, who have separated themselves unto God, and unto the door of the New Testament Tabernacle, Jesus Christ Himself!

His church consists of free citizens of the heavenly community summoned by the trumpet of the Gospel to assemble themselves together for worship, fellowship, and mission fulfillment (Phil. 3:15; 1 Cor. 1:25-26; 2 Pet. 1:10).

Not a Building or House of Worship

It is important for us to understand that the word *church* is never used to refer to a building or a house of worship. In our English usage it is often used of a building, but this usage is foreign to the New Testament concept of the church.

It is unfortunate that the *King James Version* translators have rendered Acts 19:37 as "robbers of churches." The Greek word in this passage is not "*ekklesia*" but the Greek word usually translated "temple." The church consists of the people of God that are built together into a spiritual building for God's habitation (Eph. 2:20-22).

The church meets in a building or house, but it is not a material building itself (Rom. 16:5). The people of God are a *spiritual* house, and if we make the mistake of thinking of the church as a natural building, we will become building worshipers. We will be much like the religious leaders of Jesus' day who admired the stones and materials out of which their natural buildings were constructed (Mark 13:1; Matt. 24:1-2).

The tragedy is that we can have the view that the church is a building and miss the true church. We can put all of our energies into glorifying a natural facility and miss the responsibility that we have before God to give our energies and time to the edification of the people of God who, after all, are the true spiritual house that God is indwelling (Heb. 3:6).

The actual building in which the people of God meet is only an auditorium or "sheep shed." We have to be very careful that we put the emphasis where God does. This mistake could cause us to hold the material building (sheep shed) above the spiritual building (the sheep).

Not a Sect, Denomination, or Organization

It is also important for us to realize that this word *church* in the New Testament is never used to refer to a sect, a denomination, or an organization. In our day we talk of "the church" or "our church" indicating a form of ecclesiastical system, but this concept is also foreign to the New Testament.

The church is "His" church. He is the central authority to whom all New Testament churches must relate. The church on earth is bigger than any one denomination, sect, or organization. By making this mistake we can make God's church narrower than it really is and exclude ourselves from a vital participation with part of Christ's spiritual body.

JESUS ON THE NATURE OF THE CHURCH

Jesus only referred to the church in specific terms on two occasions, and yet in those two places he tells us a great deal about both the universal and the local expressions of the church. In the first instance He spoke prophetically of the broad overreaching expression of the church sometimes referred to as the universal, invisible, or mystical church.

The universal church is that spiritual body of believers from all generations both living and dead who have separated themselves unto God and have aligned themselves with His purposes.

Jesus referred to the overcoming nature of this universal church in Matthew 16:17-19, where we find these words:

Jesus answered and said to him, "Blessed are you, Simon Bar-Jonah, for flesh and blood has not revealed this to you, but My Father who is in heaven. And I also say to you that you are Peter, and on this rock I will build My church, and the gates of Hades shall not prevail against it. And I will give you the keys of the kingdom of heaven, and whatever you bind on earth will be bound in heaven, and whatever you loose on earth will be loosed in heaven."

In this passage Jesus implied a great deal about what the nature of the invisible church was to be. Jesus implied that (1) God Himself is the architect of the church, (2) Jesus Christ is the builder of the church, (3) Jesus Christ is the owner of the church, (4) Jesus Christ commissioned the church, (5) the church is a living and spiritual organization, (6) the church will represent the authority of Christ on earth, (7) the church will be a unified church, and that (8) the church will be a victorious church.

THE LOCAL EXPRESSION OF THE CHURCH

In the only other passage in which Jesus discussed the church, He referred to the local or visible expression of the church. In Matthew 18:15-20 Jesus said:

"Moreover if your brother sins against you, go and tell him his fault between you and him alone. If he hears you, you have gained your brother. But if he will not hear you, take with you one or two more, that "by the mouth of two or three witnesses every word may be established." And if he refuses to hear them, tell it to the church. But if he refuses even to hear the church, let him be to you like a heathen and a tax collector. Assuredly, I say to you, whatever you bind on earth will be bound in heaven, and whatever you loose on earth will be loosed in heaven. Again I say to you that if two of you agree on earth concerning anything that they ask, it will be done for them of My Father in heaven. For where two or three are gathered together in My name, I am there in the midst of them."

The local church can be defined as that local expression of believers who gather together regularly. It involves a specific group of people in given localities that are marked out by confession of faith, discipline of life, obedience in baptism, gathered to the person of Jesus Christ, having gifted ministries, and keeping the memorial of the Lord. They are always spoken of as complete units within themselves, which may voluntarily cooperate and fellowship with other local churches.

The local church is the emphasis of the New Testament. Out of all of the references to the church in the Bible, nearly 90 percent refer to the local, tangible expression. It is the focus because it is in the local congregation of the saints that the people of God will walk out the admonitions of the Scriptures concerning our relationship to one another and our ministry to the world.

Jesus tells us much about the local church in Matthew 18. Some of the truths and implications that we can extract from Jesus' words include the following:

1. The local church is composed of brothers and sisters (vs. 15)

In other words the local church is meant to be a family setting. It is a place where people are related to one another by Christ's redemptive blood the same way natural brothers and sisters are related through a natural bloodline. The local church in this sense is to be a place of close relationship and belonging. Just as every single person should be rightly related to a natural family, every true believer should be rightly related to a specific spiritual family.

2. The local church is not perfect

When Jesus talks of the local church, He talks about it in the context of conflict. There is no such thing as a perfect church. Some people refuse to commit themselves to a local church because they see problems and potential conflicts. Just as the members in the natural family, members of the local church will have conflicts. In fact, there will be difficulties to work through until Jesus comes.

However, if we are to succeed as the church we must be committed to each other on our imperfect state and to the process of conflict resolution. The solution to our problems or conflicts is not to write the church off but to do everything in our power to make it better, because it is God's instrument on the earth to accomplish His purpose on the local level. God has provided the process whereby conflicts can be resolved and the local church can be unified.

3. The local church is a place of discipline

The local church is not a loosely-knit group having no responsibility or accountability to one another. It is a place where the individual members get involved in each other's lives. It is a place where sin is confronted and discipline is administered. It is a place where believers are matured and difficulties are addressed. Many Christians have no such accountability in their lives because they are not submitted or committed to a local church.

4. The local church is a defined body of believers

In order for Jesus to make the statements He did regarding the local church, it is clear that the local church is a place where you are known to be a part or not to be a part. Jesus indicated that the local church is a place from which you can be expelled. You are either a part of a local church or you are not part of a local church.

Actually the whole concept of a believer's enjoying the benefits of salvation without being a part of a local assembly of believers is foreign to the New Testament. Usually when a known believer was not a part of the local assembly, it was because they were under discipline from the local church.

5. The local church is a channel of God's authority

The same power to bind and loose that was given to the universal church in Matthew 16 is given to the local church in Matthew 18. What Jesus is actually saying is that the authority of God (heaven) is invested into the local church. In other words the local church is a place where God places His authority, and He supports the official actions of the church, especially in the case of discipline. To be disciplined by the church is to be disciplined by Christ.

6. The local church is to be a place of unity and agreement

Jesus puts such a high emphasis on conflict resolution because the unity of the local church is so critical to its fulfillment of the divine commission.

The church's power is dependent on its unity. Where there is unity and harmony among the members, the power and presence of God is released in the midst of it.

7. The local church is to be a place of fellowship in faith and prayer

Jesus seems to indicate that the church will be a gathering place where His people come together to approach God as one body. While every true believer is to have a personal relationship with the Lord, every true believer also should be a part of a corporate body of believers where they assemble together.

In this assembling together there is a corporate function, a corporate asking, and a corporate expectation for God to act.

8. The local church is a place where Christ promises to dwell

While we know that God is omnipresent and that there is no way we can ever escape His watchful eye (Ps. 139:7-9), the Bible also seems to indicate that God does at times manifest a localized sense of His presence and power. Jesus indicates that this localized manifestation can be expected as the local church gathers together in His name. This is not to imply that the believers cannot feel God in the comforts of their own homes. However, there is a much greater power of His presence manifest as the people of God gather together corporately.

9. The local church is a gathering identified with the name of Christ

The local church is to bear the name of Christ in its community. It is to be His representative. It carries the authority of His name and should be the vehicle through which Christ touches the region in which it finds itself. The local church and its members are to be the expression of Christ to its community and provide for that community what Christ Himself provided for those with whom He came into contact.

10. One person cannot make up a local church

The very word *church* in the New Testament implies that there are many who made up the church. It is a gathering of those who have been called out and separated unto the Lord.

Jesus used the expression "two or three gathered together." Some have taken this to imply that all it takes for a genuine local church to exist is for me, my family, and a couple of others to gather together in a living room and read the Bible and pray together. Jesus' words in Matthew 18 imply much more about this assembly than that. There are many ingredients that make up the local church, and all need to be present.

11. The local church is to be a place of order

The local church is not a loosely-knit group of people with no formal structure. Jesus implied that there is government, process, a plan, and a strategy for implementation. Paul told the Colossian believers that when he looked at their local assembly, he admired their order (Col. 3:5). He told the Corinthians that they should do everything decently and in order (1 Cor. 14:40). The local church is not a place were each member does whatever he or she "feels led" to do. They can do that in their homes. When the church comes together, it to be an orderly expression where all can be edified.

12. Until the church is completed, there is going to be a great need for love, patience, and a lot of forgiveness

In the context of the local church Jesus talks about believers offending believers. Of course, Peter picked up on it right away in the following verses when he asked a perfectly legitimate question, "Lord how often shall my brother sin against me, and I forgive him? Up to seven times?" (Matt. 18:21).

Peter thought he was being generous. But Jesus, wanting to make the point to Peter, responded, "I do not say to you, up to seven times, but up to seventy times seven" (vs. 22).

It is amazing how many people will leave their local church offended over the smallest of issues. Because there are so many local-church options, people begin to feel that the local church must meet all of their personal needs, and if the church does not do it just right, they will go somewhere else. It is not difficult to see why many local churches never come to a place of strength.

Jesus injected the dynamics of love, patience, and forgiveness into the context of the local church so that it would have the tools necessary to walk through the difficulties of life and maintain covenant relationship for the sake of a higher purpose. Just like the marriage relationship that is based on covenant, the local church is based on covenant. When we think in terms of the local church in the book of Acts, the believers had no options. They had to work out their difficulties because there was no other local church to attend.

When a young couple shares their marriage vows, it is with the understanding that there will be some challenges in the unforeseen future. For this reason they make vows regarding sickness verses health, riches verses poverty, and better times verses worse times. What they are in essence saying is, "Whatever life throws at us, we are going to walk through it together." Members of the local church need to be aware that problems will arise, other people will offend us, we will not agree with everything that we hear and see, but we are committed to the process and to our future together.

Does this mean that it is never appropriate to get a divorce or leave a local assembly? That is not what I am saying. I am saying that we must do everything in our power to make the relationship work. We cannot control what others do, but we can control what we choose to do. Our highest priority should be to work through rather than run from our difficulties. Since there is no such thing as a perfect local church, a believer who runs from these situations will be on the run forever.

It is amazing that Jesus says so much in such a short passage. Jesus is not only interested in our becoming identified with the Body of Christ worldwide, but He is also very much interested in our becoming identified with its local expression for our own protection, well-being, and growth.

THE CHURCH UNFOLDS

In Jesus' teaching we have the foundation on which the New Testament church is built. On the Day of Pentecost that church was inaugurated. In the years that followed, the church and man's concept of the church grew and matured as the early leaders faced problems, crises, and opposition.

As the church developed, the local expression of the church became more easily definable. This church can be seen in direct relation to what Jesus taught about the church. In the book of Acts we see the local church as:

- A congregation or assembly of people in a given locality (Acts 8:1)
- An assembly of believers in Christ (Acts 5:14)
- A place of teaching and discipline (Acts 11:26)
- A complete unit in itself with corporate authority (Acts 15:22)
- Built by Christ Himself (Acts 2:47)
- Part of Christ Himself (Acts 5:14)
- A place where the Lord, not man, adds people (Acts 5:13)
- Disciplined by Christ Himself (Acts 5:5)
- Structured, having individuals ordained in positions of authority to exercise leadership, discipline, and oversight (Acts 14:23; 20:17-28)
- A place of manifold ministry (Acts 13:1; 15:4)
- Joined in voluntary fellowship with other local churches (Acts 15:3-4)
- A place established in the faith (Acts 16:5)
- A place from which ministry was sent out (Acts 13:1-4)

The whole thrust of the New Testament is the local church. Each book of the New Testament demonstrates how God uses the local church to bring His people to maturity and completion. Nowhere in the New Testament do we have an alternative plan suggested. God wants us to emphasize what He emphasizes and get excited about what He is excited about.

THE BELIEVER AND THE LOCAL CHURCH

Every believer should be rightly related to the Lord and at the same time rightly related to a local church. Everyone who considers himself part of the invisible or universal church should also demonstrate that fact by being a committed part of the visible or local expression of the church. Every believer should be able to answer these questions as it pertains to his or her life in the Lord.

- Who is over me in the Lord (Heb. 13:17)?
- When I was added to the Lord, in what way was I added to the church (Acts 2:41, 47)?

- When I gather together with the disciples, with whom do I gather (Acts 14:27; 1 Cor. 5:4)?
- With whom am I allowing God to perfectly join me (1 Cor. 1:10; Eph. 4:16)?

All believers should be committed members of a local body of believers where they can fulfill their obligations to other believers on an individual as well as on the corporate level.

On the individual level there are many responsibilities that Christians have to one another. A commitment to a local church makes it possible for the believer to fulfill these responsibilities. As Christians we are to:

- Love one another (1 Pet. 1:22)
- Comfort one another (1 Thess. 4:18)
- Exhort one another (Heb. 10:25)
- Build up one another (Rom. 14:19)
- Admonish one another (Col. 3:16)
- Serve one another (1 Pet. 4:10)
- Forgive one another (Eph. 4:32)
- Submit to one another (Eph. 5:21)
- Bear one another's burdens (Gal. 6:2)

Where is the context in which we do these basic Christian duties to one another? It should be in relationship to those with whom we are specifically joined in our local church.

In addition to this, there is a commitment that God wants us to express on a corporate level. What does it mean to be committed to a specific local church? When believers are committed to a local assembly, it means:

- They consider themselves to be planted by God (Ps. 68:1-6).
- They are willing to come under the authority/leadership of that church (Heb. 13:7, 17, 24).
- They are willing to give their time and energy to that local church.

- They are willing to gather when the local body gathers.
- They are willing to give their financial support to their local church.
- They are willing to bear the burdens of the house and be committed to its vision.

The local church is the means by which the purposes of God will become a reality (Eph. 4:1-16). There are two aspects of truth relative to the church. There is the universal church that focuses on our relationship to the Lord. The key to the church being the church in the universal sense is for every believer to be in harmony with the Lord of the church.

Then there is the local church, which focuses on our relationship to our brothers and sisters in Christ. The key to the church being the church in the local sense is for believers to be in harmony with other believers.

These two aspects of the church represent the two planks of the cross. The cross is the key to both the universal and the local church. The vertical plank represents our Godward relationship. The horizontal plank represents our manward relationships. Jesus died both to reconcile man to God and to bring harmony and peace between all people.

Chapter Nine

MINISTERING
TO ALL LEVELS

KEY #7—*If a church is to grow and prosper from generation to generation, that church must determine to build up the saints on all levels.*

The church of Jesus Christ is called to be multigenerational in nature. That means that when it comes to the ministry and function of the church, every person, no matter what their age, should find strengthening, equipping, challenge, and ministry in the context of the local church.

Too often the program of the church is aimed at a certain age group. Sometimes the attitude of those in a particular church can hinder certain age groups from coming to the Lord and finding a sense of direction and purpose.

RELATING TO THE CHILDREN

The disciples of Jesus had an attitude that Jesus found repugnant. The disciples seemed to have more time for adults than they had for children. In fact, when mothers were bringing their children to Jesus, the disciples actually rebuked these mothers, implying that Jesus had no time for children

(Mark 10:13-16). This is a scene that is almost unthinkable. How could the disciples be so insensitive?

I was raised in a local church that seemed to have the attitude of the disciples. They didn't rebuke mothers and their children in such an obvious way. However, in the way that they functioned, the message still came across. While children had their little classes to keep them busy while the parents were meeting, there was no real effort made to involve children in the program of the church. There was even less of an effort given to the youth of the church.

As a result, as soon as the children were "of age," they walked away from the church, leaving the church to their parents. As I have watched that church for the last thirty years, I have seen the church shrink in size and increase in the age of its membership to the point that a "young person" in the church now is anyone under the age of fifty!

That church, which was once quite large, is now very small. It is also very weak because no one has any energy to do anything. I hate to say it, but that church is a few years away from totally dying off. When funeral services outnumber any other of the special services of the church, you know that the church is in trouble.

This attitude, however, is not just reflected in some of the more historic churches, it can also be reflected in the contemporary churches of our day. I hear this often when discussing such things as cell groups. "What do you do with the children during the meeting?" The answer usually involves some form of babysitting in another room or eliminating children from the meetings altogether.

Actually our entire society can lend itself to this kind of thinking. Children are often seen as being in the way of career development and other of life's pursuits. Babysitting and daycare have become big business. Many children live lives of daycare or school during the day and babysitter at night while the parents work and play.

This attitude can be seen in the terminology that is often used to describe children behind their backs and to their faces. Teenagers can face the same sense of neglect or intolerance when the word "teenager" is used in a derogatory way. When someone says, "I have three teenagers," they are to be pitied or prayed for. The impression is that they are a problem, a challenge, and an irritation to the adults.

Unfortunately, many local churches today reflect the same set of priorities found in the disciples. Everything in the church caters to the adult population or could we say "the tithers."

Children's programs do exist in most of these churches, but they are in many cases nothing more than a legitimate way to get the kids out of the parents' hair so that they can enjoy the service. Children are hard to deal with in an adult-orientated service so we take them to another room for something that will hold their attention.

In some of the more seeker-sensitive approaches, the main service for the church is actually designed for adults only. In some of the more extreme cases, children under a certain age are not even allowed in the main service. I know of one church where a person is not welcomed into the main service of the church until they reach high-school graduation. In fact, in one case, parents who were attempting to take their child into the main service of a particular church were actually stopped by ushers and prohibited from doing so.

Is it any wonder why children do not make an easy transition into the "adult world" of the church? Is it any wonder why so many of them do not "find their place" and end up walking away from the church in or immediately following their teen years?

CHILDREN'S ACTIVITIES

This wrong priority is also seen in the activities that are prescribed for the children while they are out of the service. Too often the focus of these programs is on entertaining the children for an hour or two. The measure of success is that there were no riots and everyone had a good time. Little effort is made in many programs to teach the Word of God to them at their level. Little effort is made to include children in active ministry and ministry projects.

Youth programs can be just as empty of content. The focus of many youth groups is keeping the youth occupied, off the streets, out of trouble, and entertained. The youth activities of many church groups center on social events, games, outings, and summer camps. There is often very little effort made to teach doctrine, equip them for ministry, and challenge them to become contributing members of the church.

I remember hearing of one couple being asked by an elder board to work with the teenagers of the church. However, before the elders made a final decision, they wanted to hear what the vision of this couple was for the youth and their ministry to them. The couple shared how they had a vision to see the youth discipled, taught, equipped, and released to function in the life flow of the church and evangelism.

One of the board members was shocked at this vision. This was not the definition of youth ministry with which he was familiar. He was accustomed to youth leaders who planned socials and other activities for the youth. Finally he blurted out while this couple was sharing, "It sounds to me like what you want to do is to pastor them!" To this board member that was a novel thought but he wasn't sure how he felt about it.

I heard another story from a person who was an elder of a church whose specific charge as an elder was to serve as "the children's pastor." He would often attend pastors' and leadership conferences with the other elders and leaders of the church. His testimony was that whenever he would be engaged in a conversion with another pastor or leader, everything would be fine until they asked the question, "What do you do in relation to the church?"

The answer to this question would prove to be fatal to the conversation. As soon as he would say, "I am over the children's ministry in our church," the conversation would be over. The person who was conversing with him would turn to another minister and initiate dialogue or he would ease himself out of the conversation quickly and just walk away.

Praise God not every church has this attitude. Many have the attitude of Jesus that suggests that children are extremely important and that they are a priority for Him in the extending of His kingdom. Many have God's value system when it comes to children.

GOD'S VALUE SYSTEM

What is God's value system as it relates to children? What is a child worth? What is the value of a child?

This is so important because we tend to treat things that we truly value in a special way. If we value an automobile, we take extra good care of it. If we value an heirloom, we may give it a special place of honor or protection. Unless we see things from God's perspective, it will be very easy for us to give major attention to minor things.

I daresay that a child is the most valuable thing in the universe. Children are the only eternal things that have been placed as a stewardship into our hands. All of our possessions will one day be destroyed, but our children will live forever in heaven or hell. They are eternal entities.

Our children are also the future of the church. It has been said that any local church or even the church worldwide is only ever one generation away from extinction. If we do not pass on our experience of Jesus and transmit our faith to the next generation, the church will cease to exist.

The Bible makes it clear that children are the heritage of the Lord (Ps. 127:3-5). They are a reward and are to be treated like arrows in the hands of a skillful hunter. As such those arrows are to be shaped, sharpened, aimed, and shot into a place of destiny where they will end up in "the gates" of the city. They will end up in the places of authority preparing the next generation of warriors.

The Bible also teaches that every member of the Body of Christ has significance and is needed by every other member of the body. This includes children as well as adults. Children have something to contribute now. They are not just in a spiritual "holding pattern" until they finally arrive at a place of usefulness.

As a pastor I have worked with so many adults that are so set in their ways and so resistant to change that it is refreshing to work with the younger members of the Body of Christ who are so easily shaped, molded, and adjusted. Statistics seem to bear out that about 75 percent of people who receive Christ do so before the age of twenty. If that is true, wouldn't it make sense to make those age groups a priority?

How you treat children, youth, and their associated ministries in your church reflects the value that you place on them. Do these ministries get a fair portion of the ministry budget? Do they get the cream of the ministry staff? Is working with the children considered to be a high and noble calling? Are those who work in children and youth ministry treated with honor in the assembly?

All of these things indicate the value that we place on children. All of these things speak loud and clear about our priorities.

I so appreciate the attitude and spirit of Dick Iverson and his wife, Edie, who served as my pastors for many years. It was their ministry philosophy to place the strongest, most able-bodied ministers over the children and the youth. They made sure that teachers were well trained, curriculums were well chosen, and that the facilities related to these ministries were seen as prime spaces. They also made sure that children were provided with places of service and given direction for ministry opportunities.

When the young people in the church are treated with respect, trained for the future, and included in the ministry of the church, they grow up and naturally become active, contributing members. When the day comes for them to lead the church, they are equipped and ready. On the other hand, where youth ministries have been babysitting ministries, the young people still grow up, but when they do, they have no regard for the church or what the church does.

RELATING TO THE "SENIOR SAINTS"

Thankfully, this negative treatment of the young is not a problem that is shared by every local church. There are many churches that have made children's and youth ministry keystones in the life and development of their church. As a result there are many children, youth, college age, and young married couples in those churches who are excited about God and walking in His purpose.

At times these youth-orientated churches can face another kind of challenge. Some of these churches can be so youth orientated that there is no respect for or attempt to touch the older generation. The older ones are seen as cranky, slow to change, and critical of anything that is new or outside of their past experience.

Older people in many churches can get the feeling that the church is for the young people. They see the structure and style of things in the church as geared for the young people. When they voice complaints about the volume of the music, the length of time standing in the service, all of the new songs, or their own age-related needs, they are often passed off as "over the hill" and "out of touch" with what God is doing today. They can easily feel that their concerns are not being taken seriously because it is difficult for them to keep pace with the youth of the house.

The cry of many people of age is that of David. David was a man who had accomplished much for the Lord in his youth. As he got older, it was more difficult for him to contribute in the same way to the program of God. He still had a heart after God, but the body didn't always cooperate with what the heart desired to do. David pleaded, "Do not cast me off in the time of old age; do not forsake me when my strength fails" (Ps. 71:9).

One of the tendencies in society that must be resisted in the church is the disregard or neglect of older people. Rest homes are full of people who have been cast aside. As a result many people fear old age. People do everything they can to push signs of age further and further into the future. This reality has translated into a multibillion-dollar industry including cosmetic surgery, creams, potions, and hair formulas.

Biblically speaking, old age is to be seen as the reward of living a righteous life (Deut. 5:33; 11:21; Prov. 10:27; 3:2). It should be a time to enjoy the fruit of years of godly labor (Isa. 65:22). But it is also to be a time of continued fruit bearing (Ps. 92:14).

God instructed His people to as to how to treat those who were advancing in years. People of age were to be treated with dignity and respect. White hair was not something to be hidden but to be considered a crown (Prov. 16:31) and a thing of beauty (Prov. 20:29). In addition God gave special promises to those who are old that He would be with them through it all (Isa. 46:4).

If that is the attitude of God (and it is), it should also be the attitude of the church. Members of the early church were instructed to receive teaching and practical insights from the older members of the church (Titus 2:2-5). Older people exist in the church to be functioning members. They are to be sources of wisdom and counsel (Ezek. 7:26; 1 Kings. 12:6-8), they are to assist in guiding the younger generation into the purposes of God, and they are to give stability to what is happening in the present (Deut. 32:7).

The attitudes of the younger members of the church will either make this a reality or not. The young are instructed to give honor and respect to the older ones (Lev. 19:32). They should seek out and listen to their counsel (Prov. 1:8). They should follow the faith of those who have gone before (Heb. 13:7).

YOUNG AND OLD TOGETHER

Times of restoration and blessing should be characterized by the flowing together of both the old and the young. Jeremiah prophesied of days of restoration when both young men and old men would dance together (Jer. 31:13). Joel prophesied that when God poured out His Spirit on His people, young men would see visions, and old men would dream dreams (Acts 2:17; Joel 2:28). The house of God is a place for all ages.

But how is this reflected in the program of the church? Are there ways in which the older saints can be more fully integrated with the younger ones? So often all of these groups of people are ministered to in isolation from each other. The young have strength. The old, hopefully, have some wisdom. Can these two be blended together for the optimum result?

I am not saying that there should not be separate programs for the various age groups within the church. But I am saying that the ages do not need to be separated at all times. God is calling for creativity on the part of his leaders in these days, that as we build the church, we can utilize the full potentiality of every member that God has placed in His church.

CONCLUSION

If a church is to grow and prosper from generation to generation, that church must determine to build up the saints on all levels. The babies need milk, grounding in the first principles, and foundational teaching. The young children need to be built up and given responsibilities. The young need meat (Heb. 5:12-14). The older ones need to be valued, respected, and utilized.

Chapter Ten

STRENGTHENING
THE FAMILY

KEY #8—*If a church is to grow and prosper from generation to generation, that church must determine to strengthen all of the families of the church.*

E ven though the traditional definition of the family is being challenged in our society today, the nuclear family is still the basic unit of society. The family is to society what the atom is to the universe. It is the cornerstone on which everything is built. Even though many world and national leaders do not like to admit it, the history of civilization has proven that any society that allows the family unit to collapse will itself eventually fail.

Gibbon, in his classic work, *The Decline and Fall of the Roman Empire*, lists five main reasons why Rome fell. The first reason that he gives is the undermining of the dignity and sanctity of the home.

It is no different in the church. The church is no stronger than its individual families. If the families are weak, the church will be weak. If the families are strong, the church will be strong and flourishing as well. When God restores the home, He gets the church as well.

For this reason pastors and church leaders must put a high priority on bringing order to the families of the assembly. In addition, the church itself must be family-friendly so that the purposes of the church and the purposes of the family are not conflicting in any way.

Today there is an all-out attack on the family. People are coming into the church broken, abused, abandoned, and fragmented. Parents are having trouble with their children. Children are having trouble with their parents. Relationships between husbands and wives reflect an all-time low.

There is no point in working on restoring the church if we are not working just as hard to restore the families represented in the church. The family is still the basic unit of society, and the church must bring solutions to the individual families and indeed to society itself.

Revival and spiritual encounters are not the only answer for the family. If we are not careful, we will rely too heavily on great services, anointed speakers, and prophetic encounters to solve every problem. The truth is, if a man does not know how to be a good husband and father, if he has never seen a biblical model of Christian manhood, or if he has never learned the "how-tos" of parenting, all of the power encounters in the world will not make him a great father or husband.

When people drive home from our church services where they have met with God, they still go home to live the rest of the week in right or wrong relationship to each other. If families are going to be strengthened and we are going to see change in the life of the church, practical tools must be put into the hands of every man, woman, and child.

THE FAMILY IN GOD'S PURPOSE

When God established the family, He established it as a vehicle or instrument of His eternal purpose. God established the family as a context in which man would realize the eternal purposes of divine image and dominion for which he was created (Gen. 1:26-28). The family, therefore, is a God-ordained context for the establishment and development of:

- God-centered relationships and fellowship
- God-like character
- God-ordained ministry and function

- Natural and spiritual reproduction
- Natural and spiritual dominion

It is in the family that the true principles of relationship to God and to man are laid down. It is in the family that true God-like character will be produced (2 Tim. 1:5). It is in the family that all ministry and function will be tested and proven (1 Tim. 3:4-5; 5:4; Titus 2:5). It is through the ministry of the family that the family of God will be enlarged.

A good biblical definition of the family is given in a book that was authored by a team of which I was a part titled *The Restoration of the Family*. This definition reads, "The family is the God-ordained basic unit of society having parental headship and discipline which is established for the purpose of enjoying a common life together through working, caring, sharing, serving and ministering to God, to others and to itself."

THE FALL OF THE FAMILY

This definition reflects God's original purpose for the family. It reflects God's ideal. Yet we know that the introduction of sin in the Garden of Eden altered the family significantly and made it difficult for it to fulfill its God-ordained purpose.

When Adam and Eve fell into sin, the first family lost God's image. Man and woman who had been in perfect harmony with the ways of God crossed God's will and thus separated themselves from God. When Adam fell, man became a sinner (Ps. 51:1), his mind became defiled (Titus 1:15; Col. 1:21; Rom. 8:5-8), he became a slave to sin (Rom. 6:17), he became an enemy of God (James 4:4), and he began to walk in a way that leads to death (2 Thess. 1:6-10).

This fall had a direct bearing on the family's ability to fulfill its purpose because it introduced some factors that the family did not previously have to face. It introduced disrespect for and rebellion against authority (Gen. 9:20-27). It introduced hatred and envy among family members (Gen. 4:1-8). It introduced improper and unprincipled relationships in marriage (Gen. 4:19; 6:1-7). It introduced self-centeredness and dishonesty in marriage (Gen. 12:10-20). It introduced a lack of respect and love for children (Gen. 19:18).

In addition, it introduced the issues of husbands and wives having divided interests (Gen. 25:5-17, 28), parents favoring one child over another (Gen. 25:28), and a lack of proper parental discipline of children (I Sam. 3:11-14).

The family, which began as God's vehicle for the development of relationship, character, ministry, and fruitfulness in man was rendered ineffective by the introduction of sin.

GOD'S ANSWER

God's answer to the fall of the family is Calvary. When Christ hung on the cross, he was not only reconciling man to God, He was making it possible for the family to be restored to God's original purpose. What a thrill it must have been in the early church to see entire families come to Christ and find new life in Jesus (Acts 10:1-2, 44-48; 16:14-15; 16:31-34).

The Family as a Miniature Church

In Christ, God wants the family to be like a miniature church. There are many things that the local church and the natural family have in common.

1. Both the local church and the family are to be instruments of God's eternal purpose.
2. Both the local church and the family have similar members and similar relationships (fathers, mothers, sisters, and brothers).
3. Both the local church and the family have defined memberships.
4. Both the local church and the family have a plural leadership team.
5. Both the local church and the family are autonomous social units (i.e. self-governing, self-supporting, self-propagating).
6. Both the local church and the family are to be places of covering and protection.
7. Both the local church and the family provide a context for discipline, training, and instruction.
8. Both the local church and the family are to be centers of spiritual life including worship, prayer, fellowship, and ministry in the Word of God.

9. Both the local church and the family are to be places of love and commitment.

10. Both the local church and the family are to be evangelistic and missionary in focus.

THE CHURCH AND THE HOME ARE NOT IN COMPETITION

It is clear that the church and the home are not in competition. In fact, they are to complement each other in fulfilling their destiny as instruments of God's eternal purpose in the earth.

Because this is not fully understood by everyone at all times, there are occasions when some churches are not necessarily "family-friendly" in their programs and schedule. At the same time, there are occasions when parents do not make the church the kind of priority that it needs to be in relationship to their family.

God wants a balance. God wants both the church and the home to be strong and to support each other. He wants the strength of the home to support the work of the church, and He wants the strength of the church to support the home.

THE FAMILY-FRIENDLY CHURCH

If this is going to happen, the members of the family must fully cooperate with God's plan for the church. Children should be raised with concepts of church attendance, tithing, volunteer service, responsiveness to what is being preached, and submission to local church leadership.

At the same time each local church should carefully examine itself to see if it is truly family-friendly. Are we assisting parents and family members in establishing the divine principles of family life in the home? Are we standing alongside of God's intended purpose in the family, or are we standing in the way?

There are at least four things that a local church can do to make sure it is family-friendly.

1. The church needs to examine its schedule to be sure that it is not putting unrealistic demands on its membership, particularly its core.

Without even thinking about it, it is so easy to schedule some kind of church activity on every night of the week. Especially as the church increases in size, the church can become a veritable beehive of activity. When you couple this with the fact that most churches have a core group of people who do almost everything in the church, it is not difficult for some families to have meetings, services, or some other activity nearly every night of the week for at least one of the family members.

The pastor or pastors of the church can find it especially difficult to find a night to really have quality family time. It is not hard to see why many children of pastors feel cheated by or jealous of the church.

One minor solution that we found over the years in our local church was to schedule a family night where no group in the church was allowed to schedule a meeting or gathering unless it was designed for the entire family. It occurred every Monday night, and the families in the church were encouraged to honor it with a real sense of purpose and diligence.

We cannot preach family values and then not give people time to work them out in their experience.

2. The church needs to publicly address issues related to the family in its public teaching and preaching.

Most people have not had the luxury of good teaching and good role models in the realm of parenting. In fact, most people get more hands-on instruction when they purchase a pet in the pet store than mothers and fathers get when they have children.

In addition, we cannot direct people to the pediatricians and child-rearing authorities of this world for that kind of help. Don't get me wrong. There is much information about the care of the physical body that we can utilize from these sources. But when it comes to raising children in the ways of the Lord, these experts are not going to be a lot of help.

Because of this, the church must step up and equip parents. While this includes providing classes, counseling, and other support for family members, it also includes using precious Sunday-morning service time to instill godly values and give practical instruction.

Classes in and of themselves have minimal impact. The problem is that the parents who need the classes the least (i.e. those that already care a great deal about their parenting skills) are the ones who sign up for the classes. Those parents who really need the classes have not made the family a priority in their life, and they will not attend the classes provided. Teachers of such classes often find themselves "preaching to the choir."

Pastors must therefore use the main service of the church to motivate and equip parents in these areas. Teachers of children and youth ministers must also reinforce family values in the programs and the teaching that they offer.

3. The church needs to provide activities that help men, women, and children to discover their God-given roles in respect to one another.

At times it is helpful to provide activities that minister to specific groups and specific family-related needs. Such activities might include men's meetings where men can be taught their responsibility before God and how to be good fathers and husbands. It might involve women's meetings where the women can discover their role and function as it relates to being good wives and mothers.

Other activities that reinforce family and family values in our day might include marriage seminars, childrearing classes relating to different age groups, specific ministry to single parents, blended families, and those recovering from a divorce.

Actually, all of the youth and singles ministries of the church should also focus on godly principles of dating, courtship, and marriage. Singles need to know how to find a spouse in our culture, how to manage money, and how to prepare for the future.

All of these things can assist people in practical areas so that they can be strong for the Lord and a living testimony to those outside of the church. Our people themselves should be able to provide an answer to the tremendous need in our world today.

4. The church needs to be sensitive to making the church programs family oriented not always by dividing but rather by seeking how to integrate groups of people.

All of the departments of the church need to cooperate with the vision to see the family whole and functioning with God-ordained purpose. That means that youth, children, young-adult, and senior-saint leaders alike must be looking for creative ways of bringing families together. This does not mean that every activity must be a family activity. But it does mean that at times we do things that reinforce the church's vision to see members of the family brought closer together.

THE MINISTRY OF THE FAMILY

When the family is in divine order fully functioning the way God intended, it can be a tremendous support to the church and its ministries. The home can actually become a ministry center where the vision of the church is carried out.

So much is said in the New Testament about the homes of believers. Christians were expected through the ministry of hospitality to utilize their homes for the furtherance of the Gospel. Each home represented in the church can be a lighthouse to radiate the message of the Kingdom of God in its particular neighborhood.

In the New Testament, the home was a place of refreshment (Acts 10:6), a place where believers gathered (Acts 12:12), a place of teaching and preaching (Acts 5:2; 20:20), and a place where churches were started (Acts 18:7, 11).

God wants every home to be a place where the principles of the Kingdom of God are lived out. Each home should be a showcase for Christian living. In this way our homes will become a pattern of good works that will attract the lost (Titus 2:7-8), a testimony to those who are outside of the church (2 Cor. 8:21; 1 Tim. 3:7), a place where people will come for answers (2 Pet. 3:15-16), and a true manifestation of the wisdom of God (Col. 4:5; Eph. 3:10; James 3:13).

God wants every home to be a place from which we can reach into our neighborhoods. He wants every home to be stretching out and reaching out to the poor and needy. As such, our homes will actually become the greatest tools for evangelism that we can find in the church. People want a Christianity that works. If it is working on the home front, it has an attraction to the world that nothing else has.

SUMMARY

If a church is to grow and prosper from generation to generation, that church must determine to strengthen all of the families of the church. The church and the family are on the same team to see Christ's Kingdom come and His will be done on earth. The family that fosters a strong love for and committed relationship to the church in its daily practice will be much the stronger for it. The church that focuses on strengthening the family will also benefit greatly.

Furthermore, as we all put forth effort to do what is best for the home and the church, we will ensure that our local church is not just effective in the present tense but will continue to be effective long into the future to the many generations that will follow.

Chapter Eleven

RELEASING GIFTS
AND MINISTRIES

KEY #9—If a church is to grow and prosper from generation to generation, that church must determine to develop and release the gifts and ministries of its membership.

The church must be a place where people can get a vision for their lives and discover the purpose for which they were created. Not only must they receive this vision, but they must also be developed, mentored, and given opportunities for the release of these gifts and ministries.

Part of this process involves making people aware of God's purpose in their lives. Another part is to help define spiritual gifts and biblical ministries so that people can measure themselves accordingly.

The church of today needs the supernatural element embodied in the gifts of the Spirit. The church needs the word of wisdom, the word of knowledge, healing, miracles, prophecy, and the other gifts if it is going to do the works of Christ on the earth. The church needs all of the ministries of Christ functioning in our day if the church is going to complete the ministry of Christ. The church needs apostles, prophets, evangelists, pastors, teachers, showerers of mercy, healers, intercessors, encouragers, and givers.

THE CHURCH AS THE BODY OF CHRIST

It is clear from the New Testament that if the commission that Christ gave to the church is to be fulfilled, the church must not only preach the doctrine of the church as the Body of Christ, but it must see the Body of Christ fully released to function. We must be clear in our day that the work that Christ began two thousand years ago will be completed by His church or His Body. Christ's Body is not merely composed of the leadership of the church but includes every single member of the church. Every single member of the church must be activated toward the goal of commission fulfillment.

THE INITIATION OF THE BODY OF CHRIST

When Christ ascended into heaven, He ascended to become the Head of the church, which is His Body (Col. 1:19). After His resurrection from the dead He ascended to the Father having completed His assignment. In doing so He received from the Father the promise of the Holy Spirit and in turn poured out that Spirit upon the waiting disciples (Acts 2:1-4; 33). When He did this, He gave of the grace and gifts that were in Him to those who would make up His Body (Eph. 4:11-13).

What happened in the natural realm on the Day of Pentecost in Acts 2 was symbolic of what was taking place in the spiritual realm. As one studies the language of Acts 2, it is apparent that several things occurred. There was a great sound, there was a manifestation of fire, and there was the miracle of speaking with other tongues. Each sign had its own significance.

The manifestation of fire is of particular interest in this context. The original language seems to indicate that this was a "distributing fire." This is picked up in various translations of this passage. The NIV says, "They saw what seemed to be tongues of fire that separated and came to rest on each of them." J.B. Phillips says, "Before their eyes appeared tongues like flames, which separated off and settled above the head of each one of them." Moffatt says, "They saw tongues like flames distributing themselves, one resting on the head of each."

It appears that what they saw was a manifestation of fire, which appeared above them. This major manifestation of fire then broke up into smaller tongues of fire that rested on the head of each of them until the whole of the fire was distributed.

What an incredible image! And what a perfect picture of that which is described for us in Ephesians 4:11-13. Jesus had ascended on high as the fullness of the Godhead bodily. Jesus was the fullness of grace and truth as He walked on the earth among us (John 1:14; 3:33-35). He was the embodiment of all ministry and divine function. But if He was to complete His ministry on the earth, the Holy Spirit would have to be sent to His followers, and the gifts and ministries that were in Him would have to be dispensed to them.

The fullness that was in Jesus is represented by the manifestation of fire in the Upper Room. The individual flames that came to rest on the head of each one represents the measure or part of Christ's ministry that was given to each one.

This is an accurate picture of what was taking place in the spiritual realm. When Christ ascended to the Father, He dispensed the fullness that was in Him to the individual members of the church. No one person has experienced the fullness, but each member of the Body of Christ has received a portion of Christ's ministry to the world.

As a result of this, Christ is able to continue His powerful ministry on the earth. The only difference is that now Christ functions through the church, which is His Body. Christ was the apostle, the prophet, the evangelist, the pastor, the teacher, the showerer of mercy, the healer, the comforter, the encourager, the giver, the helper, and the intercessor. He had it all. Now He has given an aspect of His ministry (our own personal flame) to each believer who has been born of the Spirit.

In this present age, if we want to experience Christ's ministry in one of these areas, we must experience it through those who have received Christ's ministry gift in that particular area. It is only when we rightly relate to the Body of Christ that we can experience the fullness that is in Christ.

The Body of Christ comprises unity in diversity. There is one body, but many members. There is one vine, but many branches. There is one army, but many soldiers. There is one temple, but many living stones. There is one family, but may children (sons). There is one sheepfold, but many sheep.

Each member of the Body has a place in that Body, a place to function (Rom. 12:1-8; 1 Cor. 12:1-31). There is no such thing as a nonfunctioning member. Regardless what some may think, regardless of our natural under-standing, everything was made with purpose and design.

God, not man, has set the members in the Body (1 Cor. 12:18). No one got to see a list of options before they were born to decide what they wanted to be when they came into the world. God has assigned ministries to people as it has pleased Him (1 Cor. 12:11). We must believe that God knows exactly what He is doing and that He does all things well.

RELEASING THE BODY TO FUNCTION

Pastors and church leaders must place a high priority on releasing others into ministry. Sometimes we have exalted the leadership ministries listed in Ephesians 4 above the other ministries of the body. Sometimes we have functioned as if God's purposes were going to be accomplished when the ministry of these leadership gifts were fully activated and the people released their leaders to function fully.

The opposite is actually the case. The purposes of God are going to be realized when the leadership ministries rise up and serve the other ministries in the Body of Christ in maturing, training, and releasing them to function fully. The leaders are the ones that God has ordained to train, build up, equip, and release into ministry with the goal that every single member of the church is doing what God has indeed called them to do.

It is not difficult to see the mentality of the leadership of churches when I go to visit them. Do the leaders see the people as those who exist for them? Are the people in their minds a platform for the release and full expression of their personal ministry? Or, do the leaders see themselves as existing for the sake of the people? Do they see themselves as the ones who are to lay their lives down? Do they see their primary function being to strengthen the hands of the members of their church so that they can fully function as God has ordained?

Until there is a major shift in the philosophy of many in the leadership of the church today, the purposes of God are going to be hindered by a lack of spiritual manpower. It is going to take the full ministry of Christ to accomplish the task, and that full ministry will not be experienced until every member is indeed functioning in his or her God-ordained place.

Without this the church will be much like a V-8 engine operating on four cylinders. It will be underpowered and ineffective to accomplish the Designer's purpose. The commission of Christ to the church is simply too grand to be able to be accomplished by a handful of spiritual giants.

There is no better illustration for us than in Acts 6 when the apostles and early church leaders were faced with the limitations of their own humanity. They were the leaders in the church, and they were trying to do it all. As a result the church suffered in every area. The needs of the people were not being met effectively, and the preaching of the Gospel itself was suffering.

When the leaders realized the need to release other capable people into the work, the murmuring stopped, and the preaching of the Gospel rose to a whole new level of effectiveness. God never intended for a small group of people to do it all. He gave many gifts and many ministries in the church, and everyone is there for the purpose of divine function.

A NATION OF PRIESTS

If we are not careful, we will go back to a system where the official delegate of the people will perform all of the ministry functions of the church. Such a priest would perform rituals in the presence of onlookers whose principle function is to witness the ritual by their presence and support the efforts of the one performing by their giving.

This is one of the concepts that Martin Luther rebelled against. He believed that every believer was called to be a priest. The New Testament confirms that believers are to be a nation of priests unto God (1 Pet. 2:5-9; Rev. 1:5-6; Exod. 19:5-6). Unfortunately, in many cases this concept has been restored to the church from a doctrinal perspective but is still awaiting restoration from an experiential or practical perspective.

ENTERING INTO THE DOCTRINE

If the church is going to grow and prosper in our day, there must be a major shift in the philosophy and practice of the church. This shift must first take place in the hearts of leaders. Leaders can enjoy being in the spotlight. They can enjoy being placed on a spiritual pedestal. They can enjoy getting most of the credit for victories. They can enjoy the fruits of their own people's spiritual ignorance. Sometimes their own insecurities in relation to their own call can keep them from truly releasing others.

Whatever the case, progressive leaders in today's church must make member activation a principle concern and a central focus. We need to define our goal. Do we want a nice church body that has few problems that takes good care of its pastor? Or do we want a well-trained, well-equipped army of people who are able to affect their communities and reach out to the world?

If all we want is to fulfill Christ's charge to the church, then we will do everything we can to assist every single member in finding his or her place. This means ministering to those working for the church and those working outside of the church. This means producing a Christian community that is ministering within the four walls of the church but at the same time has a vision to take it to the streets. This means seeing a full release of every gift, every ministry, and every grace that was found in Christ as He functioned on the earth two thousand years ago.

Often people do not respond properly because they have not been taught properly. Paul was concerned about the issue of ignorance when it came to the knowledge and function of ministry (1 Cor. 12:1). The first step in the process of change is giving people truth from which to draw. The Holy Spirit will work in the lives of people with the word of truth that has been sown into their hearts.

HINDRANCES TO THE FUNCTION OF THE BODY OF CHRIST

There are at least three classical, nonformal teachings in the church that have crippled the church's ability to function as a body. One of them is that being a preacher of the Gospel is the highest calling there is. A second one is an overemphasis on "full time" ministry that gives the impression that getting your salary from the church is somehow superior to having a "secular" job. And the third one is that ministry is what takes place behind a microphone in the corporate gathering of the church.

All three of these nonbiblical concepts have kept too many players out of the real game. Too often the church has been like a football game. There are twenty-two players on the field desperately in need of rest and forty thousand fans in the stadium desperately in need of exercise. Let's look at these three misconceptions.

Preaching Is Not the Highest Calling

I have heard preachers make this or similar statements from the pulpit on a variety of occasions. In a moment of great anointing a preacher makes the declaration that "Bless God! Being called to preach the Gospel is the greatest of all professions." Of course, the preacher is speaking out of his own sense of calling, and in a sense this is most likely true for him.

Unfortunately, this statement can have a very negative effect on those in the congregation listening to it. They can have two negative responses. First, they can feel inferior in whatever calling they possess, knowing that they can never be number one or in the "highest" calling. This can, in effect, demoralize them or cause them to devalue their own callings and giftings.

Second, they can feel that if their life is going to amount to anything, they must go to Bible school and try to become preachers. For this reason we have many people aspiring to be preachers who have not been called by God to be one. These people mean well, they make major sacrifices, but they rarely become successful and fulfilled at what they do.

If the Body of Christ is going to be activated, we need to know that all ministries are needed and vital to the overall success of the church. Even the ministries that seem to be less important are essential to the well-being of the body. We need to realize that God will not judge us on the basis of the ministry that we had; He will judge us on how faithful we were to do what God called us to do.

The highest calling or the greatest ministry is the one for which God has called someone. To the preacher, preaching is the highest call, and that should be his or her attitude. However, to someone who is called by God to serve in some other way, it would be foolish to pursue preaching. In fact, it could actually be walking in disobedience to pursue preaching.

When people understand this, when they understand that no ministry is more important than another in God's eyes, they will take pride in what God has called them to do and not belittle or minimize it. God has called each one to an important task. He has made each individual perfectly suited to the ministry to which He has called them. Everything about them is consistent with that purpose, and their great goal in life is to discover and enter into that purpose.

This is what Paul refers to as pressing toward the mark of the high calling in Christ Jesus. Paul was trying to apprehend the thing for which he was apprehended. When God put his hand on our lives, He did it with purpose in mind. Our goal is to discover that purpose and enter into it.

Full-Time Ministry Is for Everyone

The second great misconception among Christians is that somehow working for the church is spiritual and working outside of the church is secular. Often when you hear people talking about their situation, they get rather boastful about the fact that they are in full-time ministry. What they mean is that they draw their salary from the church. Unfortunately, it has nothing to do with how hard they work, just the fact that the church pays their salary. In point of fact, there may be many people who are working much harder than they are but are not drawing a salary from the church, and they may be more effective.

This misconception comes from a wrong definition of ministry. Too often we think of ministry as a title rather than a function. We hear people refer to "the ministry." Usually they are referring to a position in the church. They are "full-time ministers" if they have both the position and the salary that goes with it. This is a usage of the term ministry that is totally foreign to the Bible.

Unfortunately, when people in the congregation hear concepts like this, there is a tendency for them to feel almost ashamed of what they are doing because they are in the "secular" world.

The biblical concept of ministry is serving. It is taking the gifts, talents, and abilities that God has given to you and using them to serve God and others. Anytime you take something that God has given to you and use it to honor God and touch someone in need, you are ministering, and that activity is spiritual. It makes no difference if you are getting paid to do it or not. In fact, if you are getting paid to do it, the service you render may be less of a ministry than if you are not being paid and you still do it.

Leaders must be careful not to exalt what they do to the level that members of the body have a low regard for what they do and settle for being attendees of and financial donors to their program or "ministry."

Actually everyone is a minister because everyone is to be a servant. In addition, everyone is to be a full-time minister. That is, everyone should be a full-time servant with their eyes wide open at all times to see the needs that God has placed before them. They should have sensitive and caring hearts to take the resources that God has given to them to touch the lives of others and so minister as Christ would have in that given situation.

Ministry Occurs Outside the Church Service

Often those who participate in the services of the church, whether it be through song leading, praying, ushering or preaching, view their involvement as their ministry. Too often we feel that our ministry should find expression in the corporate gathering of the church or we don't really have a ministry. For this reason people who feel they have the gift of exhortation or prophecy feel stifled if they cannot "perform" in the public meeting of the church. People who feel uncomfortable in front of people settle for being spectators.

The truth is that the public gathering of the saints is to ministry what the locker room is to a football game. It is the place where we get encouraged and inspired. It is a place where we go over our game plan so that when we leave the locker room and play the game, we will have the best possible chance of winning the game.

Our church services are the same. For most of the people the church service is not meant to be the place where ministry functions. It is to be the place of equipping, encouragement, inspiration, and challenge in relation to the real game that takes place as soon as they leave the worship service. Ministry begins when the saints walk out of the door and into the real world.

There will never be enough opportunities in the context of a worship service for every saint to exercise some gift or fully function in some way. Only a small group of people will be able to participate. But there is plenty of room to function if we see ministry as something that takes place during the week between the locker room meetings. The gifts of the Spirit and the ministries that have been put into God's people are for the street.

When you follow the life of Jesus and see where He did most of His teaching and preaching, it was not in the context of the synagogue meeting. It was as He walked along the trails of life. Jesus wants to continue to function the same way He functioned when He was here on the earth. He still wants to touch the tax gatherers, the women at the well, the man lying in the street seeking healing, the children by the side of the road, and the multitudes that are in desperate need. We encounter them every day. We rarely encounter them in our church services.

LEADERS MUST DECREASE

There is something that plays to the ego of leaders when people believe that what they do is more holy, is higher and nobler, and is special in God's eyes. But if the Body of Christ is to arise in these days, leaders must be willing to decrease. John the Baptist saw it in his day. He realized that he only existed to prepare the way for Jesus. When Jesus came, his usefulness was gone. He had done his job. Now it was time for him to decrease and for Jesus to shine.

In a similar fashion, the purpose of leaders is to equip the Body of Christ to function. There is something nice about being treated like God's "man of the hour, full of faith and power." But what God wants to do today is not going to be done by a few big-time ministers who come on the scene in the last days. The work of the Kingdom is going to be done when leaders lay their lives down for the saints, equip them, and release them into their areas of function. It will get done by this many-membered entity called the Body of Christ functioning fully as God has intended.

Chapter Twelve

BIBLICAL STRUCTURE

KEY #10—*If a church is to grow and prosper from generation to generation, that church must determine to structure itself with a biblical expression of team ministry.*

The New Testament does give us a structure for government in the church. The church is not a one-man operation or dictatorship. It is not a democracy where every member gets an equal vote. It is not to be ruled by committees composed of those willing to serve.

God has a form of government outlined in the New Testament that could best be described as team ministry. The church is not to be led by one person but is to be led by a team of called individuals who meet the biblical qualifications for leadership. This team is led by a set-man or chief elder who gives vision and momentum to the group.

Church structure is certainly not to be our daily focus, but if the church is going to have the ability to be led by the Head of the church, the Lord Jesus Christ, its government must be of such a nature that the will of the Lord may indeed be done.

THE SKELETAL STRUCTURE

Church structure can be compared to the skeletal structure of the human body. Every person has one. Every person's skeleton is very much alike. Every person's skeleton is vital to the body's ability to fulfill function. However, in day-to-day life we don't really focus on a person's bone structure. What we tend to focus on is the way the flesh is arranged on the structure and the personality that is expressed by the individual. The skeleton is quietly going about its job, and it is only noticed when there is a problem. It is rarely noticed when everything is functioning according to design.

Church government is much the same. If you would ask the average church member what form of government their local church practices, they most likely would not be able to tell you. If you asked the average church member if they had ever read the constitution and by-laws of the church, most of them would probably say, "No!" As a rule, people are not interested in all of that "dry stuff." They are interested in the life and personality of the church. What interests them is the preaching, the pastor, the friendliness of the people, the children's ministry, or some other program of the church. They don't want to think about church government.

Yet in the overall scheme of things, church government may be the most important part of the church. The government of the church will either hinder or enable the church to do what God has called it to do.

The issue of church government is an issue that historically has distinguished one church from another. To some it has been important enough of an issue over which to either establish or break fellowship.

When one studies the names of various churches or church groups, it becomes clear that their names are based on several things. Their names can be based on the person who founded the church or group of churches (e.g. Lutheran, Mennonite, etc.). It may be based on a particular belief or distinct doctrine that they uphold (e.g. Baptist, Pentecostal, etc.). It may be based on what they believe about themselves (e.g. Assembly of God, Church of God, etc.). Or it may reflect their form of church government (Presbyterian, Episcopal, Congregational, or Independent).

In any case, the fact that churches are named after government styles shows the importance of this area in people's minds and the fact that people have been willing to establish or break fellowship over governmental issues.

The government of the church can be the most important aspect of a church's life. Your government will affect many things. It will affect the local church's ability to fulfill the will of God. It will affect a church's ability to reach the vision that God has given to its leaders. It will affect a church's ability to be led and directed by the Holy Spirit.

If the leaders of the local church (i.e. those who are responsible to make decisions) are not personally under the authority of the Holy Spirit in their lives, listening to the voice of the Lord, and submitted to His Word, the church will not be able to be led and directed by the Lord of the church. Christ exerts His headship through God-anointed and God-appointed leaders.

God has established government in His house (the church)

Most people will acknowledge the fact that there is government in the family realm (Eph. 6:1). They understand that children are to obey their parents and respond to their authority. Most people will also acknowledge authority that exists in the realm of civil government (Rom. 13:1). They understand that they are to be subject to the governing powers because they are established by God. But many of those same people do not see the local church and its leaders as an authority in their lives. They see the authority in the local church as advisory in nature at best.

The Bible indicates that there is authority in the local church that is to be an important aspect of every believer's life. It indicates that believers are to respect and respond to those who have the rule over them (Heb. 13:17).

THOSE WHO RULE
IN THE LOCAL CHURCH

There are those who rule in the local church. The concept of ruling includes directing, managing, exercising control over, regulating behavior, and influencing the affairs of something. It includes setting and promoting goals, establishing and enforcing boundaries, and producing and maintaining order, all for the sake of accomplishing vision and purpose.

The local church has been called to achieve a great purpose. For this to be accomplished, God has given leaders to the local church. He has established government. There are those who rule in the house of God (Heb. 13:17, 7, 24; Rom. 12:8). With no such government there will be a lack of order (1 Cor. 14:40; Col. 2:5).

God has a plan and pattern for government in His house

Not only has God established the local church as a place where order is present, He has prescribed the order for it. God has a plan. He did not find it necessary to consult with His creation regarding that plan. He simply lays it out for us. The local church is God's idea. He is the architect. He is the one who will live in it. He is the Lord of the church, and He has a workable plan (Refer back to chapter 6 and principle 4).

God identifies the rulers in His house as elders (1 Tim. 3:5; 5:17)

All throughout the Bible, both Old and New Testament, God's leaders are referred to as elders. In the local churches that Paul established, he set in elders who would function as the pastors, teachers, and leaders. These elders were always plural in number and seem to have worked as a team with a senior or chief elder.

There are many forms of government that God could have chosen. God was not short on ideas. He was not limited in his understanding or limited by history to a few options.

FIVE FORMS OF CHURCH GOVERNMENT

There are five main types of government or variations of them seen in various churches in the world today. The first one could be called *dictatorship* or *one-man rule*. No one would ever say the government was a dictatorship, and certainly on paper it would not use the word "dictator." But in actuality that is how many churches operate.

The leadership of such a local church would consist of a board made up of the senior pastor, his or her spouse, brother, uncle, and best friend. While business is conducted as needed (usually just a couple of times a year), it is clear that one person really makes all of the decisions, and the board is really nothing more than a rubber stamp for those decisions.

Dictatorship is a very simple form of government. Decisions can be made very quickly. No one has to get "bogged down" in lengthy discussions and frequent meetings.

Often the leader of such a church would refer to the church government as a "theocracy" or a church ruled by God. Unfortunately, it is not always

God who is making the decisions but "Theo" (the senior pastor). In these cases, decisions are not usually up for discussion because "the Lord told me." No one wants to argue with "the Lord." The authority in this system is usually supported by heavy teaching on "the anointed of the Lord" and warnings about touching "the Lord's anointed." Well-meaning people line up behind such a leader to hear the voice of God to them.

The problem is, however, that no leader is perfect. Even in the best of cases no one has perfect wisdom at all times. Since the dictatorship is built on one person, the local church is only as strong as that person. If the leader falls, the church falls with him. Dictators have few (if any) checks and balances to ensure that they and their churches will stay on track. Too much power in one person has the tendency to corrupt even the best of leaders. In addition it does not prepare adequately for the future. Often when such a leader steps out of that role because of age, health issues, or death, the church is left in a very difficult situation. The church was really built on a singular personality.

Democracy

Another form of government in many churches today is *democracy* or *"rule by the people."* Sometimes, because we see democracy as a viable or superior form of government in the world order, we want to bring that same government into the church. God was not ignorant of such a form of government when the local church was established. He simply did not want to subject His plan and purpose to popular opinion. Simply stated, the majority is not always right.

The local church was built for growth. In a growing church the new people (those who have been saved or have come to the church) will always outnumber those who have been Christians for a long time. As a result, democracy ends up being a "rule by the immature" since they will always have the swing vote.

New converts do not always have the ability to hear from God clearly. Sometimes they do not have the ability to do the difficult thing. One experiment in democracy, the Laodicean Church (Laodicea means "people's rights" and was a city that became an experiment in democracy) was characterized by lukewarmness.

Democracy would never work in the natural family, and it will not work in the local church. I can't imagine submitting all of the decisions of my household to a vote of the family members. My wife and I have three children. Now that they are grown and have families of their own, they are making great decisions. However, had they had the power to enact decisions for the family when they were young, we would have eaten ice cream every night, stayed up to all hours, and eaten off paper plates in the messiest house you have ever seen.

In addition, all of the members of the household would have been sick, and when the money ran out (since no one wanted to work), we all would have ended up a liability to society.

Central Control or "External Control"

A third from of local-church government that is widely practiced in the church world today is what I call *central control* or *external control.* This is government that comes from outside of the local church. While the local congregation may have some latitude on decision making and the development of vision, the primary or critical decisions in these churches are in the hands of those who are not a part of the local scene.

Many denominational churches are structured in this way where control is exercised by a headquarters or central agency. This external board maintains its ultimate control by several means. They maintain control by owning the physical building, ordaining, licensing, and placing the ministers, maintaining a central board for all missions and mission funds, and educating leaders through a central seminary or Bible school.

Often churches under this system operate fairly independently of the central board when it comes to the day-to-day affairs. Where control is seen most clearly is in the case where a local church bucks up against the headquarters' policy, strays from a central doctrinal position, or has a serious problem particularly as it relates to removing or replacing leaders. In such cases local assemblies must submit to the outside authority or face the possibility of losing their building or license to minister.

While the outside support of such organizations can appear to be a great benefit, this form of government can hinder the local church in tailoring its programs to the unique nature of its city or community. It can also inhibit leaders from following the voice of the Holy Spirit in the growth and development of that local assembly. It assumes that one size fits all in church programming, that we have complete understanding of all that God has for us in biblical revelation and understanding, and that God has nothing more to say to us concerning His plan.

Local churches should be as unique as people are. Yes, there are many things that every person has in common that makes them part of the human race. But every person also has a uniqueness about them that makes them particularly suited to the individual ministry that God has given to them. True biblical local churches will have much in common. These common things are those structures and elements clearly revealed to us in the Bible. But beyond this, local churches must be free to respond to the individual leading of the Holy Spirit as they attempt to fulfill the Great Commission in the city where God has placed them. God may have a unique strategy for them that is not part of anyone's instruction manual.

Local churches in the New Testament were not controlled by other local churches or outside boards. Some would attempt to use the meeting in Acts 15 as an instance where the Jerusalem church was acting as a central authority and issuing decrees to the rest of Christendom. When you study what was actually happening here, you realize that people from the Jerusalem church were preaching without commission in churches that Paul had established, causing a great deal of doctrinal confusion. The only way to solve the problem was to take the problem to the source of the problem, Jerusalem, and let the leaders of that church discuss it and see if they could help to undo some of the damage caused by these teachers who claimed to be ministering in the name of the Twelve. The result was that the Jerusalem church sent some of their key leaders to many of the churches to help clarify their position and rectify any damage.

Church Council or Deacon Board

The fourth type of church government that is commonly practiced is what could be called rule by a *church council* or *deacon board*. The board may be referred to in several ways including board of trustees, financial board, the deacons, or simply, the board.

This form is often seen in churches that have some form of external control as well. It is characterized by a church board that is elected by the members of the congregation. Usually members of such a board are selected from among the congregation by a nominating process. They may or may not have any specific qualifications apart from the fact that they are members of the church and have a desire to serve in this way.

Members of such a board are often seen as faithful members who have natural talents in the financial and business areas. They usually serve a term of office of one to three years with limitations on how many successive terms they may serve. This board often serves alongside a pastoral team or even what are called elders, but this group has the financial power in the church. Whoever controls the finances of the church controls the vision of the church.

In these situations there may or may not be biblical or spiritual qualifications for those who serve. Whether or not these individuals can hear the voice of God is not usually necessary to nominate them to the office. Whether or not the senior pastor of the church feels good about the nomination is not often considered.

In most cases it is this board that has the power to hire and fire the pastor. As a result, the board often sees their main responsibility as keeping the pastor in check or protecting the people from abusive leadership. Usually decision making is a fairly long process, and the spiritual leadership of the church must come "hat in hand" to the board to have their vision approved.

With board members rotating and pastors coming and going, the local church has a difficult task sustaining growth and vision over a long period of time. People are often coming and going as well, and usually the church has a difficult time stretching for growth.

Some would use the servants who were appointed in Acts 6 as an indication that deacons were appointed in the church to control the natural affairs of the church. The truth is, the word *deacon* is never used to apply to the seven in Acts 6. In addition, the job description of these individuals who were appointed was to distribute food to the needy.

There is no evidence in the New Testament that a group of deacons met as a board with any corporate function. There is especially no evidence that elders (spiritual leadership) had to submit their vision to a second board that controlled the finances of the church. When Paul wanted to talk to those in authority in any local church, he called for its elders (Acts 20:17). When Peter addressed the leaders of the local churches, he addressed the elders of the church (1 Pet. 5:1-4).

Eldership Management or Team Ministry

God could have chosen any form of government for His church that He so desired. God did not choose any of the forms that we have discussed to this point. God chose what I would call *eldership management* or *team ministry*.

When the New Testament talks about authority in relation to the local churches of that era, it talks about it in terms of a group of individuals called "elders" (1 Tim. 5:17).

Elders were the pastors and teachers of the local assembly much like elders who were established in the Old Testament community and in the Jewish synagogues of Jesus' day. Elders of the local churches were its bishops or, literally, overseers who were responsible for giving guidance and direction to the affairs of the church, pastoring the members of the congregation, protecting the church from corrupting influences, and teaching the congregation the good word of God (Acts 20:28-31).

It is clear that once local churches had been established by apostolic ministry, the goal was to set in elders to give ongoing guidance and leadership to the assembly (Acts 14:23; Titus 1:5).

When setting in such elders, the early church leaders never set in just one elder. Elders of the church are always referred to as plural in number (Acts 20:17; 1 Tim. 5:17; James 5:14). Actually, in order to have some checks and balances, there needs to be at least three elders established in a church to function effectively.

New Testament local churches had many elders, but at the same time they had one senior or chief elder (Acts 12:17; 15:4-7, 12, 13, 22; Phil. 4:1-3). There are some today who are trying to establish an eldership form of government where there is no such head elder or senior pastor. These efforts usually end in failure. They usually end up with three or more visions, with the congregation choosing their personal favorite (1 Cor. 1:12).

In situations where this form of government is attempted, the eldership is of necessity limited to a small number of individuals, because to have a coequal plurality would be difficult with five, ten, or twenty individuals. With this type of government it is easy to get to a stalemate or to find some measure of power struggle within the group. Eventually if this system works at all, it is because one of these individuals is recognized officially or unofficially as the principal voice.

God's plan for the church is plurality of elders with a chief or senior elder. This has always been God's form of government. God has always used plural leadership with one of those leaders placed as head (see chart on page 157). There is a sense of equality among the leadership team with a recognized head to be the official leader or spokesperson for the team.

EQUALITY AND HEADSHIP IN THE GODHEAD

God demonstrated this principle for us first in His own person and nature. God has revealed Himself to us in a divine mystery. He is three yet one. There are three distinct persons of the Godhead who are distinguishable but indivisible.

There is the Father, the Son, and the Holy Spirit (1 John 5:7). The Bible clearly teaches that the Father is God, the Son is God, and the Holy Spirit is God. There exists within these persons an equality of person (Phil. 2:6), and yet there is at the same time an order of headship (1 Cor. 11:3). The Father sent the Son, the Son sent the Spirit. The Spirit bears witness to the Son and the Son bears witness to the Father. The Father becomes the ultimate figure in the Godhead (1 Cor. 15:27-28). For the sake of mission fulfillment each person of the Godhead recognizes His particular function and role responsibility.

EQUALITY AND HEADSHIP IN THE FAMILY

When God established the natural family, He followed the same governing principle (Gen. 2:24). Each natural family has plurality of ministry or team ministry. Each natural family is led and directed by two mature ones (elders) who are established as the parental authorities in that home. The man and the woman are equal before God. And yet for the sake of mission fulfillment, God has given differing role responsibilities to each one.

Within this equality is an order of headship. The husband is the head of the wife as Christ is the head of the church (Eph. 5:23; 1 Cor. 11:3). This does not mean that the husband is more important than the wife or that he leads as a dictator independently of the wife. It does mean that for the sake of order and the ability to function, one of the members of this team has been placed in a position of headship as the chief elder.

EQUALITY AND HEADSHIP
IN ISRAEL AND THE SYNAGOGUE

This is the same form of government under which Israel walked during the wilderness wanderings. In Israel, God established His chosen senior leader or "set man," Moses. Along with Moses a team of elders served to give leadership to and care for the needs of that nation (Num. 11:16-17; 27:16-17).

This is the same pattern that the Jews used in the synagogue (Acts 13:15; 18:8, 17). Each synagogue had its group of elders who presided over the affairs of the community. Within that structure there was a chief elder who served as the set leader or team captain among the elders.

EQUALITY AND HEADSHIP
IN THE LOCAL CHURCH

As has already been stated, a team of elders (Titus 1:5; 21:18) led each New Testament local church. Even though the Bible seems to imply that various elders had different functions or anointings, they all seemed to function as a group. But as with the other patterns mentioned above, they too had a senior elder or general overseer.

The clearest pattern for this seems to be the Jerusalem church, the one about which historically we know the most. The twelve apostles seemed to have served as the initial eldership for this first church. After some time, however, other elders joined their ranks and served with them to form the leadership team (Acts 11:30; 15:2). Among their ranks one person emerged as the leader of that team. It is interesting that the leader was not one of the original twelve apostles but James, the brother of the Lord. As you read through the pages of the book of Acts, it is clear that James functioned as the senior elder or senior pastor of the church at Jerusalem.

In Acts 12 when Peter escaped from prison by divine intervention, it was James to whom he felt personally accountable (Acts 12:17). In Acts 15 when the church leaders met to discuss how to handle Gentile converts, it was James who made the final judgment and brought a conclusion to the discussion (15:13-19). In Acts 21 when Paul was bringing a relief offering to the church in Jerusalem, he presented it to James in the presence of the other elders (21:18).

The Jerusalem elders worked as a team, but James acted as the first among equals who assisted in bringing resolution and impetus to their efforts. This seems to have been true of other churches as well. When the Lord addressed the local churches in the book of Revelation, He addressed His letter to the set-man or the "angelos" (messenger) of each of the churches (Rev. 2:1).

MODEL	EQUALITY	HEADSHIP
The Godhead	Three Persons	Father
The Family	Two Parents	Husband
Israel	70 Elders	Moses
The Synagogue	Elders/Rulers	Chief Ruler
The Church	Elders	Chief Elder

QUALIFICATIONS FOR ELDERS

God determines the kind of individuals that are to be rulers in His house (1 Tim. 3:1-7; Titus 1:5-9). Through the apostle Paul, He gave us very specific guidelines for identifying those who would serve in this capacity. Strict adherence to the guidelines given in the New Testament is the only thing that will ensure this form of government being any better than any of the other forms of government that we have discussed.

In fact if these guidelines are not strictly adhered to, eldership can be an even worse form of government than some of the others that we have discussed, because with an eldership you could have the wrong people in office and have no ability to remove them.

These qualifications that Paul gives are to ensure that the leaders of the

church have demonstrated through their personal lives that they are personally submitted to Christ, are an example for others to follow, and have a track
record of hearing from God. It is these qualities that make them candidates
for leadership. Christ is to be the head of the church. He exercises His headship through His leaders. Christ can rule through these kinds of leaders.

We can summarize the qualifications listed by Paul into four categories:

1. Potential elders must be people with **proven character**. That is,
   they have allowed the work of sanctification to take place in their
   lives and they manifest the fruit of the Spirit.
2. Potential elders must be people of **spiritual vision**. That is, they
   have a vision to see God's purposes established, and they have
   the maturity to make sacrifices in the present to see those purposes come to pass.
3. Potential elders must be people with their **homes in order**. That
   is, they have demonstrated their ability to rule and provide pastoral covering for the church by virtue of the fact that they have
   established the Kingdom of God in their own homes.
4. Potential elders must be people with the **spiritual gifting** for this
   ministry. That is, they are not only good people, but they have a
   gift of leadership or the "charisma" needed to enable them to
   teach and to exhort and convince those who oppose the Gospel.

It is interesting that these are in essence the same qualifications that were
laid out in the Old Testament for the elders who served under Moses. God's
leaders were to be "able men, such as fear God, men of truth, hating covetousness" (Exod. 18:21).

A Corporate Function

While each elder's ministry focus may be different (i.e. some may be
apostolic, prophetic, evangelistic, or pastoral), all of the elders working
together have a corporate function or job description. The eldership team's
main responsibility is the general oversight and care of the church. This
responsibility involves three main areas: ruling, pastoring and teaching.

Ruling

The elders of the local church are the rulers of the assembly (Rom. 12:8; 1 Thess. 5:12-14; 1 Tim. 5:17; Heb. 13:17, 24). The word *rule* means "to be over, to superintend, to preside over, to care for, and to give attention to." Elders are to the church what parents are to a home. As rulers, therefore, they stand accountable before God for the state of the assembly (Heb. 13:17). This ruling, however, is to be done with a proper spirit and attitude. Elders must remember that they are servants of the people, not lords (1 Pet. 5:2-3) who are set up by God to provide an example for the saints to follow (Heb. 13:7). This ruling may at times call for the exercise of discipline (1 Thess. 5:12-13; 1 Tim. 3:5), but every action taken by the elders is to be with the best interest of the souls of the people in mind.

Obey those who rule over you, and be submissive, for they watch out for your souls, as those who must give account. Let them do so with joy and not with grief, for that would be unprofitable for you. Hebrews 13:17

Pastoring

One of the charges that is consistently given to elders is that of shepherding or tending the flock of God (Acts 20:28). In doing so they are to watch out for wolves (Acts 20:29-31), they are to help the weak (Acts 20:35), they are to minister to the sick (James 5:14-15), and they are to go before the sheep with their good example (1 Pet. 5:3). Paul gives this charge to the elders at Ephesus:

Therefore take heed to yourselves and to all the flock, among which the Holy Spirit has made you overseers, to shepherd the church of God which He purchased with His own blood. For I know this, that after my departure savage wolves will come in among you, not sparing the flock. Also from among yourselves men will rise up, speaking perverse things, to draw away the disciples after themselves. Therefore watch, and remember that for three years I did not cease to warn everyone night and day with tears. So now, brethren, I commend you to God and to the word of His grace, which is able to build you up and give you an inheritance among all those who are sanctified. I have coveted no one's silver or gold or apparel. Yes, you yourselves know that these hands have provided for my necessities, and for those who were with me. I have shown you in every way, by laboring like this, that you must support the weak. And remember the words of the Lord Jesus, that He said, "It is more blessed to give than to receive."   Acts 20:28-35

Instructing

Elders are responsible to teach or instruct the church (1 Tim. 3:2; Titus 1:9). They are the ones that are going to give stability to the church and help bring a unity among the local body of believers. As such it is essential that their teaching be firmly based on the Word of God (Heb. 13:7; 1 Tim. 5:17; 2 Tim. 2:2). In their teaching they should be able to convince those who oppose the Gospel (Titus 1:9). A real priority should be placed on the eldership's coming to a place of doctrinal unity on questionable areas so that they can speak as one person (1 Cor. 1:10).

Appointment and Term of Office

Elders or bishops in the New Testament were not elected by a vote of the people. Elders were to be chosen by the Holy Spirit (Acts 20:28) and recognized and appointed by leadership (Acts 14:23).

In new churches it seems to have been the ministry of the apostle who founded the work or his representative to ordain the initial elders in that work. After a work was established, new local elders were undoubtedly set in by the decision of the functioning elders of that local assembly.

There is no specific mention in the New Testament concerning the length of an elder's stay in office. It is abundantly clear that they did not have one-, two-, or three-year terms of office as is so common today. We must believe, therefore, that unless a person voluntarily withdraws from the position, can no longer do the work, no longer desires to do the work, or in some way disqualifies himself by the same qualifications that were initially required for the office, the person remains in the office indefinitely. It would seem likely, however, that elders who are particularly aged may only function in an advisory capacity due to a lack of physical strength, but their wisdom should always be highly valued.

Regardless of the term of office, every elder should have a specific assignment and a specific work to do in connection with their eldership. I might add here that periodic evaluations of a person's eldership would be in order to assist in measuring the person's willingness and fitness for this important position. Nothing can destroy the momentum of a church quicker than a sluggish eldership.

The Honor of Elders

The elders have a serious charge before the Lord, and God holds them accountable on a very strict scale. The elders who have been given a charge by God but fail to fulfill their responsibilities will be dealt with by God. But it must be remembered that the elder is not the only one who has responsibility in this relationship. Not only does the elder have an obligation to the congregation, but the congregation also bears responsibilities toward its leaders. Those responsibilities are as follows:

1. **The people are to "know" those who are over them** (1 Thess. 5:12). In this sense the people are to appreciate the true value of their leaders and seek them out.

2. **The people are to esteem them very highly** (1 Thess. 5:13). This esteem is not to be based on one's inner feeling or sentiment. It is a respect that is calculated and deliberate. It is having a respect for the office that God has established in the church.

3. **The people are to submit themselves to God's anointed and appointed leaders** (Heb. 13:17). The elders will not be able to be what God has called them to be without the submission or, could we say, the cooperation of the people.

4. **The people are to support the elders financially** (1 Tim. 5:17; Gal. 6:6; 1 Thess. 2:6, 9; 2 Cor. 11:7f; Phil. 4:10f; 1 Cor. 9:11-14). This may not be immediately possible in every situation because of the size of the church. However, this should be seen as a long-range goal. How much support is given may vary from place to place, but whatever the arrangement, it should be such as to remove from the leaders' mind all cause for worry over financial support.

5. **The people are not to hastily charge an elder with wrongdoing.**
   By the very nature of their office, elders are often exposed to mis-representation and unjust criticism. For this reason God protects them by warning His people not to rebuke an elder (1 Tim. 5:1) and not to receive an accusation against an elder except in the mouth of two or three witnesses (1 Tim. 5:19). It should be noted, however, if the elder does sin and is in fact guilty of something worthy of rebuke, an elder is to be rebuked openly that others may fear (1 Tim. 5:20). The public nature of their office demands public discipline.

6. **The people are to remember their leaders and pray for them**
   (Heb. 13:7; 1 Thess. 5:25). Elders are ordained by God to exercise the general oversight and care of the local church. They need all the prayer support they can get. It is a great responsibility before the Lord.

SUMMARY

If a church is to grow and prosper from generation to generation, that church must determine to structure itself with a biblical expression of team ministry. If you would like more teaching on this subject, I encourage you to get the following books from the same publisher.

Team Ministry by Dick Iverson
The Local Church Today by Bill Scheidler
The Vanguard Leader by Frank Damazio
The Church in the New Testament by Kevin Conner

Chapter Thirteen

———

DISCIPLINE

KEY #11—*If a church is to grow and prosper from generation to generation, that church must determine to exercise spiritual discipline relative to its membership.*

C hurch discipline is almost unheard of in today's church world. Confronting another church member about his or her sinful lifestyle is not only neglected, the very thought of it is despised by most church members.

It is interesting that the only time Jesus talked directly about the local church was in the context of discipline (Matt. 18:15-20). He seemed to indicate that there would be problems in the church, and that these problems would not go away by themselves. He actually gave a rather specific procedure by which such confrontation was to take place.

What would happen in the natural family without any discipline? There would be chaos. Selfishness would be the rule of the day. People would function on the basis of feelings rather than principle. There would be a tendency to only do what had to be done to get by. Sounds a little like some churches!

The church is to be more than a loosely-knit group of followers. It is to be a disciplined army on the march against the powers of darkness. Followers are to become disciples. Disciples are to become warriors. Warriors are to become overcomers.

When Jesus commissioned his followers, He gave them some tall orders.

If you examine all of the charges that Jesus gave his followers between His resurrection from the dead and His ascension into heaven, you will find the church's marching orders for all of the church age. Putting all of the verses together, we will arrive at a multifaceted commission. The disciples were to:

- Be witnesses (Acts 1:8).
- Preach the Gospel or evangelize (Mark 16:15-20).
- Preach repentance and remission of sins (Luke 24:27).
- Make disciples (Matthew 28:19-20).
- Baptize the disciples (Matthew 28:19-20).
- Teach the disciples (Matthew 28:19-20).
- Feed the lambs (John 21:15).
- Tend the sheep (John 21:15).

This list is obviously more involved than simply "getting people saved," getting them to tithe, and getting them to attend the services of the church. God's goal is that His people be a disciplined army pressing forward and reclaiming that which the enemy has taken away.

THE FOUNDATION FOR DISCIPLINE IN THE LOCAL CHURCH

The foundation for discipline in the church comes from two important instructions given to us by Jesus Himself. Jesus gave a commission to the church that involves making followers of Christ into "disciplined ones" (Matt. 28:19-20). Obviously, if the followers of Jesus are going to be entrusted with the keys of the Kingdom and the awesome responsibility of storming the "gates of Hades," they will have to be a disciplined group.

In addition, when Jesus referred specifically to the local church, He gave clear instructions as to how to handle difficulties that arise between members of the church (Matt. 18:15-18). He was implying that accepting Christ as Lord and Savior would not solve everyone's problems for all time, but that the church would need a process by which those who professed to be believers actually lived like believers.

One of the greatest indictments against the church today is that members of the church do not live like true Christians. Some church members have a terrible testimony in the business world. Some church members have as much trouble with lying, immorality, divorce, cheating on the job, and covetousness as nonbelievers. As long as there is no difference in the lives of those who profess Christ, the church will be powerless to effect the commands of Christ and fulfill their commission.

WHY DISCIPLINE IS OFTEN NEGLECTED

Discipline in the church is a very neglected aspect of modern day pastoral ministry. It is neglected primarily because of four things: fear, ignorance, lack of true covenantal love for the sheep, and lack of faith on the part of church leaders.

Fear

Church discipline is neglected because of fear of various sorts. The first fear that must be overcome is a *fear of confrontation* in general. No one enjoys confrontation. It seems that people would rather talk to anyone else about someone's problem than the person who is directly involved. No one likes to tell someone that what they are doing is wrong and that they need to change. We don't like the uneasy feeling that comes with such confrontation. We would rather do anything else than say something negative to someone. We would rather pray in private, tell someone else or simply "let it go." Jesus was willing to become uncomfortable for our betterment. We must be willing to lay our personal lives and preferences down for others for their betterment as well.

A second fear that will hinder us from our biblical responsibility to exercise discipline and accountability toward another believer is the *fear of being unpopular* among people. We all have a desire to be liked by others. We can be afraid that if we confront someone regarding an issue in their life, they will hate us forever (2 Chron. 18:7). Every time we speak into someone's life, we run this risk. But we have to be willing to put our relationship on the line for others to save them from themselves. If a person was about to be hit by a speeding car, we would not think of our personal popularity as we pushed them out of danger even if in our exuberance we bruised them in the process. Sometimes people do not appreciate our actions until much later.

A third fear that pastors can have if they discipline a member of the church is the *fear the church will become divided* or polarized over the discipline. They fear that members of the church will try to defend or take up the cause of the person being disciplined. This is a realistic fear. People tend to be extremely tolerant of certain kinds of sin and often want to extend more grace to people than they really ought to have. People tend to have fewer facts at their disposal, which inhibits their ability to render accurate judgment. Perhaps they feel that if they side with the person being disciplined, it will go better for them if they ever get into a similar situation.

Just like a child in a family can get upset with the parents because they discipline a sibling, members of the church can take up the cause of sinning members. The reality that these things happen does not change the fact that the church needs pastoral care or that parents are responsible to discipline their children. Failure to discipline will not produce spiritual heath in people's lives any more than failure to discipline children will produce health in the home.

A fourth fear that can hinder the pastor is a *fear of reaction outside of the church* or in the local community. We do not want to get a reputation for church discipline. It is amazing how many people in a small community can be aware of what is going on in a local church even though they have never attended any of its gatherings. The pastor and leaders of a church are trying to get people interested in the church, not drive them away.

Pastors and leaders need to realize that they already have a reputation in the community. Actually, if the pastors and leaders do not discipline their members who are sinning, that message will also reach the community. It is interesting that the unsaved community seems to have a pretty good idea of what a Christian should look like. If they are aware of someone who is openly living in a way that is against the teachings of Christ, they know something is wrong. If the person involved is a member in good standing in a local church and nothing is being done to confront the sin in this person's life, the community knows something is wrong. In such a case the church itself will lose its testimony, and the community will have little or no respect for its leaders.

Finally, pastors and leaders can be hindered by the *fear of a lawsuit* against them or the local church. There is no question that we are living in a society with litigation frenzy. People are suing for everything imaginable. If we are not careful we will be afraid to do anything because of a potential lawsuit. We hear the horror stories where other local churches have lost thousands of dollars over such suits.

The court systems of our day do not always sympathize with pastors over their biblical mandates, especially when they render judgment concerning things that are not illegal and are openly practiced in society by "consenting adults." The court systems in the days of the early church were not always sympathetic to the commands of Jesus as the disciples preached the Gospel openly. But at some point, for the sake of the higher commission, we must stand and declare with the disciples of Jesus, "We must obey God rather than men" (Acts 4:20-21; 5:29).

Certainly we need to use wisdom in exercising any form of discipline and take all of the appropriate precautions even to the point of consulting legal counsel ourselves, but we cannot cease to do what God has clearly commanded us to do because of the fear of man. We must fear God more than man. If we do not, we will never be able to take the Gospel into a hostile world.

Ignorance

In addition to fear, ignorance can keep us from exercising biblical discipline. We can have ignorance of the necessity of discipline, thinking that if we love God, are sincere as leaders, and we pray about it, everything will work out in the end. The sad fact is that is why God gives leaders to the church. Leaders are the answer to such prayers. We are often asking God to do things that He has commanded us to do. We are waiting for Him to act, and He is waiting for us to act.

I was in a church for a season a few years ago assisting them in developing their cell-group ministry. While there, I noticed that every Sunday morning during the prayer time before the service, people were praying for backsliders by name. After a few Sundays of similar prayer I asked the pastor, "Is anyone going to these people to confront them face to face about their condition?" He indicated that no one was doing so.

The assumption that was being made was that if members of the church prayed hard enough, then God would do the work for us. Unfortunately, in those cases the parties being prayed for were not listening to the Holy Spirit. If they were, they would have already returned. They are in reality ignoring the Holy Spirit Whom they cannot see, and they need someone that they can see to get in front of them and tell it like it is.

Just as parents cannot expect God to discipline their children for them, church leaders cannot expect God to do the work of pastoring for them. God set parents in the home and gave them a charge. He set elders and pastoral leadership in the church for the same reason.

In addition to our ignorance concerning the importance of discipline, we can also dwell in ignorance regarding the practice of discipline in the church. It is possible to grow up in the modern church and never see discipline administered in a godly way. Many times when we have seen discipline administered, it was practiced in an unbiblical way or a vindictive way that did not produce good fruit and did not lead to restoration.

We cannot choose to remain in ignorance because we have had some negative experiences. We must be willing to see the heart of God and be instructed in His ways. Fortunately He has given us clear guidelines for this important area of church life.

Lack of Covenantal Love

Too often we relate to people out of a sense of self-preservation. Pastoral ministry involves a daily laying down of one's life for others. This is the model of Jesus. In order to fulfill the commands of Jesus in the area of discipline, we must have a love for people that goes beyond the positive feelings that they produce in us or what they can do for us personally.

We have to ask God to place His love in us. His love is a covenant love that reaches beyond self interest to a realm that is sacrificial and purposeful in relationship. It is the Lord's covenantal love that motivates Him to discipline His children. It is because He cares so much about us and our future together that He is willing to do whatever it takes to bring us to a place of prosperity (Heb. 12:6-7).

Christ has demonstrated this kind of love in that while we were sinners

He set His affection on us. He cared so much for us that He was willing to do whatever it took to see us restored to God.

Many years ago when I was a young pastor, I had a couple under my care that were quite a bit older than I was. The husband had some personal problems that were seriously affecting the marriage and the life in the home. Things seemed to be gradually getting worse. I was young and dreaded the thought of talking to this man about his marriage and family.

Finally I realized that if I didn't confront him, no one else would. I scheduled an appointment with him knowing that if I shared what I knew I needed to share with him, he would hate me for the rest of my life. He came in, I prayed with him, and then I told him what I had observed. I felt the Holy Spirit was speaking through me to him in a clear and very direct way.

I was immediately amazed. Rather than getting mad at me and storming out in a fit of rage, tears began to well up in his eyes. After I finished sharing, he said to me, "I wish someone would have loved me enough to have told me these things years ago." Somehow he understood that what I was sharing with him was out of love and that I was willing to risk our relationship and step out of my personal comfort zone to help him to a place of prosperity. That couple is doing well to this day.

I wish I could say that all of the confrontations that I have had with people have gone that well, but I believe God was helping me in this case to see that true discipline is important if people are going to be able to achieve their personal destiny.

Lack of Faith

It must be extremely difficult for a farmer who has planted an orchard to go out the first time and prune the trees that he has so faithfully planted, watered, and nurtured into a place of fruit bearing. Will he damage or even kill the tree? It certainly looks like he is attacking it. However, because of what he has been taught in the gardening manual he is willing to take the risk for the sake of the promise of "more fruit."

Discipline is part of the fruit-bearing process in people's lives. As pastors and leaders we can neglect it because we do not have that spirit of faith that we need to trust the gardening manual of God's Word. We are afraid that we might kill the tree.

If you have ever seen a fruit tree that is old but has never been pruned, you will fully understand what I am talking about. A tree left to itself will become sickly, and what fruit it does produce will be virtually inedible.

We must have faith as parents that as we follow God's instruction manual in the rearing of our children, they will turn out in a way that will bring glory to God. We must have the same faith in God's instruction manual for building the church. Discipline will not kill the church; it will improve it and bring it into the realms of greater fruitfulness.

REASONS FOR CHURCH DISCIPLINE

Church discipline will help the church to be strong and to grow. It counteracts the spirit of lawlessness of our age. It evidences a standard of biblical conviction for living that the Christian is commanded to uphold. It has the potential for bringing about change and growth in the individual's life when nothing else will. It helps the individual member to deal with sin in himself that by himself he has been unable to eliminate. It underscores the value of righteousness as the basis for all relationships in the body.

In addition, it prohibits the leavening influence of sin from gaining a foothold in other members of the congregation. When sin is left to sit in the congregation, others will be tempted to do outwardly what they have only been tempted to do inwardly. When leaders fail to deal with obvious areas of sin in the church, their silence becomes tacit approval of the activity in question.

No Disciple Will Create Problems

Churches that fail to exercise any discipline end up having serious problems over the long term. Without church discipline there is no clear standard of right and wrong among the congregation. Without church discipline sinning members go on sinning, destroying their own potential fruitfulness in God. Without church discipline the spiritual life of the body as a whole becomes greatly weakened. Spiritual vitality and life seep out, and a progressive, spiritual stagnation sets in. Without church discipline confidence and respect for the church leadership is lost.

Discipline Involves More Than Excommunication

Often when we talk about the subject of church discipline. it is easy for our minds to go directly to the ultimate form of discipline, that is, excommunication. In reality, excommunication is only a small part of discipline as it relates to the church. In fact if more attention were to be paid to the other issues of discipline, perhaps there would be little or no need for excommunication.

There are many biblical admonitions to leaders regarding how they are to relate to their people in areas of discipline. These admonitions deal more with the regular or daily life of the church. Some of the main words used in this area include reprove, rebuke, admonish, correct, judge, or warn. These have nothing to do with cutting an erring member off from fellowship. They have to do with the ongoing spiritual tune-up that every believer needs from time to time. To some degree every believer has a responsibility to every other believe. Members of the church are to be each other's keepers.

Reproving

Paul wrote to Timothy who was the pastor of the church at Ephesus that he was to **reprove** or convince (Gk. *elenko*) with all authority (2 Tim. 4:2). He gave the same admonition to Titus who was also a pastor (Titus 2:15). The word that he used here literally means "to convict, to expose, to bring to light, to call to account, to show one his fault (demanding an explanation)."

This is the same word that Jesus used when he exhorted brothers and sisters in the church who felt that they were sinned against. Jesus instructed them to go to the offending party and show them their fault or demand an explanation (Matt. 18:15). Jesus did not say if someone has offended you, tell everyone else about it including the pastor of the church. He encouraged believers or members of the covenant community to go to the person in private in an attempt to resolve the issue.

Jesus indicated that this kind of reproof was a measure of His love (Rev. 3:19). This kind of reproof is the measure of a true friend (Prov. 27:6). This kind of reproof is part of our responsibility to each other as covenant partners (Luke 3:19; John 3:20; 8:9,46; 16:8; 1 Cor. 14:24; Eph. 5:11,13; 1 Tim. 5:20; 2 Tim. 3:16; Titus 1:9,13; Heb. 12:5; James 2:9).

Rebuking

A second word that indicates a form of discipline in our relationships in the local church is the word **rebuke** (Gk. *epitimao*). This word is a little stronger than the word described above. It means "to tax with a fault, rate, chide, reprove, censure severely."

Jesus used this word in respect to our interpersonal relationships. In Luke 17:3 He said, "If your brother sins against you, rebuke him; and if he repents, forgive him." Paul instructed Timothy that this type of activity was part of what leaders do in pastoring a church (2 Tim. 4:2, See also Matt. 12:16; 16:22; 17:18; Luke 9:55; Jude 9).

Admonishing

A third word that is used in the New Testament relating to leaders and their people is the word **admonish** (Gk. *noutheteo*). This word means "to admonish, warn, or exhort." Paul indicated that such warning or admonition was a major part of the function of elders in relation to their pastoral duties (1 Thess. 5:12). Paul tells pastors that they are to warn the unruly (1 Thess. 5:14). He tells leaders to reject those who do not respond to two or three admonitions (Titus 3:10).

Pastors see people all of the time who are living beneath their potential and are doing things that will hurt them in the long run. Often in the counseling ministry, pastors work with people who are resistant to come under the authority of God's Word and change their negative life patterns. Part of the counselor's duty is to warn people of the consequences of such resistance (Acts 20:31; Rom. 15:14; 1 Cor. 4:14; 10:11; Eph. 6:4; Col. 1:28; 3:16).

Correcting

A fourth word that carries within it the concept of discipline is the word **correct** (Gk. *epanorthosis*). This word means "to correct, to restore to an upright or right state, to raise up again, to reform, to restore, to reestablish" (2 Tim. 3:16).

This word highlights the fact that the purpose of all discipline is to bring about the restoration of the believer to God's intended purpose. It also points out the fact that sometimes people need assistance in coming back to an upright position. This is what covenant relationship means. This is how true brothers and sisters respond to each other in the Body of Christ (Gal. 6:1-2). When one of our company falls, we reach out to pick him or her up. We do not shoot our wounded.

Judging

A controversial word that enters into this concept of discipline in the local church is the word **judge** (Gk. k*rino*). How many times, when someone is involved in some sort of confrontation, don't we hear the phrase, "Who are you to judge?" Or we hear people say, "Judge not, lest ye be judged!"

Many believers have the concept that in the church we have no right to make judgments when it comes to the behavior of others, because, "No one knows the heart." Nothing could be further from the truth. They are correct when it comes to judging the world or the unbeliever (1 Cor. 5:12-13), because that is the work of the Holy Spirit (John 16:8).

However, when it comes to members of the local church, we are required to make judgment. Leaders especially must do so if they are going to be able to fulfill their responsibilities to their congregations.

The word *judge* means "to separate, put asunder, to select, to approve, to determine, to decree, to judge, to pronounce an opinion concerning right and wrong, to rule, to govern, to preside over with power of giving judicial decisions." Pastors and leaders who refuse to make judgments will face a multitude of problems that will continue to mount up because problems do not just go away by themselves (1 Cor. 6:2-31; 14:29).

KEY BIBLICAL VERSES CONCERNING CHURCH DISCIPLINE

As you read through the pages of the Bible, it is clear that God has a lot to say about the area of discipline. As with most truths in the Bible, there are key passages that deal very specifically with this subject. I would like to take a closer look at some of these key texts.

Matthew 18:15-20

These verses give us the only passage where Jesus dealt directly with the local church. It is interesting that Jesus did not have any unrealistic expectations concerning the local assembly. He indicated that there would be problems. He said, "If your brother *sins* against you..." Perhaps we could say "*when* your brother sins against you." If you live with people long enough, offenses will come.

The word Jesus used for "sin" here is the word meaning "to miss the mark." We all have experienced times of weakness where we fail in some area of personal relationship. Thankfully Jesus understood this and gave us guidelines as to how to function in the event that such things happened.

Jesus said that when an offense occurs, the responsibility is on the offended party to go to the offender alone and "show him his fault." The Greek word here is "*elenko*," which means to bring it out in the open, point out the fault, and perhaps even demand an explanation. Sometimes an explanation is all that is needed. Sometimes the problem was simply the result of bad communication. In this case it can be cleared up easily and quickly. In this case perhaps no one else needs to be drawn into it.

Jesus goes on in this passage to give us a process for situations where the results are not so positive. We will discuss this process later because it is so absolutely essential if we are to find success in the area of church discipline. Suffice it to say at this point that the process is gradual, attempts are made to keep the problem as private as possible, and the extent of the discipline is totally dependent upon the response of the person being disciplined.

1 Corinthians 5:1-13

In 1 Corinthians 5, Paul is addressing a serious problem in one of the churches that he personally fathered. He is concerned because a member of the church is living in open sin and no one seems to be too terribly concerned. In fact, it is clear that the people in the church are rather proud of their tolerance and absence of a "judgmental spirit" (vss. 1-2).

Paul lets them know in no uncertain terms that their tolerance is ungodly and that he doesn't have to know all of the details to know that something serious needs to be done both to save this man and to preserve the congregation from further pollution.

Paul gives several specific instructions to the church. They were facing a drastic situation, and it would call for drastic measures (Matt. 5:29). He instructed them that this man should be "taken away from among you" (vs. 2); that they should "deliver such a one to Satan for the destruction of the flesh (vs. 5); that they should "purge out the old leaven" (vs. 7); that they were not to "keep company with sexually immoral people" in the church (vs. 9); that they were "not even to eat with such a person" (vs. 11) and that they were to "put away...that wicked person" (vs. 13).

All of this is pretty serious. But Paul's concern is for the rest of the church. He knows that if the church leaders do not take their responsibility to judge those who profess to be believers (vs. 12), and they continue to tolerate sin in the congregation, it will eventually affect other believers (vss. 6-8).

2 Corinthians 2:5-11

Evidently, the leaders of the church "saw the light" and followed through on the discipline that Paul had recommended to them. Paul referred to this discipline in his second letter to the church at Corinth and described this action as "the punishment which was inflicted by the majority" (2 Cor. 2:6). In other words this discipline was an action of the entire church.

Unfortunately, the church that had been so tolerant of sin among them now had gone to the other end of the discipline spectrum. Now, after their discipline had accomplished its intended purpose and the man actually repented, they did not want to receive the disciplined man back into the congregation. Paul had to challenge them now to reaffirm their love to this man (vs. 8). He gave great instructions to them on how to receive someone back into fellowship and how to see them restored. He told them to forgive, comfort, and receive this man back so that Satan would not win in this situation.

It is so typical among God's people. We tend to like extremes. It is so easy for us to swing from one end of the spectrum to the other. We can be all law or all grace. Somehow Jesus was able to be full of grace and full of truth all at the same time. All discipline should be mixed with grace. All grace should be tempered by truth.

Romans 16:17-18

Paul makes it clear in Romans 16 that discipline does not always involve areas of moral impurity or disorderliness. Sometimes discipline may be called for when someone is sowing discord in a local church by the persistent teaching and dissemination of false doctrine. He encouraged the believers in the Roman church to "note those who cause divisions and offenses, contrary to the doctrine which you learned" (vs. 17). He spoke of those who used "smooth words and flattering speech" to deceive individuals who were not grounded in truth.

Paul makes reference to an initial posture toward these people by encouraging people to "note them" and "avoid them" (vs. 17). It is clear, however, from later passages that should people persist in sowing division, it could lead to more severe measures.

2 Thessalonians 3:6-15

Paul seems to be referring to the same kind of scenario when he writes to the believers in Thessalonica. He instructs the church to "withdraw from every brother who walks disorderly and not according to the tradition which he received from us" (vs. 6). Here Paul seems to be talking about issues of lifestyle. He speaks of people who are lazy and refuse to work, who are disorderly in behavior, and who are busybodies (vs. 11).

He goes on to challenge them to use his epistle to bring some adjustment to these people, and if they do not respond, the leaders should "note" them and "not keep company with" them. This is all with the intent that they might be "ashamed" (vs. 14), repent, and change their behavior. The church leaders are cautioned, in this case, not to treat these individuals as enemies but to admonish them as fellow Christians.

1 Timothy 1:20

Paul writes to Timothy about a couple of men by the names of Hymenaeus and Alexander. We do not know too much about the situation of these men. They were most likely leaders who had been discipled by Paul. They seem to have rejected the faith and a good conscience and refused to respond to Paul's personal admonitions. Paul, in a sense, had given up on them or realized that these men would not respond to his leadership in their lives. As a last resort Paul had delivered them to Satan "that they may learn not to blaspheme" (vs. 20).

Just exactly what Paul meant by this is uncertain from this passage alone. Other passages in the New Testament seem to suggest some form of church discipline or excommunication. In any event it is important that whatever this action entailed, it was for the purpose of bringing about change in the lives of the disciplined parties.

Titus 1:10-13

When writing to Titus who was also pastoring a church, Paul makes reference to those who are insubordinate, idle talkers, and deceivers who are teaching false doctrine and undermining the work of God. These individuals are evidently using their teaching as a way to gain disciples to themselves and make a living by what they are doing.

Paul indicates that these individuals should be rebuked "sharply" (vs. 13). The word "sharply" used here means "abruptly, curtly, or severely with uncompromising hardness." Paul understood that there were certain individuals who were doing damage to the local church. Paul could be very direct with such people.

The thing to note here is that when it came to the protection of the Bride of Christ, the church, Paul was very motivated. It is one thing when someone has a diverse opinion about something. But when these individuals insist on disseminating their opinions in a way that brings harm to others or leads others astray, they must be stopped. Paul told Titus that sometimes you have to "rebuke with all authority" (Titus 2:15).

Titus 3:10-11

It is interesting that it is in what have been called the "pastoral" epistles of Paul that we find so many admonitions about how to deal with problem people. Sometimes we have the idea that to be "pastoral" is to be conciliatory to everyone so as not to be offensive. The truth is that one of the instruments in the hands of the shepherd was the rod. This rod was used to defend the flock against those who would do harm whether it was from outside the flock or inside the flock (Acts 20:29-30).

Paul warns Titus of "divisive" men. He instructs Titus to warn a divisive person once, then warn him a second time. If he does not respond, have nothing to do with him (vs. 10). Paul indicates that such people who do not respond are "warped and sinning, being self-condemned" (vs. 11).

THE PURPOSE OF DISCIPLINE AND CONFRONTATION

All discipline that takes place in the local church is purposeful. It is never vindictive. It is never self-serving. In fact it takes a lot of courage and love to exercise biblical discipline. The exercise of discipline is redemptive in nature. Yet it is important to see that as leaders we must realize that there is more at stake than the individual that it being disciplined. There are three main concerns that must be kept in balance as discipline is administered. First of all, we must have a deep love for the individual who is at fault. Second, we must do what is best for the entire local church. Third, we must remember that God has some issues in this situation as well.

Discipline as it relates to the Individual

Discipline has an important place in the life of the members of any family. In the same way, every believer needs some discipline or accountability in his or her life. Discipline in the life of the individual has a ninefold purpose. For the sake of space I will simply list these with the biblical references. Discipline is applied…

1. To keep people from going astray (Ps. 119:67; Hosea 7:11-12; Jer. 10:23-24; Prov. 10:17; 1 Cor. 5:5).
2. To keep people from the calamity of the wicked (Ps. 94:12; 1 Cor. 11:32).
3. To bring people closer to God (Isa. 26:16).
4. To make people wise (Prov. 22:15).
5. To bring people to a place of abundant life (Heb. 12:9).
6. To help people deal with sin and grow in righteousness in areas where they have been personally unsuccessful (Heb. 12:9-12).
7. To teach people the right ways of God (Ps. 119:71).
8. To produce greater fruitfulness in the lives of people (John 15:2).
9. To restore the repentant believers (Gal. 6:1; 2 Cor. 2:7-10).

Discipline as it relates to the local church

Discipline is not just about the individual who is involved in the problem. It is very much about the rest of the local church as well. It may even have implications to the entire Body of Christ. For this reason, discipline has a purpose as it relates to the church. I will also simply list these purposes with biblical references. Discipline is applied...

1. To bring the church to maturity (Eph. 4:12-16; 1 Cor. 3:1).
2. To deter others from similar sins (1 Tim. 5:20; Titus 3:10).
3. To protect the reputation of the church and its leaders (1 Cor. 5:1).
4. To protect the church from further contamination (1 Cor. 5:6-7).
5. To prove that leaders love and care (2 Cor. 7:12).
6. To affirm each member's responsibility to be his brother's keeper (Heb. 3:13).
7. To cut emotional ties with unrepentant Christians (1 Cor. 5:11).

One of the things that we will see when it comes to discipline is that most believers will not be able to do what they are supposed to do in this area without the standard being set and action being taken by those in the leadership. When the action is affirmed by the whole believing community, it is easier for people to take the matter out of the emotional side of their life and place it into the principled side of their life.

Discipline as it relates to God

Discipline in the local church is also very much about God. The local church is not only God's representative to the community, but it has a responsibility to reflect back to God His heart. In other words we have a responsibility to handle the situation at hand the way God would handle it. We cannot be more gracious than God is. We cannot be more tolerant than God is. We must function in a way that is consistent with who God is. Discipline has a purpose as it relates to God. Discipline is applied...

1. To affirm the authority of God and His Word in our lives (2 Cor. 2:9).

2. To maintain the honor of God (Rom. 2:24).

3. To maintain the purity of the Scriptures (Titus 1:10-11).

THE KINDS OF SINS THAT ARE
TO BE DISCIPLINED BY THE CHURCH

It should be obvious by now that discipline takes on many different forms and has many different degrees depending on the severity and scope of the issues involved. Bill Gothard in his advanced seminar described three areas that should lead to discipline by church leaders. Those three categories are as follows:

> **Irresolvable** disputes between members (Matt. 18:15; 1 Cor. 5:11)
> **Persistent** teaching of false doctrine (Titus 1:9-11; 3:10-11; Rom. 16:17)
> **Continuing** immorality and disorderliness (2 Thess. 3:6; 1 Cor. 5:11)

The thing that all of these areas have in common is a persistence on the part of the disciplined person to continue in sin even after the initial confrontation. People who are in the place of discipline are in full control. If they respond to discipline, there will be healing and restoration. If they persist in their sin, there will be further steps of increasing severity.

THE LEVELS OF DISCIPLINE
(MATTHEW 18:15-20)

In Matthew 18, Jesus describes a process for discipline in the church. While there is some debate over the actual steps and how they should be applied, it is clear that it is God's intention that the church should be a place of unity where conflicts are laid to rest and the power of God can be released.

Private

The first observation that we can make from Jesus' instruction is that privacy is always attempted. In other words, God is not interested in embarrassing anyone. The first step involves believer to believer where the situation can be handled as privately as possible (Note: A possible exception to this is dealing with those in leadership who have been found to be guilty of a sin of disqualification [1 Tim. 5:19-20]).

We often miss this step in the process. In general, members of the congregation are reluctant to confront another member whom they see sinning. Unfortunately, as a result, small issues become large issues. Pastors must teach their people that we are a covenant community that shares in a mutual accountability and that we are our brothers' keepers. Most people who are sinning are not doing so in the purview of leaders in the church. When they are around leaders in the church, they are at their best. Often it is the members of the congregation who will first see the problem.

If the people of God would follow Jesus' first step and go to another brother and sister alone, perhaps there would not be as much need for more serious discipline to be applied.

Semi-Private

It is clear, however, that if sinning members of the church will not respond to the gentle admonition of another believer, the situation will progress to another level. Two or three others may have to be brought into the situation. The whole idea is to get others involved to exert more pressure on the erring brother or sister to repent and change.

Who should be brought in at this level? I do not believe that we should grab any three people in the church that we can find to bolster our case. If our goal is restoration, we should seek to include people who have the most power and influence in the life of the erring party. Perhaps we would choose a close friend of that party, a parent, an official church leader, or some other key individual in the person's life. The goal is to get them to do the right thing.

Public

Once the person being disciplined responds in a biblical way, the need for further levels of discipline is eliminated. However, if the erring party refuses to respond at any level, the circle of those involved widens. At this point there is some disagreement as to what is meant by "tell it to the church." It is my view that the next step would be to tell it to the leadership team or the elders of the church. The elders are the official authority of the church, and as such they are responsible for all affairs that affect the well-being of the local assembly.

The elders at this stage may make an official confrontation of the situation. If the person still remains obstinate, a formal declaration of discipline may have to be made, and the entire congregation will have to be brought into the process.

This of course is the most severe form of discipline and hopefully will rarely need to be exercised, especially if the other forms of discipline are faithfully administered.

PREREQUISITES FOR EFFECTIVE CHURCH DISCIPLINE

Before a local church can begin to discipline at this level, there must exist the proper climate for that discipline. Elders and other church leaders cannot "all of a sudden" step up in this area. Too often pastors and church leaders read books or attend conferences where they are challenged to make some changes or implement some programs. The pastor comes home with great resolve to put into practice all that he has been taught.

Unfortunately, the people in the local church have not read those same books or been to those same meetings. They do not know what is coming and may resist change because that change has not been properly sown into their hearts.

It can be much like parents who attend a seminar on childrearing and realize they have been inconsistent and have not disciplined their children in a biblical way. They cannot come home and immediately implement all they have received. They must talk to the children, repent of their past negligence, and instruct them regarding how it is going to be in the future. Only then can they proceed on the enlightened path.

The same is true in the local church. If church leaders have been negligent in the areas of church discipline, they need to repent to their congregations, teach and lay the foundation for biblical discipline, and gradually implement the truth at all levels, especially the early levels.

Before pastors and leaders can exercise discipline in the local church, there must be the establishment of a biblical standard in the life of the church. If leaders are not living holy lives, if there are not true biblical standards of right and wrong, it is hypocritical and ultimately arbitrary to discipline issues in the congregation.

Before pastors and leaders can exercise discipline in the local church, leaders must teach the membership concerning discipline. I know that we do not like to preach on the subject of discipline in the church. We are trying to get people to come to our churches, not drive them away. Somehow the subject of discipline does not look good on the church reader board in the front lawn of the facility. However, people must have truth to draw upon if we are to expect right behavior. I heard one pastor say one time that if my people are not responding in the way that I think they should, it is because I have not taught them properly.

Before pastors and leaders can exercise discipline in the local church the leadership must be willing to set the example in all areas of living. Parents who are violating the law will not have the respect of their children and lose the moral authority to discipline. The same is true in the local church. Pastors and leaders must lead by example. They must be willing to live by the preached standard and they must demonstrate that they accept the authority of Christ in their personal lives.

Before pastors and leaders can exercise discipline in the local church, they must be committed to all the levels of confrontation, especially the first level. It is wrong to jump directly to the ultimate level of excommunication when other levels of confrontation have not taken place in a timely manner. In some cases, I think we actually owe our people an apology for not taking our pastoral charge seriously and neglecting to confront them sooner.

EXCOMMUNICATION

Excommunication is the most serious form of discipline in the local church. It is exercised when all else fails. Excommunication is the public removal of a church member from membership and a severing of fellowship with the believing community.

What effectively takes place in excommunication is that when a person refuses to respond to the earthly authorities in their life, they are referred up to the higher authority. God has divested his authority in the local church.

If people will not respond to that authority, God will step in Himself.

It is not unlike a woman who is having trouble with her children not responding to her or not submitting to her attempts at discipline. She may say, "Wait until dad gets home!" Of course no dad wants to come home to that situation, but the principle is the same. Jesus is the head of the church. If you don't respond to His ordained leaders, you will answer directly to Him. There is no question that God has a "bigger stick" than church leaders when it comes to discipline.

In excommunication the sinning member is placed outside of the spiritual covering of the church. The sinning member is turned over to God for direct discipline. Since God fully respects the authority of the local church, it is the official action of the church that initiates this ultimate stage of discipline.

When a person is placed outside of the church, they not only come under the direct auspices of God, but the covering or protection that they had previously experienced by being rightly related to authority is removed, exposing them in a fresh way to the attacks of Satan.

People need to know that God cares enough about His people that He will use any means that He can to bring them back. And God has things at His disposal that earthly leaders do not. It is a fearful thing to fall into the hands of the living God.

I remember one person who was excommunicated by our church for perpetual immorality. He had violated his marriage covenant and was seeing another woman. The day following his public excommunication, he was in a car accident, he lost his job, and a couple of other calamities occurred. He came back to the elders the next day pleading to be restored. He is living in right relationship with his family today. Excommunication works! It does not always work that fast, but it accomplishes what it is intended to. It works especially well if the congregation does its part in the process.

The Congregation's Part in Excommunication

What is the congregation's part in the excommunication process? Actually, the congregation plays a vital role. If they do not cooperate with the discipline, they can undermine and prolong the process. But their cooperation will ensure that the greatest possible pressure is exerted on the offending party.

The congregation has three parts to play in the process. First of all, they are to refuse to fellowship with the sinning member. This withdrawal of fellowship is designed to put pressure on the person and help him to understand what he is losing by persisting in his sin. If the congregation continues to treat the person like everything is normal, it takes the teeth out of the discipline.

I remember an incident that was shared with me many years ago about a man in the church who was behaving badly toward his wife and family. He was an avid hunter, and many of the people in the church, including some key leaders, enjoyed going hunting with him because he always got his catch. Because of the man's hunting prowess, these leaders tended to overlook his less-than-Christian lifestyle, and the man had little or no motivation to change his behavior.

Finally, one of the leaders realized what they were doing. They were in essence caring more about their hunting than they were about this man and his family. They decided to confront the situation in a different way than they had done in the past. They determined that they would no longer fellowship with this man or hunt with him until he made some significant changes. It worked! The man had also loved to be with these Christian friends. When his friends cut him off, it put the kind of pressure on him that he needed to make some serious changes in his life.

The second responsibility of the congregation is to urge and implore the offending party to repent. The Bible teaches that we are to treat the person like a heathen. This does not mean that we refuse to speak to them. We are friendly, but when we speak to them, we only have one aim in our conversation and that is to implore them to repent. This is not the same as fellowship. This is not the same as hanging out together. This is taking every opportunity to speak truth into the life of the disciplined member, keeping the pressure on them until they do the right thing.

The third responsibility of the congregation is to pray for the disciplined member that they might see the light, repent, and be restored. As you can see, the members of the congregation must be on board with the discipline because they have such a powerful role in its effectiveness. Therefore, it is essential to determine before someone is disciplined whether or not the discipline is for something that is generally considered to be wrong by the congregation.

Restoring the Repentant Member

Ideally, the day will come when all of this pressure produces the desired fruit and the erring member repents and turns his life back to God. When there is sufficient evidence that true repentance has taken place, the Bible makes it clear that this repentance should be cause for great rejoicing. Now is the time for the congregation to do their part to open their arms of comfort to the person, forgive him both privately and publicly, and reaffirm love to this individual (2 Cor. 2:6-8).

THE ATTITUDE OF A RESTORER

Throughout this process, the attitude of those who are handling the issues of discipline are critical to its overall success. The leaders of the church are not to be judgmental, vindictive, or harsh in their approach to sinning members. On the contrary, the Bible is very clear about the attitudes that must be possessed by those enforcing discipline. These attitudes involve six aspects.

- The restorer must be motivated by love (Heb. 12:6; Rev. 3:19; Eph. 4:15; 2 Thess. 3:15).
- The restorer must function with gentleness (1 Thess. 2:1-9; Ps. 141:5).
- The restorer must have a spirit of meekness, recognizing that except for the grace of God, we would all be in trouble (Gal. 6:1-2).
- The restorer must be ready to extend mercy and forgiveness (2 Cor. 2:6-8).
- The restorer must have the heart of a father (1 Thess. 2:10-12; 1 Cor. 4:14-16).
- The restorer must reprove in wisdom (Prov. 25:2).

Like an earring of gold and an ornament of fine gold is a *wise reprover* to a listening ear. (NAS)

PRACTICAL STEPS OF CHURCH DISCIPLINE

The following notes are some that I gleaned from a pastors' conference held by Bill Gothard. I think that they represent a good, practical process for the leaders of the church.

1. Thoroughly investigate charges (Matt. 18:16; 1 Tim. 5:19; Deut. 13:14; 19:18; Prov. 25:9; 18:13).
2. Work with parents and other authority figures whenever possible.
   a. Parents still have much influence (Deut. 4:9; Prov. 23:22).
   b. Parents can give background information.
   c. Parents should be first to get involved (Eph. 6:1; Deut. 21:20).
3. Prepare the church for public discipline.
   a. In teaching
   b. In prayer, fasting and self-examination (2 Cor. 7:11)
   c. In reminding them of the purpose and place of discipline in the church
4. Inform the church (Matt. 18:17).
   a. Read a prepared and approved (lawyer and leadership) statement. Statement should be brief, factual, and project no malice.
   b. The church should be called to continued prayer for and appeal to the sinning members.
   c. Scriptural love, not avoidance, should be followed.
5. Be ready to restore the person when repentant (2 Cor. 2:7-11).

PUBLIC ANNOUNCEMENT

"It has come to the attention of the board that a member of our church must be dealt with by church discipline.

The church board has carefully and thoroughly investigated the facts, and has confirmed that discipline is necessary.

The parents and the board have appealed to the one who has sinned. All attempts have so far been rejected.

Scripture now instructs us to inform the church so that the united prayer and obedience of the members to the scriptural steps of discipline may be used of God to bring this person to repentance and to a life of victory over sin.

Before naming this person we are asking each member to set aside a time of personal self-examination, confession of sin, and commitment to God's instructions of church discipline and restoration.

We are doing this so that Satan will be given no opportunity to bring confusion or division on this matter and that God may be free, because of our obedience, to accomplish His purpose in the life of the one who has sinned."

CONCLUSIONS ABOUT DISCIPLINE

If a church is to grow and prosper from generation to generation, that church must determine to exercise spiritual discipline relative to its membership.

Discipline is an important aspect of the church. Discipline is a demonstration of faithfulness (Ps. 110:75; Prov. 27:5-6). It is for the purpose of restoration and salvation (James 5:19-20; 2 Thess. 3:15). Discipline is a means of instruction (Ps. 94:12). It is designed as a means of grace, not of destruction. Discipline is important for the protection of the rest of the church body. It is gradual and totally dependent on attitude and response of the person being disciplined. Discipline is designed as an evidence of love, not of hate or of fear.

Chapter Fourteen

———

TITHING AND GIVING

*KEY #12—If a church is to grow and prosper from
generation to generation, that church must determine
to promote the biblical concepts of faith and sacrificial giving.*

omeone has said, "vision is spelled m-o-n-e-y." There is a truth to
that statement. If the church is going to be all that it is to be, God
has got to be able to deal with the "love of money" issue in the hearts
of His people. At the same time, God has got to help ministers to understand that it is very spiritual to talk about money issues.

Many true pastors and leaders shy away from the issue of money. They
are true shepherds and not hirelings, and they do not want to be misinterpreted. Jesus, the apostles and Paul were not so hesitant. They were not afraid
of the money issue because they understood that money and the proper use
of it have a lot to do with the spiritual condition of people. They understood
that the purpose of money is to establish the kingdom and purpose of God
(Deut. 8:18). They also understood that the use of one's money is a reflection
of one's heart (Matt. 6:21). Perhaps this is why there are more warnings about
money and the use of money in the Gospels than any other single subject.

The truth is, it is going to take a lot of money to fulfill the Great
Commission. The early church saw money as a tool. It was one of the
resources that God had placed in their hands to fulfill their spiritual charge.
They were willing to lay these resources at Jesus' feet much like the woman
with the alabaster box (Acts 4:35-37).

189

If the church is going to influence society, it must be touched by a spirit of generosity and a spirit of contentment. God wants to bless His people with much more than they need, but not for the purpose of building bigger barns or houses or driving more expensive cars. He wants to bless them so that they can be a blessing to the world (Gen. 12:1-3).

GOD'S FINANCIAL SYSTEM

To better understand God's financial plan for the local church, it is necessary to be familiar with God's financial system in the Old Testament. This does not mean that the New Testament church must follow all of the Mosaic admonitions in regard to finance, but it is significant that there is only one financial system that God ever gave to any nation in the world, and that is the system of the tithe that God gave to the nation of Israel. We have to assume that this system at least reflects God's heart in principle form.

The concept of the tithe was not new with the Mosaic system. Long before Moses' ascent to Mount Sinai, Abraham had offered tithes to Melchizedek, priest of the Most High God (Gen. 14:18-10). Jacob, also in a time of consecration to the Lord, had vowed to give God a tenth (Gen. 28:22). But it is with Moses that God gave a detailed definition of what He desired for His people in regard to the tithe. God was very concerned about the plan of giving in the nation of Israel. God prescribed certain offerings, sacrifices, and tithes that constituted His plan for their giving.

The principal area of tithing in Israel's economy was referred to as the "Lord's tithe" (Lev. 27:30-33). This tithe consisted of 10 percent of all their increase before anything else was taken out. It was used primarily for the support of the Levites or ministers of the congregation (Num. 18:21-24).

In Israel's history the tithe was not always maintained, because the people themselves were not always stable in their personal relationship to God. When Israel backslid, their neglect in the area of tithing was usually one of the first symptoms of their declining spiritual condition. In these times of backsliding it was not uncommon for the Levites to have to go to work at civilian jobs because giving was so low (Neh. 13:10-12; Mal. 1:7-14).

When God's people did not honor Him in their tithing, it released the devourer, and calamity ate up whatever they would withhold (Mal. 3:7-12).

However, it is equally important to note that whenever there was spiritual revival in Israel, there was also a restoration of the spirit of tithing (2 Chron. 31:5-12; Neh. 10:37).

In the Old Testament the Lord's tithe was only the beginning of their giving. They had an additional tithe that was to be set aside to be used for religious observances (Deut. 14:22-26). In addition to this, every third year they were to give an additional tithe for the poor and needy (Deut. 14:28-29). For this reason the third year was called "the year of tithing" (Deut. 26:12-14). Beyond the tithes, which were mandatory, there were a variety of free-will offerings that were entirely up to the individuals (Deut. 12:6).

OUR PRESENT RELATIONSHIP TO THE TITHE

To understand our present relationship to the tithe, we must first understand Jesus' relationship to the law. We know that the Law and the Prophets were until John, and after that the Kingdom of God was preached, and every man was to press into it (Matt. 11:12-13). Jesus came as the King of that Kingdom.

As the King of the Kingdom, He was also the Lawgiver. In Matthew 5, Jesus fulfilled this ministry, and even as Moses had received the law on Mount Sinai in the Old Testament, Jesus set Himself on a mountain and laid down principles or laws that were to govern the Kingdom under His rule and authority.

In every case Jesus began from the Law of Moses and moved to the principle behind the law. By so doing, He magnified the law and made it honorable (Isa. 42:21). He later summarized the whole of the Mosaic Law into the command to love God and love your neighbor (Matt. 22:36-40). This new commandment of Jesus did not make the Mosaic Law any weaker. In fact, it made it stronger and much more difficult to practice. Jesus summarized the Mosaic Law into one higher law—the law of love.

In the New Testament when we fulfill the higher law of love, we automatically fulfill the requirements of the Mosaic Law. If the royal law of love does not allow me to hate my brother, then that law more than covers the Mosaic admonition against killing my brother. If the royal law of love does not allow me to lust in my heart after a woman, then that law more than covers the admonition not to commit adultery.

In the New Testament, Jesus seems to take this same attitude toward tithing. First of all, He confirms the truth contained in the Mosaic Law by supporting and fulfilling it (Matt. 23:23; Luke 20:25). He then teaches on principles of giving that stand behind the law (Mark 12:41-44; Luke 6:38). Finally, He institutes a higher law to cover the principles of New Covenant giving. He teaches us that all we have belongs to God and that it is more blessed to give than to receive (Acts 20:35).

For this reason the epistles never explicitly command tithing. We do, however, find an outline of the higher law that is prescribed by God. Before the law, tithing was done voluntarily. Under the law, tithing was compulsory. In the New Covenant, tithing or giving is to be done willingly and cheerfully. The net result is the same. The difference is that a higher law motivated by love has been introduced. Love in its very nature is giving. Love gives and gives and gives again well beyond the demands of the law.

THE HIGHER LAW

The New Testament principles of giving reflect this higher law. Giving of our substance to the Lord begins by giving ourselves to the Lord (2 Cor. 8:5; Rom. 12:1-2). Once we have done that, we are free to fulfill the New Testament requirements of giving, which encourage us to give in the following ways:

- Generously (2 Cor. 8:2; 9:6)
- Willingly (2 Cor. 8:3,12)
- Proportionately (2 Cor. 8:14-15; 9:6)
- Lovingly (2 Cor. 8:24; 1 Cor. 13:3)
- Cheerfully (2 Cor. 9:7)
- Thankfully (2 Cor. 9:11-12)
- Sacrificially (Heb. 13:16; Mark 12:44)
- As unto the Lord (Matt. 25:40)

Paul, in his second letter to the Corinthians, outlines some of the principles of New Testament giving that were intended to release this great church into the realm of faith. These principles can serve as a model and admonition for the church today. It should be noted from the very outset that Paul was addressing a local church that had needs and was going through what could be termed as "affliction" (2 Cor. 8:1). Our natural circumstances should never dictate our faith.

Note the following principles taken from 2 Corinthians 8-9:

- Giving in faith requires a grace from God (8:1-2). When we walk in the law of love and have a godly desire to give, God will favor us to be able to give generously even when all of our personal needs are not met.
- Giving in faith requires giving willingly beyond our natural ability (8:3). If we only give what we know we can give, it requires no faith on our part.
- Giving in faith views giving as a privilege, not as drudgery, even to the degree that we may plead with a recipient to receive our offering (8:4).
- Giving in faith requires giving of ourselves totally to the Lord first so that we will be able to be obedient to His leading in our giving (8:5). If Christ is the Lord of our lives, He is the Lord of our finances as well.
- Giving in faith requires having a desire to excel in this act of grace (8:6-7). To excel is to go beyond the expected measure. It means to outdo or surpass the normal limits.
- Giving in faith is based on love that is willing to put the needs of others ahead of our own so that they might be made rich by our sacrifice (8:8-9).
- Giving in faith involves making commitments of faith and then following through with those commitments (8:10-11).
- Giving in faith is determined by the willingness and the sacrifice involved, not on the actual size of the gift (8:12).
- Giving in faith requires a willingness to stretch out in faith, believing that God will supply what we need in the future through the proper functioning of the Body of Christ (8:13-15).

- Giving in faith will be tested by circumstances that come against the commitments that we have made (9:1-5). True faith will, however, give us the courage to follow through on our promises.
- Giving in faith involves a generous sowing of seed, realizing that unless there is a significant deposit there can be no significant return (9:6).
- Giving in faith is done cheerfully because it springs from a deep appreciation and spirit of thanksgiving for everything that the Lord has done for us (9:7).
- Giving in faith recognizes that God is a debtor to no one and that He will be generous with us beyond our generosity to Him (9:8-11).
- Giving in faith is a testimony to others of the grace of God in our lives that will not only inspire faith to rise up within them but will cause them to praise God in greater ways (9:12-13). In other words, generous faith is contagious.
- Giving in faith will inspire others to participate in what we are doing through their encouragement and prayer support (9:14).

Any New Testament church that follows these basic New Testament principles of giving will never have a financial problem. They will have plenty for salaries, missions, and all of the other regular functions of the church. In addition, their members will begin to experience the blessings of God on their lives in a new and exciting way.

It is tragic when local church leaders have to argue over every nickel and dime in the extension of the Kingdom of God. What a release that comes when we instill principles of faith into the hearts of the people of God and they begin to take on the impossible in the work of the Lord.

Church leaders who fail to teach biblical principles of giving to their membership are robbing the people of the blessing of God that can only come when God's principles are followed (Mal. 3:6-12). This applies equally to megachurches or to small missions that are established in poor countries. Whenever poverty-stricken people are deprived of biblical teaching concerning giving, they are being deprived of the very means that God uses to bless His people financially. When we fail to teach any portion of God's Word, we are hurting people and not helping them.

The wealthiest person in the world today is not the head of some computer company. The wealthiest "person" in the world today is the Body of Christ! When we allow Jesus to be the Lord of our finances, the local church will grow and expand in an amazing way. We have the resources that we need. Faith will release them into the harvest.

Chapter Fifteen

THE PRESENCE OF GOD

KEY #13—*If a church is to grow and prosper from generation to generation, that church must determine to focus on those things that promote the manifest presence of God in its gatherings.*

God's presence is still the key to the church's success. The thing that made Israel distinct among the other nations was the pillar of cloud and the pillar of fire. Israel was a nation that was covered by the manifest presence of God. Just so, the church is to be the place where God's presence is manifest. Jesus indicated His desire to be in the midst of the church (Matt. 18:20).

I am fully aware of the doctrine of the omnipresence of God and that there is a sense in which we are always in His presence and cannot in this same sense escape His presence (Ps. 139:7-12; Jer. 23:24). But I am also aware that the Bible seems to promote the idea that God at times manifests His presence in a personal, a powerful, and a manifest way. David did not want to lose this sense of God's presence in his life (Ps. 51:11).

GOD'S DWELLING PLACE

The whole purpose in God creating man was so that God could have an intimate relationship with His creation. God has always had a desire to dwell among His people. This desire is first seen in the warm relationship that existed between God and the first human beings in the Garden of

Eden before the terrible breach that was caused by the fall (Gen. 1:3).

Even after the fall of man into sin, God continued to demonstrate His desire to dwell together with His creation in His relationship to the patriarchs and His provision for them in the altars of stone (Gen. 8:20; Exod. 20:24-25). With the coming of Moses and the formation of Israel as a nation, God was more specific about that desire. While Moses was on Mount Sinai, God gave him specific instructions for a tabernacle in the wilderness.

And let them make Me a sanctuary, that I may dwell among them.
Exodus 25:8

As God walked with man throughout Old Testament history, His manifest presence went from "tent to tent, and from one tabernacle to another" (1 Chron. 17:5), but the one thing that remained constant was God's great desire to dwell among His covenant people.

God continued in the Old Testament to make provision for His dwelling among His people in the tabernacle of David (1 Chron. 15) and the temple of Solomon (1 Kings. 8:8, 13). All of these dwelling places prepared the way for God's greatest expression of this desire, the Incarnation.

When Jesus came among us, He came as the Tabernacle of God. John declared that the Word was made flesh and dwelt or "tabernacled" among us (John 1:14). Jesus declared that He was the temple of God (John 2:19-21). However, Jesus was not the final dwelling place or house of God.

Jesus came to build another house. That New Covenant house is the church. The church is the present provision of God for His dwelling among His covenant people (Matt. 18:20; 28:20). The church will one day give place to the New Jerusalem where we will experience the highest expression of God's dwelling among men.

And I saw a new heaven and a new earth, for the first heaven and the first earth had passed away. Also there was no more sea. Then I, John, saw the holy city, New Jerusalem, coming down out of heaven from God, prepared as a bride adorned for her husband. And I heard a loud voice from heaven saying, "Behold the tabernacle of God is

with men, and He will dwell with them, and they shall be His
people, and God himself will be with them and be their God."

Revelation 21:1-3

One thing that must be noticed in each of these dwelling places that were provided by God is that God's dwelling with man has always been on His terms and according to His pattern. David had a tremendous desire to see God's presence once again in the midst of Israel. God's desire was to be in the center of His people as well. But when David tried to make the desire work with an approach other than the God-ordained approach, the results were not as he desired. In fact, it brought death to the camp (2 Sam. 6:1-9).

As we desire to see God's presence manifest in the midst of the church, or God's house today, we need to learn from the experience of David. We want God's power among us, but in order to see it released fully, we must build God's house, God's way.

GOD'S PRESENCE IN THE CHURCH

If the church does not have a supernatural touch upon it created by an awareness of God's presence, it is no different than any other social organization. The church is not like another social organization. It is the temple of the Living God! It is God's dwelling place.

When the people of God gather together in one place, they make a habitation for God by the Spirit where they can potentially have a very real experience of His manifest presence (Eph. 2:19-22; Matt. 18:20). That is the most exciting thing about the corporate gathering. God shows up and ministers to His people in ways that they cannot minister to each other.

When we gather in the corporate assembly, it is not for the choir. It is not for the entertainment factor. It is not so we can see all of our friends together. While all of these things have their value, our principal goal is to meet with God and experience a dynamic of His presence that we cannot experience alone in our living room in front of the television.

I think it could be said that the most important aspect of the house of the Lord is the presence of the Lord (Ps. 16:11). What good is a house if the man of the house does not dwell in it? What good is gathering together unless God is in the midst of His people ruling, guiding, leading, healing, and breaking bondages?

David had the right idea in Psalm 27: 4 when he said "One thing I have desired of the LORD, that I will seek: that I may dwell in the house of the LORD all the days of my life, to behold the beauty of the LORD, and to inquire in His temple." David was a man after God's heart who had a passion to be in God's presence.

Moses understood the importance of the presence of God in his life and ministry as well. If God does not go with us, what is the point of going (Exod. 33:14-15). Moses knew the benefits and blessings of the presence of the Lord. He knew that:

- The Presence of the Lord is our defense (Zech. 2:4-5).
- The Presence of the Lord brings rest (Exod. 33:14).
- The Presence of the Lord melts mountains (Isa. 64:1-3).
- The Presence of the Lord brings refreshing (Acts 3:19).
- The Presence of the Lord causes enemies to tremble (Ps. 9:3).

The presence of the Lord is the secret of the church's strength. The church is powerless without it. What a difference, however, when the man is in the house (Mark 2:1-2). When the man Jesus enters an otherwise ordinary house, suddenly the supernatural element is injected into the situation and anything can happen. That ordinary house can be transformed into a center of healing and life.

MAINTAINING THE PRESENCE

Unfortunately, simply having Christ's name over the door of our church does not ensure that He is manifestly present in our gatherings (Rev. 3:1). As individuals, we can lose out on His presence when we do not cultivate a right heart. Adam and Eve hid from the presence because of sin (Gen. 3:8). Cain lost access to God's presence because of pride and a lack of true repentance (Gen. 4:16). Jonah ran from God's presence in disobedience (Jon. 1:3,10).

Sometimes we miss out on the presence of God because we do not understand the spiritual principles that cultivate the presence of God. While

God is no respecter of persons, He has established certain principles that will either hinder or promote an experience of God's manifest presence in the midst of His people.

If we practice those things that hinder the experience of His presence, we will shut ourselves out of the full benefit of the manifest presence of God. If we practice those things that promote God's presence, we will enhance our opportunity to experience that presence regularly.

THE ARK, HIS PRESENCE

What are the things that we can do that release a sense of God's presence among us in a greater way? What are the things that we can do that will elicit a response from the unlearned or the visitor that says, "God is truly among you" (1 Cor. 14:25). To discover some of these principles, we can look at the life of David who had such a deep love for the presence of God.

When David became king after the failed leadership of Saul, he had a sincere desire for change. He did not want to follow the example of Saul who seemed to have little desire to hear God's voice unless he was in some kind of trouble. David knew that he could not effectively lead God's people unless there was a way for him to be in direct contact with the Lord on a consistent basis.

Under the Mosaic Covenant, God had provided a place for His presence to dwell in manifest glory. The *Shekinah* glory of God rested between the cherubim and above the mercy seat on the ark of the covenant that was originally built for the tabernacle of Moses.* This is where God promised to meet with Moses and speak with him face to face with an audible voice (Num. 7:89; with Exod. 25:22). The presence of God was so manifest on the ark of the covenant that when they journeyed, Moses addressed the ark as "the Lord" (Num. 10:35-36).

The ark of the covenant was the centerpiece of the whole wilderness experience. The life of every Israelite was orientated to the placement of the ark in the midst of them whether they were walking or camping (Num. 2:17; 10:14-28). The ark of the covenant or the manifest presence of God

---

* While the word *Shekinah*, which means "the one who dwells," does not appear in Scripture, it does appear in extrabiblical Hebrew writing.

was the thing that made Israel different from all of the other nations of the world. The ark was key to so much. Note the following:

- The ark of the covenant led the way into the Land of Promise (Josh. 3:3-15).
- The ark of the covenant accompanied them into battle (Josh. 6:1-14).
- The ark of the covenant was a key to their victories (Num. 14:44-45).
- The ark of the covenant was the place to hear the voice of the Lord and discover His will (Jdg. 20:27-28).
- The ark of the covenant was a source of strength to the nation (Ps. 132:6-9).
- The ark of the covenant defeated enemies and strange gods (I Sam. 5:1-12).

As vital as the ark was to the people of God, there came a time in their history under the administration of Eli when the love for God's presence had waned, and the ark was lost. The sons of Eli, who had no true respect for the ark and no willingness to follow the pattern revealed in the Word for transporting the ark, resorted to the ark to get them out of a bad situation with the Philistines. They took the ark into battle, the ark was taken, and they lost their lives (1 Sam. 4). The nation of Israel lamented because "the glory" had departed from them.

Indeed, the Philistines had taken the ark captive. But it proved too hot for them to handle, and they eventually sent the ark back to Israel on a cart pulled by oxen (1 Sam. 6:1-13). The ark was now back in the land, but the people by this time did not understand the principles of the Word of God associated with it, and as a result it was not returned to the tabernacle in Shiloh.

In the meantime, life went on in the tabernacle of Moses and the service of the tabernacle as if nothing was missing. The sacrifices and offerings were continually offered in the outer court. The priests continued to minister before the lampstand and the table of shewbread. They continued to burn incense on the golden altar of incense. The only problem was that behind the veil in the Most Holy Place there was no ark. The room was empty!

I wonder how many local churches go through the motions week after week with no presence of the Lord. All of the forms look good. They are doing the same things that they have always done, and yet something is missing. In fact the most important thing is missing.

This is the way things continued in Israel under the administration of Saul. Saul seemed to have no real love for the presence of God and no real desire to be led of the Lord in his leadership. David had a completely different heart. He was desperate to have the presence of God in his life and in his administration as king over the nation of Israel.

Because of this heart, one of David's first orders of business was to get the ark back to a place of centrality in the life of God's people (2 Sam. 6:1-11). David gathered a large group of people and took them to where the ark had been for many years. They put the ark on a cart and began their trek back to Jerusalem. But something happened. The oxen stumbled, Uzzah touched the ark to steady it, and he was killed. David stopped immediately. What was wrong? Why is there death in this situation? Isn't what we are doing pleasing to God? Doesn't He want to dwell in our midst?

David was forced to seek the Lord. As he was seeking the Lord, he also read the books of the Law. In doing so, he immediately realized that there was a God-ordained procedure that was to be in place if the ark of the covenant was to be moved. David had no previous knowledge of this, but God was not going to let him get away with moving the ark the way the Philistines had done it. If he was to have the presence of the Lord in the midst of the camp, he would have to do the right thing the right way (1 Chron. 15:13).

God wanted David to be a pattern for us of a man after God's own heart. If David would be that pattern, he would have to do things the God-ordained way. Fortunately, David's love for the presence of the Lord did not allow him to give up. He would have a second run at it (1 Chron. 15-16). This time God blessed his efforts and David achieved his goal, setting up the tabernacle of David in the City of David.

PREPARING FOR HIS PRESENCE

What did David do differently the second time? What were the principles that he observed that can serve as a model to us if we are to see the presence of the

Lord in the midst of the people? David sought the Lord for direction and was able to tap into six things that brought a new release of the presence of the Lord.

1. He prepared a place for the ark (1 Chron. 15:1,3,12). If we are going to have God in our midst, we must prepare a personal place in our hearts and a corporate place in our services for God to move freely.

2. He gathered the people in unity (1 Chron. 15:3). The coming together of God's people in unity has always been a catalyst to release the power of His presence (2 Chron. 5:11-14; Ps. 133; Acts 1:14; 2:1). No one wants to dwell with people who are fighting with each other.

3. He followed God's pattern (1 Chron. 15:2,12,13). We cannot expect God to bless our best efforts unless we walk in obedience to His Word. When we build the house as He has commanded, we can expect Him to be comfortable in that house (Exod. 40:32-32).

4. He sanctified the priests (1 Chron. 15:12,14). The priests were the ones who were going to bear the ark on their shoulders. In the New Testament all believers are the priests, and every believer has a responsibility before the Lord to be separated unto the Lord.

5. He sought the Lord in prayer (1 Chron. 15:13). Prayer precedes every visitation of the Lord (Zech. 10:1; 2 Chron. 6:24-31; 7:14). As we seek the Lord, He will be found and come and meet with us (Isa. 55:6-7; Jer. 29:12-13).

6. He ministered in singing and spiritual worship (1 Chron. 15:16; 15:27-28; 2 Sam. 6:13-15). Somehow David was able to tap into a worship of total abandonment to the Lord that did not meet with everyone's approval. However, it did meet with God's approval. The offspring of Saul (the man who was happy to have a form with no presence) did not like this order of worship that seemed too showy and almost vile. It should be noted that those who despised this Davidic worship remained barren, not realizing that this worship was an actual key to growth, new life, and the presence of God in their midst (1 Chron. 15:29; 2 Sam. 6:16, 20-23).

WORSHIP AND THE PRESENCE OF GOD

Biblical praise and worship becomes an important key to the manifest presence of God, which is a vital key to true growth. I am not just referring to numerical growth here, but more importantly, true biblical worship will cause a spiritual growth among God's people. God delights in His children when he sees them enjoying Him in worship and praise. Worship is not something that is done professionally by a choir or appointed priests; worship is to be a part of the life of all New Testament priests or, should I say, every believer.

To help us better understand the role of the believer in worship, I offer the following biblical outline of our place as New Testament priests.

1.   All believers in Christ are called to be priests and have a responsibility to function as such (1 Pet. 2:5).

In the Old Testament, God called the nation of Israel to be His nation of priests (Exod. 19:5-6). In the New Testament, the believers in Christ are called to be God's nation of priests (Rev. 5:10; Isa. 61:6).

2.   All believers as priests have a responsibility to offer gifts and sacrifices unto the Lord (Heb. 5:1; 8:3-6).

In the Old Testament, the sacrifices that God required were natural sacrifices that pointed to the spiritual realities that would come in Christ. In the New Testament, the sacrifices that God requires are spiritual in nature.

New Testament priests offer five spiritual sacrifices in the sense realm.

* *The sacrifice of ourselves (Rom. 12:1-2)*

As New Testament priests, we are to offer ourselves totally to God. We are to personally get on the spiritual altar of sacrifice and willingly present ourselves to God in totality. This is the foundation for all other sacrifices and the beginning of our worship. In essence, we are doing figuratively what Solomon did literally at the dedication of the temple when he got on the scaffold himself and lifted his hands to God (2 Chron. 6:13). For the believer this should be a daily experience.

- *The sacrifice of our time (Eph. 5:16)*

As New Testament priests, we are to offer our time to God. Our time represents our life. Just as Christ poured out His life for us, we are to expend our lives for Him.

- *The sacrifice of our substance (Phil. 4:18, Heb. 13:16)*

As New Testament priests, we are to use our finances in a way that pleases the Lord and extends His Kingdom.

- *The sacrifice of our good works (Heb. 13:16)*

As New Testament priests, we are to offer the sacrifice of "doing good." Jesus is our model who went about doing good (Acts 10:38). These good works are the fruit of faith in our lives. As believers, we are to be zealous of good works (Titus 2:14).

- *The sacrifice of our fruit (Rom. 15:16)*

As New Testament priests, we are to produce spiritual fruit. In other words, we are to bring others to Christ and present them to Him as a pleasing offering. Paul offered His fruit back to the Lord because he realized it was only through the Lord that this fruit could be produced.

New Testament priests offer three spiritual sacrifices in the soul realm.

- *The sacrifice of thanksgiving (Ps. 107:22; 116:17)*

The sacrifice of thanksgiving involves cultivating a personal expression of thanks to God even in times of difficulty, understanding that God is always good and He is always faithful.

- *The sacrifice of joy (Ps. 27:6, lit. joyous shouts)*

There is a difference between the joy of the Lord and a naturally happy and exuberant spirit. The joy expressed by Christians is an inner rejoicing based on faith, not on circumstances (2 Cor. 4:8-10). It is expressed in "joyous shouts" unto the Lord that can actually have the power to change our circumstances.

- *The sacrifice of praise (Heb. 13:15-16)*

A blessing is something that you receive when you come to the house of God, but the "sacrifice" of praise is something that you bring with you. It is something that we offer to the Lord, not on the basis of our feelings or our circumstances but on the basis of our revelation of God's awesome greatness and our personal desire to honor Him.

To fully express these three sacrifices of the soul realm involves the use of our voice. As the writer to the Hebrews suggests, these sacrifices involve the "fruit of our lips" (Heb. 13:15). Therefore the believer is to offer audible thanksgiving, audible joy, and audible praise to the Lord.

New Testament priests offer one primary sacrifice in the spirit realm, the sacrifice of a broken and a contrite heart (Ps. 51:17).

God is never as interested in external sacrifices as He is in a heart that is rightly related to Him. If the heart relationship is right, none of the other sacrifices will be a problem. But if the heart relationship is wrong, all of the sacrifices will be mere forms. It is from this heart condition that true worship springs forth. True worship can only spring from a heart that has been broken before God.

3. All believers in Christ are to come before the Lord and offer their spiritual sacrifices freely to Him.

There are many things that can hinder us from offering freely to the Lord.

- *Self-centeredness* (2 Tim. 3:1-4). When we offer sacrifices, it is a self-less act on our part because we are not the objects of our sacrifice. All of us tend to be lovers of ourselves.
- *Being ruled by feelings* (Ps. 54:6). When we offer sacrifices, it is costly to our fleshly appetites. We must offer by faith not by our feelings.
- *Lack of a spirit of sacrifice* (Ps. 50:5). We usually give in order to receive. In true worship we give simply because God is worthy. Receiving can be a by-product, but it cannot be the motivation.

David had the proper attitude as he offered to the Lord. He did not want to offer God anything that did not cost him personally (1 Chron. 21:22-25).

4. All believers as priests are to offer praise and worship to the Lord.

Praise and worship are important to God (John 4:23-24). God desires worship in spirit and in truth. Worship in spirit may mean two things. It may mean that our worship must originate in our spirit (Phil. 3:3). It may mean that we are to worship wholeheartedly (Ps. 9:1).

Worship in truth has two aspects as well. It means to worship sincerely or honestly. It also means to worship according to truth or according to the Word of God (John 17:17).

Not only is God worthy of our worship (Ps. 18:3; 47:6-7; 63:3-4), but God also has commanded a certain worship that is acceptable to Him (1 Chron. 16:29; Ps. 22:23; 117:1). It is not up to us to decide what is pleasing; it is up to us walk in a spirit of obedience as His dear children.

The fact is that God never asks us to do things that are not for our good. We actually need to worship far more than God needs to receive our worship.

5. Praise and worship are important for the believer.

From man's point of view, the worship and praise of God is very beneficial.

- It helps us to become more God-centered instead of self-centered (1 Pet. 5:6; 2 Tim. 3:1-5). As we offer praise and worship unto God we are recognizing His Lordship and right to rule over us. We are humbling ourselves before God.
- It helps us to set our minds on the things of the Spirit (Isa. 26:3; Rom. 8:5-6; Col. 3:1-2). As we maintain our focus on Him, He will keep us in perfect peace.
- It helps us develop a deeper love relationship with the Lord. We are created for intimacy and relationship with God, praise and worship help us to draw near to God.
- It prepares us to reap good things from good sowing (Gal. 6:8; Luke 6:38; Job 36:26-29; 2 Cor. 9:6). While we do not want to

worship God for what we get in return, the fact is that God blesses those who bless Him.

- It helps us maintain an attitude conducive to faith. Praise and worship is the language of faith. When we believe and trust in God we will praise Him in spite of circumstances.

- It releases God's power and presence in our lives (2 Chron. 5:13-14; 20:21-22; Acts 16:25-26; Ps. 22:3). In other words, God inhabits the praises of His people.

- It helps us maintain a thankful heart (Ps. 100:4). As we worship, we are reminded of the goodness of God, and that becomes our focus.

- It purifies our hearts and minds (Prov. 27:21). God has given us His Holy Spirit, the Word of God (Eph. 5:26), and prayer to purify (1 Tim. 4:4-5) us as a people. He also purifies His people through praise.

- It helps us become more Christlike as we are changed into His image (2 Cor. 3:18). We are changed into the image of the one we worship. This can happen in a negative way as well (Ps. 115:8; 106:19-20).

- It provides a means by which God can meet with us (Exod. 29:41-42). We have God's promise that He will meet and commune with us when we offer sacrifice unto Him.

6. God has a prescribed way in which we are to worship.

New Testament worship is according to the Davidic order. David was the architect of worship in the Bible. His order of worship is reflected in the psalms. Paul seems to have worshiped according to the Davidic order (Acts 24:14). In addition, the early church used the psalms of David as a hymnbook, because it was descriptive of their order (Eph. 5:19; Col. 3:16).

The Davidic order involves exuberant, full-bodied worship reflected in the psalms. Most of the psalms were composed in relation to worship in the tabernacle of David not the tabernacle of Moses, where there was no singing. The Davidic order is characterized by the following:

Praising God with our voice or mouth (Ps. 42:4). This includes:
SPEAKING (Ps. 51:15; 63:5; 66:8; 71:8; 109:30; 145:21)
SINGING (Ps. 7:17; 9:1-2; 33:3; 40:3; 100:4; 135:3)
SHOUTING (Ps. 5:11; 32:11; 35:27; 95:1-2; 132:9, 16)

Praising God with our hands. This includes:
LIFTING (Ps. 28:2; 63:3-4; 88:89; 134:1-2; 141:2; 143:6)
CLAPPING (Ps. 47:1; 98:8)
PLAYING INSTRUMENTS (Ps. 33:2; 43:4; 92:3; 97:4-6; 150)

Praising God with our bodies. This includes:
STANDING (Ps. 24:3; 33:8; 134:1; 135:1-2)
KNEELING OR BOWING (Neh. 8:6; Ps. 95:6-7)
DANCING (Ps. 149:3; 150:4; 2 Sam. 6:14)

CURRENT TENSIONS FOR THE PASTOR IN THE AREA OF WORSHIP

When it comes to the corporate worship of the church, we are touching an area that has a huge impact on the experience of the manifest presence of God in any given service. Because it is such an important area of church life, it is an area for which we must continually contend. There will be many forces at work from personal tastes to spiritual forces that will seek to minimize this area and shape it according to man's preferences rather than God's. Every leader will have to deal with certain tensions when it comes to the worship life of the local church.

Congregational Worship Verses Private Expression

Many people want to use the corporate gathering to bring their private expression of worship before the Lord. Often this can lead to disorder in the house and a drawing of undue attention to individuals. In essence it can actually draw attention away from the Lord. When a person is in their own prayer closet, they are free to worship in any way that they deem appropriate. However, when the whole church comes together, this is a time when we lay aside our uniqueness and express our willingness to blend with others by following the music leadership of the service in our expression of worship.

Seeker Sensitive Versus Biblical Mandate

As pastors we have to face a constant tension between making the service and our expressions of worship palatable to the unlearned or the visitor. We do not want to offend people in our expressions of worship. However, we cannot take this way of thinking to an extreme, because we must also think about how God looks at our worship. We must not be disobedient to God or offend God by our lack of responsiveness to His desires. When the two issues come into conflict, we must worship the way God prefers and trust that the visitor will be inspired and challenged to come up to a higher level.

Structure Versus Spontaneity/Worshipping Our Worship

While on the one hand we want to do all things well and pay attention to the order in our worship, on the other hand, we do not want to become so structured and refined in our program that we lose the spontaneous expressions of exuberant praise that characterized worship in the New Testament church. It is possible to get so concerned about the functions or expressions of worship that we worship our forms of worship rather than God. God is still more concerned about the heart of worship than the mechanics of worship.

Platform/Electronically-Driven Versus Congregational/Voice-Driven Worship

In the world today, with the modern instruments and sound equipment that are available as a support to our worship, it is very easy for our instruments and singers to provide the primary "voice" of worship. Worship that pleases God is not an electronic sound that is produced by a few experts on the platform. Those things should only serve to facilitate, enhance, and undergird our congregational worship experience. Unfortunately, they can actually become a replacement for true worship. True worship only requires the heart and the voice of the worshiper. Everything else is an extra. If you turned off the power and shut down the instruments, could you still have a powerful time of worship? It should be no problem to do so if all is functioning in proper balance.

Worship Leader Versus the Pastor

The senior pastor and the elders of the church are those that are responsible to establish guidelines and set the tone for the corporate worship expression. Many individuals who have a gift in music feel that because of a perceived call to the area of music, they are "in charge" of the worship life of the church. You cannot separate the worship life of the church from the rest of church life. It is an extremely important part of church life that must respond to the spiritual oversight of the church, that is, the senior pastor and the elders. Worship leaders who do not respond to the elders of the church should not be placed over such an important area of church life.

Musical Talent Versus the Heart of Worship

The pastor is always torn between selecting worship leaders who have musical skill and charismatic personalities or selecting individuals who have less talent but have a stronger heart for worship. Obviously it would be great if you had a person who had both heart and gifting. Unfortunately, that is not always the case. The primary purpose of a worship leader is to bring the congregation into the presence of God, not to impress us with his gifts and abilities as a musician. The primary quality that should exist in the leader, if they are going to be able to do this, is a personal heart of worship. If the pastor must choose, then he must choose heart over gifting. The best worship leaders are ardent worshipers themselves when they are not leading the service.

Music Versus Lyrics (Theology)

Many songs are being written today by many people. Some of the people writing songs have a great understanding of music but little understanding of the Bible. As a result you can find songs that are very enjoyable musically but unscriptural in their theology. Songs are one of the ways that we teach and instruct (Col. 3:16). Therefore, it is essential that the songs we use in the worship life of the church are thoroughly biblical in their content.

Songs have a powerful ability to imbed truth deep into our spirits. Therefore, it is important for the pastor to evaluate theologically what is being sung before new songs are introduced to the congregation.

The Old Versus the New

The church is composed of people from many generations. When we gather together for the corporate expression of worship, there should be something there for everyone. Often a rift develops between the young and the old. The young tend to like songs that are new, faster in tempo, and louder. The older saints tend to like songs that are older, a little slower, and quieter in their expression. The wise pastor will have the skill to present a style that has a blending of expressions (Matt. 13:52). Using a variety of worship leaders instead of the same person week after week is one way to contribute to a variety. The pastor should also instruct the worship leaders regarding the goal in worship.

All About the Lord or All About Me

Our worship expression should be aimed primarily at exalting the Lord and focusing on Him. It is often interesting to ask concerning the body of songs sung, "Who is the subject and who is the object in the songs that we are singing?" God (Father, Son and Holy Spirit) needs to be the center of our worship, not man. Are we singing about me, what God can do for me, and how He makes me feel? Or are we singing about God's greatness and majesty, what He has done for us, and our desires toward Him? The worship of God is to draw us away from man's natural tendencies to be self-consumed.

A HUNGER FOR HIS PRESENCE

If we are going to build churches that are strong and have a true touch of God upon them, we desperately need His manifest presence in them. The local church is the house of the Lord. If He is not present in the house, that same house becomes a museum. When He is present, the secrets of men's hearts are revealed, mountains melt away, and life springs forth.

Psalm 150 (NIV)

Praise the Lord.
Praise God in his sanctuary;
Praise him in his mighty heavens.
Praise him for his acts of power;
Praise him for his surpassing greatness.
Praise him with the sounding of the trumpet,
Praise him with the harp and lyre,
Praise him with tambourine and dancing,
Praise him with the strings and flute,
Praise him with the clash of cymbals,
Praise him with resounding cymbals,
Let everything that has breath
Praise the Lord.
Praise the Lord.

Chapter Sixteen

HOUSE-TO-HOUSE MINISTRY

KEY #14—*If a church is to grow and prosper from generation to generation, that church must determine to develop house-to-house ministries.*

There are not many specific methods outlined in the New Testament concerning the program of the church. One exception to this is the apparent universal existence of house-to-house ministry in the New Testament church.

It appears that this house-to-house ministry went well beyond individual fellowship among believers. It seems to have included a certain amount of structure to minister to the needs in the churches and to reach out in evangelism.

There is no question that the fastest growing churches in the world today have some form of small-group ministry. It this just another fad? Or have they tapped into a divine principle or a pattern that should be considered by every church seeking to follow the biblical model?

THE GREAT COMMISSION

When Jesus met with His disciples after His resurrection from the dead, He spent a good deal of His time issuing orders as the commander-in-chief of the army of God called the church (Acts 1:1-3).

As you study the four Gospels and the book of Acts in relation to this time period of forty days, you will find that these commands of Jesus were a little overwhelming, especially when put in the context of the disciples' having recently exhibited a lot of fear and personal doubt.

When you put all of the verses together, it is clear that Jesus commanded them to preach the Gospel to every creature beginning at Jerusalem and ending up at the ends of the earth, to make disciples out of those who responded, to baptize those who responded, to teach those who responded to observe everything that Jesus had ever said, and to pastor His people into maturity and productivity. In their spare time they could heal the sick, cast out devils, raise a few dead people and, if they still had time left over, they could pick up a few serpents along the way (Matt. 28:19-20; Mark 16:15-20; Luke 24:27; John 21:15; Acts 1:8).

What a challenge! No wonder Jesus further instructed them to wait in Jerusalem until they were empowered from on high. They would need supernatural help if they were going to accomplish this supernatural task. With the help of the Holy Spirit, these once-fearful disciples changed the world in their generation.

The commission that Jesus gave to the disciples is a commission that is still on the shoulders of the church today. Everything that we do as a church has to be done in the light of God's commission in Genesis 1 and Jesus' commission to His disciples given after His resurrection.

The church is God's instrument on the earth today for the fulfillment of His divine purposes. There is no other plan; there is no other organization or group of people to which we can turn for its success.

A STRATEGY FOR SUCCESS

The early church was successful because of two things. First of all, they had been obedient to Jesus in waiting in Jerusalem for the empowering of the Holy Spirit in their lives. Their task could never be accomplished in their own strength. The book of Acts is really a book of the acts of the Holy Spirit in and through the church.

The early church was also successful because they appear to have had a strategy for the fulfillment of the commission. They used a two-pronged attack in fulfilling Christ's charge. This two-pronged attack is seen in Acts 5:42 where the early church leaders focused on the public teaching and preaching in the corporate gathering of the church and evangelistic endeavors, and they carried the same ministry into the homes of the believers.

They appear to have focused on the large gathering in the courts of the temple (Acts 2:46-47). They appear to have focused on smaller gatherings in the homes of believers to reinforce what was taking place on the larger scale.

This two-pronged attack made it possible for the multitudes who had received Christ in the outpouring of Acts 2 to continue steadfast in the apostles' doctrine, in the breaking of bread, in fellowship, and in prayers (Acts 2:42).

THE PRESENT-DAY CHALLENGE

It is clear that the church is approaching a day of great outpouring and harvest. Jesus made it clear that before His return there would be a harvest the likes of which the world has never seen. Perhaps this goes against your personal theology. Perhaps as you look around and see what appears to be a rise in the level of wickedness, you wonder what the last days will be like.

It is clear in the Bible that while the love of many will wax cold and many will fall away from the faith, the end times will also be marked by the greatest harvest and ingathering of souls that the world has ever seen (Matt. 13:27-30, 39). In addition to a numerical expansion in the Kingdom of God, the end times will be marked by a church that has come to full stature (Eph. 4:13-16), is without spot or wrinkle (Eph. 5:25-27), and is a sharp threshing instrument moving mightily against Satan and the kingdom of darkness (Rom. 16:20).

In other words, the end times will be marked by great visitation and revival where multitudes will be swept into the Kingdom and added to the church. Christ's parables of the Kingdom, Peter's miracle draught of fish, and Joel's vision of the latter rain outpouring all seem to indicate that the "glory of the latter house" will far surpass anything that has been seen heretofore.

What does all of this mean for today's church? What does it mean for pastors in the end times? It surely means many things, but one thing is obvious—the net of the church will have to be prepared structurally to handle what God is about to do.

THE NEED FOR A STRATEGY

Multitudes of people have always brought with them multitudes of problems. In Acts 6 when the number of the disciples multiplied, suddenly problems, murmuring, and greater needs arose.

What is the church to do? What is the pastor to do? How can the church effectively reach out and also minister to the needs of the people? Can one person standing behind the "sacred desk" one hour per week effectively get the job done? How does one person touch a community? How does one person minister to the lives of one thousand, two thousand, or ten thousand people? How can a local church handle the very thing for which it has prayed for centuries—growth?

Many churches in the world today have begun to grow rapidly. As they have, they have crossed a line where they have had to make a choice in their ministry. When the local church gets large, five changes can easily take place.

1. The church can become *program orientated* rather than *people orientated.* All of the energy of the pastoral staff must be given to keeping programs going that will hopefully touch people's lives. Soon people can get the feeling that the programs are more important than people and that they are only a small part of a massive, insensitive, and impersonal piece of equipment.

2. The church becomes guilty of *pulpit pastoring* rather than *personal pastoring.* The pastor preaches a shotgun message on Sunday morning hoping to hit the needs of most of the people, but he is never able to minister to the personal needs of any one person. The individual has no personal relationship to his pastor, and the pastor cannot even call his own sheep by name.

3. The church becomes an *assembly hall* rather than an *assembly line.* The church is to be a place where people's lives are put together and where that which is missing is put into place. In many large churches, however, it is easy to feel that church

attendance and tithing are the only important barometers of spiritual life and that the only value an individual has is to fill a certain spot once a week. As long as he is "not forsaking the assembling" together, he is considered to be doing fine.

4. The church becomes an *orphanage* rather than a *family*. It is difficult to raise children effectively in a group. One or two parents for fifty children will never be able to develop an intimate relationship and fellowship with those children. Most likely the children themselves will never feel close to either parent or to the other members of the family.

5. The church becomes a *ministry center* rather than a *ministry factory*. When a local church becomes large, it is difficult to help each person enter into his or her unique ministry. We can only offer certain general services to people that will hopefully keep them going for another week rather than effectively equipping the saints themselves to do the ministry.

God is placing a great challenge before the church in these days. It is the challenge of growth. It is fairly easy to assist a group of twenty-five people to become mature men and women of God. But how can one handle a multitude?

God wants large churches. He created the church for growth. All of the principles of God's Word must be workable for small churches and large churches alike. God is raising up an army of trained servants in these days to march effectively against the gates of hell. There must be a way to fulfill His glorious commission.

TOWARD A SOLUTION

The problem facing the church today is not unlike the problem faced by Moses when he led the people of God out of Egypt and toward the land of promise. Here was one man trying to be the chief counselor and decision maker for all three million people. It sounds absolutely ridiculous when you think about it, and yet sometimes you can be so close to a problem that you cannot see the obvious solution. It took a visit from his father-in-law to pinpoint the problem.

The problem in Israel was serious for a couple of reasons. First of all, Jethro was careful to point out that Moses was going to "wear away" (Exod. 18:23). When a pastor is ministering to a small number of people, he can do it all, and usually does. But as the number of people increases, the pastor must begin to release responsibility to others or the burden will become too heavy for him to bear.

When Jethro came to visit his daughter and grandchildren, he had no time to spend with Moses, because Moses was never home. When you pastor three million people, there is always someone in trouble or going through a difficult problem. Moses loved the people more than his own life. Therefore, he put his own personal needs and the needs of his family after the needs of the people. This left Moses with no time for himself, his family, or his personal relationship to God. When you love people and you have a desire to help them, this is usually the result.

Every morning when Moses got up, there was a line outside his tent. There were people who needed answers, people whose lives were in turmoil, people who had to make critical decisions about their life and future. How could Moses say no to these people? He didn't! Every day from sunup to sundown (even after sundown) Moses talked, shared, and counseled with the people. Day after day, week after week, month after month, it was the same. The waiting line never went away, but Moses himself was wearing away.

Jethro did not need a special revelation to know that Moses would never last at this pace. Out of a concern for Moses, his own daughter and his grandchildren, Jethro had to rebuke Moses for the sake of his life. No one man was ever meant to carry the burden of so many people. "The thing that you are doing is not good" (Exod. 18:17).

In addition to Moses' personal health and family issues, there was another reason why the situation was serious. Jethro saw that what was taking place was not good for the people. People just cannot stand in line day after day without getting frustrated and giving up. If people know that you are too busy for them, they will wait until their problems are so big that only God Himself will be able to solve them. In addition, if the people have to wait so long in line, they will be tempted to not come for help at all and give up before they see a leader.

THE JETHRO PRINCIPLE

Jethro saw that as long as Moses was by himself and continued his present approach, the job would not get done, and the people's needs would never be met. If this condition were to continue, it would ultimately jeopardize the entire plan of God to bring a believing people into the Promised Land.

Jethro proceeded to give Moses some "fatherly" advice, which later proved to be the same advice that God gave to Moses (Num. 11 and Deut. 1). He suggested three main changes in Moses' approach. First of all, he suggested that Moses needed to get back in right relationship to the Lord and learn once again how to put the government on God's broad shoulders. Often when we get busy it is so easy to let that time with the Lord slide. Unfortunately, it is that time with the Lord where we find our strength, our answers, and the grace to deal with everything else.

Second, he suggested that Moses take up the mantle of teaching on a corporate basis. Rather than individually trying to teach each person the divine principles they needed to navigate a particular situation, he suggested that Moses begin to publicly teach all of the people in three main areas, and in doing so he would equip the people to make their own decisions and to solve many of their own problems, because they would have truth upon which to draw.

He told Moses to teach the people the Word, the way to walk, and the work to do. That is, he should teach them the Word of God including the principles, commands, and precepts. He should teach them how to walk, focusing on practical principles of living as believers. And he should teach them about their personal responsibility before the Lord to be workers in His vineyard. Every member of the family of God has a work to do.

Third, he suggested that Moses bring others into the work. He encouraged Moses to select qualified individuals who had their own lives in order and delegate some of his responsibility to them. He gave him the principle of team ministry.

Jethro further suggested that Moses place these individuals over groups of people according to their individual capacities whether it be for ten, fifty, one hundred or one thousand. These support leaders would take care of the day-to-day concerns while only the most difficult issues would come to

Moses. Moses saw the wisdom in this plan and implemented the suggestion, saving both himself and the congregation of the people.

IN JESUS' MINISTRY

Jesus Himself demonstrated this same principle of ministry when He fed the five thousand (Mark 6:34-44; Luke 9:14-15). It would be difficult for one person to feed five thousand hungry people. In preparation for the miracle feeding, Jesus instructed the disciples to have the multitudes sit on the ground in companies of fifty and one hundred. Then he broke the bread, gave it to His disciples who in turn distributed it to the people. It is interesting that John's Gospel emphasizes the fact that they gave the food to those who were sitting down as Jesus had instructed (John 6:10-11).

Jesus had a plan to feed (pastor, shepherd) His people. One person could not reasonably do it all. If all are going to eat to their fill and no one is going to be overlooked, there must be a strategy. Things must be done decently and in order. Ultimately, only those who are cooperating with the strategy will be guaranteed what they need.

IN THE EARLY CHURCH

In the early life of the church, multitudes were not the problem—making sure that the pastoral work generated by the multitudes got done was the problem. Because the heart of the leadership was that of servants, it became very easy for them to want to be personally involved in every need in the church. When the number of the disciples multiplied, this became an ever-increasing impossibility.

As a result, the needs of some were neglected (Acts 6:1-6). An even worse thing occurred, however. Because the apostles were trying to meet all of the needs of the people personally, they ended up neglecting their primary call to prayer and the Word. Everyone was in effect being hurt because they were so loving. The public ministry of the Word of God was suffering.

They learned very quickly that "many hands make light work." They chose other able individuals to share the task of ministering to the personal needs of the growing church. They refocused on their primary function and, as a result, the Word of God increased and more responded to the Gospel (Acts 6:7).

TODAY'S CHALLENGE

Today the church is facing the same challenge of growth. It is exciting to see the promises of harvest coming to pass. However, as the people come, they will come with great needs. The church must be prepared in advance to minister effectively to these needs or we will limit what God wants to do through each and every local church. It is my persuasion that God will only give us the quantity that we can handle.

The solution that Moses found, that Jesus demonstrated, and that was discovered by the early church is a solution that still works today. That solution could be summarized as follows:

Concentrate in public (in the temple) on the preaching and teaching of the Word, focusing on principles of practical living, putting the tools into people's hands to be personal problem solvers.

Divide the congregation into segments as Jesus did when He fed the five thousand.

Place over these segments, individuals who are qualified to carry such responsibility.

Work to train and equip these individuals to function as leaders in their defined area of responsibility.

THE TWO-PRONGED ATTACK

The New Testament church used a two-pronged attack in ministering to the needs of the people and fulfilling Christ's commission to make mature ones of all nations. They had the public gathering, which was absolutely vital for the worship life, inspiration, and marching orders of the church. They also had smaller gatherings. They continued in the temple and from house-to-house (Acts 5:42). Paul indicates that he preached publicly and from house-to-house (Acts 20:20). The corporate gathering is important for the unity of the church and outreach potential. The smaller gatherings are important for many other reasons.

There are many aspects of church life that can be fostered by the smaller groups in any local church. Small groups are not meant to be in competition with the larger gathering. On the contrary, the small group should be a tremendous complement to the corporate assembly life. If the small group is designed in such a way that it competes with the main gathering of the church, it will become divisive, repetitious, and perhaps even boring. But if the small group is providing something that is not being touched by any other phase of body life, it will be a source of life and strength.

MULTIPLE FACES OF SMALL GROUPS

Small-group ministry will take on different forms in different settings depending on the vision of the leadership, the strengths of the local leadership team, and the primary focus for such gatherings. Strictly speaking, no plan is wrong and no plan is to be considered universal in its application. The principle of the small group is universal, but the application may vary from one place to another.

Regardless of the primary purpose of small groups in the life of the local church, they will most likely satisfy a combination of needs. Some of the primary purposes that are met by the small gathering include the following:

1. Pastoral Care and Discipleship

God has definitely given His church the burden for pastoral care and discipleship. Our desire should go beyond just birthing people into the Kingdom; it should involve providing effective covering and accountability that precipitates growth and brings people to a place of personal fruitfulness and ministry. It is impossible to pastor a crowd in any individual way. The small-group approach is a biblical way of feeding a multitude of people.

2. Building Relationships and Fellowship

It is clear that God wants the individual members of the church to be more closely linked to one another so that they can be in position to better minister to the needs of one another as the Bible clearly directs. This was a top priority of the church in the book of Acts, and the small group helps to keep individuals from being alone in the midst of a large number of people. This is more important for the more passive, reserved, and quiet personality, and yet all will benefit greatly by their personal involvement.

3. Assimilating New People into the Church

Whether people are newly saved or simply new to the church, there needs to be a means whereby they can quickly feel a part if they are going to be permanently established and genuinely committed to the vision of the local church. It takes several years to feel a part of a crowd, but in a few brief contacts in an intimate setting, people can feel loved, cared for, and needed.

4. Evangelism

God wants every believer to be reaching out to others in their spheres of influence. The small group is a perfect place to introduce new people to other believers in the Body of Christ. Through the small group, it is possible for them to gain the support and the relationships that they need for them to be established.

5. Releasing People into Their Gifts and Ministries

It is clear from the Bible that every believer has a ministry and can be used by God to reach out beyond the church walls. They also can function in gifts of the Spirit and can be used to edify the body of believers (1 Cor. 12-14). Where do the passages like 1 Corinthians 14:26 find their fulfillment in the life of a local church where everyone has something to contribute as they come together? In a large and growing church it is impossible for everyone to participate in some way. However, in the small-group setting, everyone can be involved in some way in any given meeting.

6. Identifying and Multiplying Leaders

Many people are called by God to be leaders in the local church. However, the traditional model of church ministry drastically limits the opportunity for leadership to function in the local assembly. Not only does the small-group approach open the door of opportunity to many in the congregation to lead in a significant way, but it also affords those especially gifted to be identified and released to greater areas of responsibility. A much higher percentage of the congregation could grow in their capacity for leadership if there were more opportunities open to them at their current level of ability.

7. Accountability and Personal Growth

The small group is a great place to go over the Word that is being emphasized in the corporate life of the church to assist in accountability and seeing that word established in the lives of individual believers. It is a place where the more mature believers can serve as a pattern and an encouragement to those who are not living up to their potential in the grace of God.

MODELS THAT HAVE PROVEN EFFECTIVE

Because of the obvious strengths of the small-group ministry in the local church, many pastors have come home from church-growth seminars with great plans to grow their church through small groups, only to face disappointment and, in some cases, ruin. Part of the problem is that small-group ministry or any other thing that is added to the program of the church cannot just be tacked on to an already full ministry program.

In addition, it will take a long time for the people in the church to get comfortable with a ministry that forces them to get out of their traditional comfort zone and enter into a smaller setting where they will become vulnerable to others. As a result, some pastors have given up in the process.

Some pastors have gone into such programs not being totally convinced, not counting the ultimate cost, or not laying the proper foundation for change. In order to understand how to minimize some of the negative effects, I have done a rather thorough study of those churches that seem to be doing well with small-group ministry, have been doing it for a good length of time, and seem to be having the desired success.

The reason for the study is to discover what these successful local churches have in common. I have discovered at least nine common denominators of the most successful small-group churches.

1. The small-group ministry is seen as the main program of the church.

Small groups are not an add-on to an otherwise full schedule of activities in the church. If you add small groups, you will have to eliminate other phases of church life that you presently have in motion. Otherwise there will be a constant competition for leadership, and some of the people will use their other fulfilling involvements as an excuse not to get involved in the small-group ministry.

2. The small-group ministry must be led, fanned, and envisioned by the senior leadership of the church.

It is a fact that 80 percent of the success of small-group ministry is dependent on the senior pastor of the local church. This is not an area that will succeed in a corner, and it cannot be delegated to a few fanatics who want to move out on their own in this area. In order for small groups to succeed, there must be much pulpit time given to casting a clear vision. There must be ongoing exhortations and testimonies, which will require time in the corporate gathering. This also means that the senior pastor will have to get personally involved in the training of key leaders. But most of all, it means that every leader in the church from the top down will have to be committed to personal involvement in the groups.

3. The small groups must meet fairly often.

If the small group is going to have any chance to fulfill the purposes for which it was established, it will have to meet fairly often, preferably once a week. Again this means that the senior pastor will have to look at the overall program of the church to see that the small group is not in competition with a full schedule of weekly services. When adding small groups to the program of the church, it should most likely replace one of the other happenings in the program of the church.

4. The small groups must be growth orientated.

One of the greatest difficulties that you will have is multiplying groups. Part of the problem is that people become comfortable in their group and they want things to stay just the way they like them. It's ironic, but groups that do not birth new groups end up becoming ingrown and usually dissolve after about two to three years. All groups should be open to new people at all times or have a natural life cycle because of the unique purpose of that specific group. Birthing new groups should be seen as a primary purpose from the very beginning. It is even helpful to put goals out that reflect this (e.g. six months to a year).

5. The small groups must become the vehicles through which most care ministry occurs.

Again, when you structure the church around small groups, those small groups become ministry centers. You can handle just about everything regarding ministry to the believer through this channel including: personal discipleship, visitor follow-up, pastoral care, hospital visitation, wedding and baby showers, and even evangelistic endeavors.

6. The small groups must be small in size.

If the small groups are going to succeed at the purposes for which they are designed, the smaller they are, the better. The average size of the small groups should be around ten to twelve adults. Once you get to a maximum of fifteen or sixteen adults, that group should birth a new group. If a group gets too large, most homes cannot accommodate it, you might end up with too many children, and it ceases to be conducive for adding new members. It can actually become more like a small local church, which is obviously not the goal.

7. The small groups must become the center for the release of the body ministry in the church.

The small group is the care unit of the church where the members of the group take care of the needs of one another. This is where all of the "one another's" of body life can take place. This is where the members love one another in tangible ways. They comfort one another, they pray for one another, they edify one another, and they pour out their lives for one another.

8. The small groups must exist for building relationships and a caring, nurturing community both for believers and the newly converted.

Sometimes where small groups get into trouble is when they are used as the primary means for equipping the saints and training leaders. These are functions of the five leadership ministries of apostle, prophet, evangelist, pastor, and teacher (Eph. 11:13). Not every small group will have this level of ministry within it and can end up in error if it tries to function in this way. In addition, the small group is not to become a place of group therapy or counseling. Those kinds of issues are best handled privately with proper pastoral oversight. The small groups should be focusing on serving the needs of the people coming into the groups.

9. The small group must be a priority function of all the leadership of the church and every single staff person in the church.

The small groups will not be a success if they are not fully supported by the leadership of the church and other staff members. It will soon be interpreted that if you are more mature or that you have "arrived," you no longer need the small group. Not only that, but people are more inclined to follow your example rather than your words. All leaders should be actively involved in the small-group ministry, and they should seriously consider leading such a group.

These are some of the common denominators of successful small-group ministries around the world today. Every successful program may not be true to all nine of them, but they will share in a strong majority of them.

There are a few other simple observations or issues that affect the small group's success:

- Leaders must be prepared for every meeting so that something significant takes place.
- There needs to be a strong emphasis on training of leaders, and every leader must have an intern leader who is being trained to start his or her own group.
- The focus of the corporate gathering is for worship, edification, and the equipping of the saints.

- Sermons should be geared toward equipping people to reach out in evangelism and service. Every believer should be equipped to lead someone to the Lord, to exhort and disciple them. Every believer must be equipped to minister to the felt needs of others.
- Corporate gatherings should be celebrations in honor to God and thanksgiving for the harvest.

CAUTIONS IN THE DEVELOPMENT OF A SMALL-GROUP MINISTRY

Not everyone who walks down the path of small-group ministry finds long-term success. There are often very good reasons for this. Some potential pitfalls can be avoided if we do those things that will maximize our potential for success. Here are ten suggestions that may help you to succeed.

1. Do your homework.

Find the model that is best suited to your situation. This will involve being personally aware of what you are trying to achieve in the groups themselves. Find other churches that are successfully using that model. Visit those churches and study their material carefully. Try to talk to the person who has been most directly involved with the small-group ministry and let them share their journey with you including the good, the bad, and the ugly.

2. Be convinced yourself.

Do not attempt to get others excited about this new venture until you are fully persuaded in your own mind that this is the way you want to go. First of all, you do not want to get a bunch of people excited about something that may or may not become a reality. They will only get frustrated, and you will have created another problem. Second, and perhaps more important, this must be approached as a conviction, because there will be many opportunities for discouragement along the way. Third, this cannot be something that you try for a year or two. It is a long-term commitment that may never cease. The specific form that the small groups take may change from time to time, but the idea of small groups will be with you forever.

3. Lay a proper foundation.

Do not go into this as a new function of body life without saturating your local church with the biblical basis for what you are trying to accomplish. If people are going to get on board, they must be convinced that this is a superior format to their traditional ideas about "church." You might even begin a pilot program with a select few to work out the "bugs" and arouse interest in others. This may be a good way to train some of your first leaders.

4. Go slow.

Take your time establishing this new program in the local church. There is no reason to rush. Give your people time to accommodate their thinking every step of the way. The idea is not to divide your flock. The idea is to bring everyone along with you as you go.

5. Be patient.

Results will not come immediately. It will take some time to reap a harvest from this program. It will take a lot of working the soil, a lot of sowing of seed, a lot of watering and fertilizing, and a lot of pruning. But as you are faithful, results will come. The normal experience is to begin with a certain level of enthusiasm only to see that enthusiasm wear off. The temptation will be to "shut it down." However, if you will persist through some early challenges and not give up at the first sign of trouble, the small-group ministry will eventually pay off—big time!

6. Choose leaders wisely.

Choosing leaders is a major key to success. When you release people into the hands of others, you must be confident that they will not hurt the flock. In Acts 6 they had specific qualifications for those who would minister to the needs of the people. We must have specific qualifications as well. Leaders must be people who fear God, love the local church, understand their relationship to authority, and have demonstrated a true heart of loyalty and faithfulness. This should be their spiritual condition **before** they are selected as leaders (1 Tim. 3 and Titus 1).

7. Train leaders well.

Nothing will ensure failure more quickly than to give someone a responsibility without a clear job description and the appropriate training for the task. Leaders should be prepared in advance before the program begins, and there should be opportunities for further training as time goes on. The senior leadership of the church should be directly involved in such training so that a strong bond is formed with those who will be functioning in their behalf.

8. Stay close to leaders.

Keeping a close relational tie to those who are leading the groups is essential if unity is going to be maintained. It is so easy for leaders to slip into their own worlds and lose touch with the corporate vision. Relationship is the key to success. Jesus personally spent time with his leaders so that small issues could be dealt with quickly and the needs of those leaders could be met as well. The small-group leaders will need a pastoring touch in their lives just as much as anyone else.

9. Monitor the results.

The only way that you can know if you are succeeding is to have some form of evaluation as the small groups progress. Are the groups really doing or accomplishing what you set out to do with them? There needs to be a context where reports can be received, problems can be identified, failures can be evaluated, and successes can be honored. Anything that is left to itself will eventually degenerate into something other than its intended purpose.

10. Make course adjustments as needed.

When issues arise that indicate a problem, don't be afraid to make minor adjustments along the way. No matter who you are, you will not hit the right mixture the very first try. Eventually you should get to the right mix for you, your people, your culture, and your specific community. It is important not to breed any "sacred cows" when it comes to how this program functions. Remember, in the Bible we have a general method but not the specific application of the method. The specific application may differ from one local

church to another. It may even differ in varying seasons in the life of a specific local church.

A NET FOR THE HARVEST

The Bible is clear that in the last days there will be an ingathering of souls
much like the miracle catch of fish that Peter experienced when he
responded to Jesus' command to let down the net. The local church is to be
a net that is let down into the sea of humanity, fishing for the souls of men.
If the net is going to be successful, it must be properly prepared, it must be
washed, it must be mended, and it must be cast into the sea.

Small-group ministry is a structure that will serve to catch the harvest
that God wants to bring into His house. We have an opportunity today to
get that structure (net) ready so that when God does move, the harvest will
be preserved.

Chapter Seventeen

PRAYER

*KEY #15—If a church is to grow and prosper
from generation to generation, that church must determine
to develop a strong corporate prayer life.*

When the Bible speaks of the house of the Lord, it ascribes a name to His house—"a house of prayer for all nations" (Luke 19:46; Matt. 21:13; Mark 11:17). If an organization is called "the house of" something, you would reasonably expect that "something" to be a main activity of that organization. It is not out of line to assume that at "The House of Pancakes" you will find pancakes! Or at "The House of Fabrics" you will find, of all things, fabrics!

The church is to be first and foremost a house of prayer. The early church lived and functioned in the atmosphere of prayer, not just personal prayer, but corporate prayer as well.

While personal prayer is vital to the personal life and vitality of the individual believer, corporate prayer is vital to the life and vitality of the congregation. There is no question that the devil does everything that he can to keep believers off of their knees.

Paul makes it clear that prayer is a critical offensive weapon against the forces of wickedness. Jesus made it clear from His teaching and personal example that no one is strong enough to stand on his own—we all need the strength, direction and power that comes from a life of prayer.

THE PRACTICE OF PERSONAL PRAYER

Deep in all of our hearts as believers, we know that there is nothing more vital to our spiritual lives and development than prayer. We know that our personal prayer lives will affect our fellowship with God, the power of our Christian witness, the holiness of our character, and our continued guidance from the Lord.

In spite of that, it has been observed that prayer is the most preached and least practiced disciplines of the Bible. There are many reasons for this, including our natural sluggishness, our overconfidence in ourselves, or a lack of proper priorities in our lives.

Perhaps another significant reason for our prayerlessness is satanic opposition. Satan reads his Bible too. He knows that a Christian on his knees is a powerful force with which to reckon. He knows that if believers would put this principle into practice, he would be in trouble.

Many books have been written and will continue to be written on personal prayer and its power in our lives. They will cite the example of Jesus who was a man of prayer (Matt. 14:23; Luke 6:12; 9:28). They will point out how important prayer was to the early apostles (Acts 2:42; 6:4). They will highlight all of the blessings of prayer. They will stress that all the key leaders of the Bible had personal relationships with God that were cultivated by lives of prayer (e.g. Abraham, Moses, David, Daniel, etc.).

But unless these exhortations change the behavior of the average believer, they will have no bearing on our future walk with the Lord. For prayer to be effective, it needs to be discussed less and practiced more. Prayer meetings of the church need to spend less time talking about prayer and more time actually praying.

PRAYER PRECEDES VISITATION

It can be clearly demonstrated that the prayer of God's people precedes any visitation of God. Hannah positioned herself in prayer in a day when there was a cloud over the priestly office, and God responded to her cry (1 Sam. 1:10, 12; 2:1). The offspring of her prayer would end up being God's answer for the nation (1 Sam. 3:3).

Prior to the coming of Jesus, there were those who faithfully came to the temple and spent time in prayer waiting for the consolation of Israel. God honored the faith of Anna and Simeon, who experienced personal encounters with the Lord (Luke 2:25-38).

In the New Testament age, the apostles and other early believers gathered together with a sense of expectation in response to the instruction of Jesus. They waited in Jerusalem for God to fulfill His promise of an outpouring of the Holy Spirit. It is critical to see how they waited. They waited in prayer and supplication (Acts 1:14). They did not take anything for granted. They received the reward of their faith when the Holy Spirit came in power (Acts 2:1-2).

Later in the New Testament record we find a man by the name of Cornelius who desired a visitation from the Lord. He tapped into the same principle of prayer and was visited by the Lord (Acts 10). Prayer changes things.

PRAYER MUST PRECEDE THIS VISITATION

The principles that guided the church in the past are the same that must be in operation today. If we are going to see a manifestation of God in the midst of the church, we must be a people of prayer.

Isaiah exhorted the people of God to position themselves in prayer and not give God any rest until the purposes of God are established on the earth and the people of God (the church) become the thing of beauty that God has designed it to be (Isa. 62:6-7).

Zechariah prophesied that in the time of the latter rain we should ask or pray for the rain (10:1). It is time for the church to ask for rain and the visitation of God upon the nations of the world.

The New Testament admonishes the church of the last days to be sober and to be watchful in prayer (1 Pet. 4:7). James reminds us of the prayer life of Elijah who prayed for natural rain. He indicates that we can pray for spiritual rain and receive the same result (James 5: 7, 17-18).

This is the principle that God gave to Solomon when he dedicated the temple. God indicated that when things have turned sour and the heavens are withholding rain, if the people of God would humble themselves and pray, God would hear them, He would forgive them, and He would heal their land (Compare 2 Chron. 6:24-31 and 2 Chron. 7:14).

Someone has said, "That which brings revival maintains it." In other words, prayer should not be a last resort that we use to twist the arm of God; it should be a lifestyle that characterizes God's people. If such is the case, perhaps it is possible to live in a constant state of blessing.

PRAYER IS A CORPORATE THING

No one will question the importance and the power of individual prayer for the personal growth, spiritual development, and ongoing, divine guidance of the believer. However, of equal importance for the growth, development, and guidance of the local church is the corporate prayer life of that church.

It is interesting in the nation of Israel in the Old Testament that the people of God had personal responsibility toward prayer and seeking the face of God as is abundantly reflected in the psalms of David. But the people of God in the Old Testament also had a corporate responsibility to come together as a nation corporately to seek God in a central location.

It is not good enough to have a congregation full of people who have wonderful lives of prayer through which they are developing their personal relationships with God. Each local church needs to consider how they come together corporately to seek the face of God for the corporate issues that face the church and affect the destiny of that local church.

Jesus has given special promises to the local church that agrees together in their asking (praying). In the only passage of Scripture where Jesus directly touches on the local church, He emphasizes the unique power that they have when they function corporately or in agreement.

In Matthew 18:19-20, Jesus indicates that when two or three agree together in their asking, powerful things will take place. Does this mean that if there is no such agreement these same things will not take place? That is the obvious implication!

Whenever the early church was in one place and in one accord asking corporately of the Lord, powerful things happened. This was true on the Day of Pentecost when those praying together received a powerful outpouring of the Holy Spirit (Acts 2:1-2). This was true when the disciples who had been threatened by the authorities not to speak in the name of Jesus joined with other believers to pray for the supernatural boldness of the Holy Spirit

(Acts 4:23-31). This was true when the believers gathered together and sought the Lord for the release of Peter from prison (Acts 12:5-18).

It would be easy for someone to say, "We can all pray at home individually for this need. God is not limited by space and time." But that is not the experience of the early church. They understood that the coming together, the verbal agreeing together, and the corporate crying out to God had a corporate effect that was greater than one person praying alone in the privacy of his or her own home.

There is something about the spiritual principle of agreement that transcends a natural explanation. This principle is highlighted in Deuteronomy 32:30 where the Lord indicates that when the people of God join themselves together to do warfare, they do not merely add their strength to each other—they multiply their strength.

For this reason, prayer was not a side issue for the early church. They continued "steadfastly" in prayer (Acts 2:42). To continue steadfastly in prayer means to persevere in it. It means to give constant attention to it. It means to be in constant readiness for it. It means to show oneself courageous in it.

This is why such an emphasis is placed on prayer in the book of Acts. It is one of the keys to the early church's success. It was one of the keys of the Kingdom that Jesus placed in their hands (Matt. 16:19). The early church prayed on a regular basis (Acts 3:1; 2:42; 6:4; 10:2, 4; 12:15; 16:13). But they also prayed in specific situations.

- They prayed in selecting leaders (Acts 1:24).
- They prayed as they set in new leaders (Acts 6:6).
- They prayed in the sending out of ministries (Acts 13:3).
- They prayed in the process of ordaining elders (Acts 14:23).
- They prayed in departing from friends (Acts 20:26; 21:15).

In could be said that the early church bathed every activity and function of the church in prayer.

- They prayed for boldness (Acts 4:31).
- They prayed for people to be baptized in the Holy Spirit (Acts 8:15).

- They prayed for the dead to be raised (Acts 9:40).
- They prayed for Peter's release from prison (Note: Even though they were surprised when their prayers were answered so specifically).
- They prayed for direction from the Lord (Acts 16:16).
- They prayed for people to be delivered (Acts 16:25).
- They prayed for people to be healed (Acts 28:8).

There is no question that the early church believed that the effectual, fervent prayers of the righteous make a significant difference in the effectiveness of what is done (James 5:16).

The early church was birthed in prayer, and from then on prayer was a vital key. The Christians in the book of Acts breathed the atmosphere of prayer, they believed in the power of prayer, and they began, continued, and ended all of their work with prayer. A prayerless church is a powerless church.

PRAYER AND CHURCH GROWTH

Prayer is a key to both kinds of church growth. First of all, it is an obvious key to the personal growth and development of the individual members of the church, which in turn leads to the deepening and maturity of the local church. A church is only as strong as its individual members are strong.

However, prayer is also a vital key to the numerical growth of the local church. This is something that is often overlooked.

It is interesting to note that over the last number of years arguably the most studied local church in the whole realm of church growth is the church led by Dr. David Yonggi Cho in Seoul, South Korea. He has a church approaching one million members. Many leaders who desire greater numerical growth have read his materials, traveled to his conferences, and even visited the church.

Most of them come home and try to implement a method. Most often they try to get the cell groups going. They restructure the church and begin preaching church growth through cell division only to find that the church still does not grow. What many people miss, I think, is that the key to the church in South Korea is not a method but a lifestyle. And that lifestyle is prayer.

Many local churches practice various models of small-group ministry, but very few local churches maintain the intensity of prayer that is modeled by the Korean church. One of the most amazing aspects of Dr. Cho's ministry is Prayer Mountain where around-the-clock prayer is offered to the Lord. Many visitors are impressed by what they see in relation to prayer, but very few of them make any attempt to model that aspect in their churches' lives.

When asked what was the key to his success, Dr. Cho replied, "I pray and I obey!" Perhaps that is the key to the success of his church as well—they pray and they obey!

Jesus said that we were to pray that the kingdom would come. He said that in the days of harvest we were to pray for laborers. All of these things have to do with growth and harvest. Jesus is telling us that corporate prayer makes a difference.

DEVELOPING A STRATEGY OF PRAYER

Prayer does not just happen. Perhaps because it is such a vital key, it is something for which we have to constantly contend, whether it be in our personal lives or in the corporate life of our local churches. This is not something that we can just leave to chance and believe that the innate goodness in people will prevail, and they will do what they should do in this arena.

Those who fail to plan, plan to fail. Pastors and church leaders must assist people who are willing in their spirits to deal with the weaknesses of the flesh by providing guidance and structure for this discipline in the life of the church.

A Strategy for Personal Prayer

Knowing the critical importance of personal prayer in the life of the believer, pastors and leaders need to constantly do things that will reinforce this discipline in the lives of their church members. They can do this in many ways.

Obviously, revisiting this area regularly in the public teaching and preaching is the first thing that leaders can do. This does not just include teaching on the importance of prayer, but it also involves giving people practical instruction on how to pray and on different methods of prayer that will help to enrich their prayer lives. Prayer does not have to be boring.

Other ways to reinforce the personal aspect of prayer include occasional exhortations on prayer, testimonies from people who have seen clear answers to prayer, directing them to biographies of those who triumphed through prayer, encouraging them to keep prayer journals, and using a regular Bible reading plan in the church.

In addition, leaders should put tools in the hands of parents to help them with the personal devotional lives of their families. This would include giving them practical ideas and suggested activities of prayer that they can do with their families. It would also include pointing them to other recommended resources that they can use to keep alive their family prayer activities.

Pastors need to realize that if they can get their people genuinely praying and conscientiously reading their Bibles, they will go a long way to minimizing their counseling load. People will be in touch with the Holy Spirit who is a better counselor than any church leader or pastor could possibly be.

A Strategy for Corporate Prayer

At the same time that leaders are encouraging prayer in the individual homes represented in the church, there needs to be specific attention given to the development of a prayer strategy for the corporate prayer life of the church.

If prayer is a genuine conviction, and if we genuinely believe that prayer has the power to make what we do more effective, every department of the church should be deeply involved in prayer, and every activity of the local church should be in some way bathed in prayer.

It doesn't matter if we are talking about the music department, the children's or youth ministry, the office volunteers or staff, evangelistic endeavors, or the maintenance and janitorial workers; prayer needs to permeate the entire life of the church.

From the earliest ages, children need to be taught how to pray. They do not have to wait until they grow up. The youth of the church should be mighty prayer warriors. The musicians and worship leaders must be people of prayer who spend quality time in prayer together so that they can know how to hear from the Lord and respond to His heart in their functioning together. The elders of the church should be people of prayer if they are going to be able to lead the local assembly under the Lordship of Christ, the true head of the church. Every person who functions in the church must have sensitivity to the Holy Spirit that only a life of prayer can produce.

This dependency on prayer is first and foremost demonstrated in the corporate gathering of the local church. Some begin their services with a time of prayer. Others have a strategic prayer meeting on Saturday night in preparation for the Sunday services. In either case, prayer should be seen as a main focus for an increasing percentage of those who are part of the local assembly.

Radiating out from the corporate prayer life of the church is the development of a support system of prayer, which may include some or all of the following (it may go well beyond this list as well):

- Prayer-ministry leaders
- A dedicated prayer center or room
- Ministry teams
- Prayer cells
- Prayer walks
- Personal intercessors

A Regular Prayer Schedule

The schedule of the local church should reflect a strong belief in the importance and the power of prayer. Prayer and fasting should be built into the fabric and lifestyle of the church. By making it a corporate focus, we develop a large support group to reinforce the habit of prayer.

One suggestion would be to make an emphasis on fasting and prayer with the local church where the people are encouraged to pray daily, to fast one day a week, to fast three consecutive days quarterly, and to have one extended fast of seven to ten days once a year. If the local church would schedule these times as a congregation, it would help encourage everyone to participate.

Another suggestion is to use the corporate gathering quarterly as a prayer and worship gathering. In such a service, the time that is normally given to the preaching of the Word could be utilized for focused prayer in relation to all of the areas of prayer that we are challenged to uphold. The Bible clearly instructs us to pray for specific groups of people. We are to pray—

- For one another (James 5:16)
- For all saints (Col. 1:9; 1 Thess. 2:1; 5:23; 2 Thess. 1:11)
- For leadership (Heb. 13:18; 1 Thess. 5:25)
- For missionaries and other outreaches (2 Cor. 1:11; 2 Thess. 3:1-2)
- For political leaders (1 Tim. 2:1-8)
- For the salvation of all people (1 Tim. 2:1-8; Rom. 10:1)
- For the enemies of Christianity (Matt. 5:44; Luke 6:28)

LEADERSHIP AND PRAYER

The leaders of today's church need to fully recognize that they are called to pray. It is so easy to get caught up in the tyranny of the urgent and lose our primary focus. The early apostles understood that their primary call was to the Word of God and prayer (Acts 6:4-6).

A brief study of the life of the apostle Paul makes it clear that he prayed regularly and that prayer made up a significant part of his schedule. Not only did he wait on God for personal direction and provision, but he also spent time in prayer for those under his charge. Notice how Paul prayed for people. He prayed—

- That they might live in honesty and sincerity (Phil. 1:10)
- That they might be full of the fruit of the Spirit (Phil. 1:10)
- That they might know the will of God (Col. 1:9; 4:12)
- That they might walk worthy of the Lord (Col. 1:10)
- That they might increase in the knowledge of God (Col. 1:10)
- That they might be strengthened with all might (Col. 1:11)
- That the patience of Christ might be worked in them (Col. 1:11)
- That they might fulfill God's call on their lives (2 Thess. 1:11)
- That they might bring glory to God's name (2 Thess. 1:12)
- That they might know the hope of their calling (Eph. 1:15-18)
- That they might know the power of God on their lives (Eph. 1:19)
- That they might effectively communicate their faith to others (Phlm. 4-6)

Ultimately it will be the leader's pattern and example of prayer that will draw others into a life of prayer. It was Jesus' example of prayer that aroused the interest of his disciples and led them to ask Jesus to teach them to pray. It was His personal contact with the Father that gave authority to His life and ministry.

If leaders want to see God bless what they do, they must be fully committed to this timeless principle. If a local church is to grow and prosper from generation to generation, that local church must determine to develop a strong corporate prayer life.

Chapter Eighteen

———

UNITY

KEY #16—*If a church is to grow and prosper from generation to generation, that church must determine to make unity a priority.*

U nity is one of the keys to having influence. One of the things that has hindered evangelism and church growth is the lack of harmony in the local church. When people come to a church, they can tell whether or not there is peace in the camp. People are looking for a safe haven where they can find a place of rest. They do not want to be joined to another tense situation. They do not want to be in a place where gossip, personal politics, and relational conflicts exist. The church is to be different. It is to be a place where we treat one another like brothers and sisters, where we live for one another, resolve our differences, and march toward a common goal.

Unity is important in the local congregation, but it is equally important in the greater Body of Christ if we are going to see the nations touched. One of the greatest hindrances to the spread of Christianity is the division within Christianity. One group is at odds with another group, Christians tearing down other Christians. It is rare in a community for pastors to be united in purpose to reach their city together. Pastors are too often busy competing with other pastors for the same few people while the harvest is lost.

God wants to change our concepts in these days. He wants to bring pastors and leaders together for a common harvest. He is giving key leaders a vision of the Body of Christ and the Kingdom of God that will help to unite them and break down long-existing barriers. The prayer of Jesus will be fulfilled prior to the return of the Lord for His completed bride.

THE PRINCIPLE OF UNITY

God is a God of principle. When He established the natural universe, He put certain principles in operation that govern it. As long as you function within the parameters of those principles or natural laws, you will find success. However, if you try to function outside of those natural laws, you will surely fail. You may have wonderful motives, but without taking into account the natural order, good motives alone will not be sufficient to ensure success.

Just as there are principles or laws in the natural realm, there are spiritual principles or laws that govern the Kingdom of God. They are just as sure as the laws of nature. If you tap into these laws and cooperate with them, you will find success. If you work against the laws, you will not find the success for which you are searching.

One of the laws that governs the Kingdom of God is the law of unity. Unity is a key to experiencing the blessing of God upon our lives, our ministries, our local churches, and the church worldwide. Where unity exists, the blessing of God exists. Where unity is in short supply, the blessing of God is in short supply.

The priests in the Old Testament were able to tap into the principle of unity when they were dedicating the temple of Solomon. As they were all gathered together with a common purpose and were as one in their expression of worship to the Lord, God came down in visible manifestation. His presence was so strong among them that they were not able to stand (2 Chron. 5:11-14).

The early apostles also tapped into the spiritual law of unity. On the Day of Pentecost when they were waiting for the outpouring of the Holy Spirit, they were all in one place and in one accord. In this atmosphere the Holy Spirit descended in power. God loves to dwell together with His unified people.

On the Negative Side

As we study God's dealings with His people in both the Old and New Testaments, it is clear that unity is a powerful force. This is true whether the unity among men is for the purpose of good or the purpose of evil.

In the book of Genesis, God was upset with the people of Babel who were attempting to establish a false religious expression and build a tower into the heavens. His observation from heaven was that unless He did something dramatic to thwart their efforts, they would be able to achieve all that they had set out to do. They were not going to fail because they were one in spirit, one in purpose, and one in speech (Gen. 11:6).

God did not want this tower completed. So why didn't He just strike it with lightening? Why didn't He create an earthquake to destroy it? Because He knew that they would just build it again. He knew that there was a more lasting way to thwart the work. If he wanted them to cease to build and cease to be able to complete the task, all He had to do was to take away their unity.

This is what happened when God confounded their language. All of a sudden these people could not communicate on the same level. As a result, the people scattered in all directions as they tried to sort out with whom they could communicate and with whom they could not (Gen. 11:8).

On the Positive Side

Unity is just as powerful a force on the positive side. Jesus said in the context of the local church that there is power released when there is unity and harmony in a local church. In the Amplified Bible, Matthew 18:19-20 reads:

> *Again I tell you, if two of you on earth agree (harmonize together, together make a symphony) about—anything and everything—whatever they shall ask, it will come to pass and be done for them by My Father in heaven.*

Perhaps this is why Paul was so concerned about the believers in Corinth and why he exhorted them to be of the same mind and same judgment (1

Cor. 1:10). He knew that their lack of unity, which was precipitated by their own spiritual immaturity, was hindering their witness and power.

JESUS PRAYER FOR UNITY

Jesus knew how important unity would be for His people if the world was going to believe (John 17:20-24). This is why He made the unity of His people the focus of His prayer. The Lord's prayer for His followers was that they would all be one that the world might believe the message.

It is pretty hard to convince the world that we have a superior message if we are constantly fighting with one another. The average person in the world does not need more strife. The average person in the world is turned off by politics in the church. The average person in the world is looking for peace on earth not another battlefront.

Sometimes when you arrive at the home of someone who has invited you to dinner, you enter an atmosphere that is very hostile. Perhaps the husband and wife were in the middle of an argument just as you arrived. As soon as you walk in the door of the house, you can feel it. There may be a pleasant aroma coming from the kitchen, but there is another odor emanating from the people. What do you want to do? You want to back out as quickly as you came in.

Many local churches are like this. When people enter, they can feel the strife in the air. I am quite sure they are thinking, *I have enough problems in my life, I do not need this!*

UNITY DRAWS PEOPLE IN

On the other hand, where there is unity, there is peace—it is inviting. If you go into a home where there is true love, forgiveness, and acceptance, you can feel that too. You are actually drawn into such a setting.

The same is true in a local church. If the members of the church demonstrate a genuine love for one another, speak well of each other, act like they really enjoy one another, and look forward to being with each other, there is something very contagious about that atmosphere. So many people are looking for a spiritual family. They are looking for a safe place of refuge from the stuff that goes on in the world. They are looking for a place of affirmation where they will not be betrayed for silver.

UNITY IS WORK

Satan learned a lot about strategy by watching what happened at the Tower of Babel. He knows that he can thwart the program of the church if he can destroy the unity of the believers. And so he goes to work. He uses seven things to destroy the unity of the church. He uses scandal (Prov. 17:9), back-biting (Rom. 1:30; Ps. 15:1-3), slander (Prov. 10:18; Num. 14:36), whispering (1 Cor. 12:20; Rom. 1:29; Prov. 16:28), gossip (Ps. 41:6), discord (Prov. 6:16-19) and talebearing (Lev. 19:16; Prov. 20:19; 29:20) as weapons to bring the church to self-destruction.

Unfortunately, most believers are willing pawns in his plan. They are envious of one another, they are unforgiving, they are critical and judgmental, they revel in the failure of another, and rejoice in calamity. How sad!

No wonder Paul told the church at Ephesus to endeavor to keep the unity of the Spirit in the bond of peace (Eph. 4:3). The word *endeavor* means "to work at." It means to labor for. It means be diligent about. Any church that wants to be effective will have to work at the unity of the believers who make up its membership. We must realize that unity is more important than our personal opinions or goals. If we treasure the harvest, we must be willing to allow ourselves to be molded together for a common purpose.

THE VICTORIOUS CHURCH
WILL BE A UNIFIED CHURCH

The church is a complex organism that has a tremendous unity in the midst of diversity. Unity does not mean uniformity. Uniformity implies a loss of identity and individuality. In the unity that exists in the church we maintain individuality, personality, unique expression, and a variety of function; and yet we come into a corporate identification where we forfeit our rights to act independently of the rest of the members. This relationship is seen in various New Testament pictures of the church.

- The church is **ONE** body with **MANY** members.
- The church is **ONE** temple with **MANY** stones.
- The church is **ONE** flock with **MANY** sheep.
- The church is **ONE** nation with **MANY** citizens.
- The church is **ONE** vine with **MANY** branches.

- The church is **ONE** family with **MANY** brothers and sisters.
- The church is **ONE** army with **MANY** soldiers.

This kind of unity exists nowhere else in the world and is the source of tremendous power in the church. It is this unity that will be a witness to the whole world of the truth of the Gospel (John 17:20-24). It is the unity of the people of God that will be their defense in the days of storm. It is this kind of unity that is foundational to all that God desires to do through His people.

TWO KINDS OF UNITY

The church of Jesus Christ will experience two kinds of unity, and the first is foundational to and must precede the second, or it can lead to division.

First, God desires there to be a *unity of the Spirit* (Eph. 4:3). This is the kind of unity that is created in each member of the Body of Christ the moment he or she is born again. However, this type of unity must be cultivated and maintained, for Paul tells us that we are "to endeavor, to make an effort, to labor, to be diligent, to be prompt to keep the unity of the Spirit in the bond of peace."

The only way we can give ourselves to this goal of unity is to keep before us a picture of the Body of Christ as God sees it. God is calling His Body to unity in these days so that His glorious purpose might be fulfilled through it. If any church body is going to be effective, it is going to have to be unified.

Second, God desires to establish a *unity of the faith*. Paul tells us that Christ gave ministries in the church to help adjust the saints to do the work of serving, but also to establish the unity of the faith (Eph. 4:3).

Paul writes as if he firmly believed that the day would come when there would be a unity of faith. This involves a doctrinal unity. This was somewhat of a lofty dream for Paul because doctrinal unity was not the reality that we sometimes think it was even in his own day. Paul knew that he differed doctrinally from others (Gal. 2:6-12; Acts 15:7; 2 Pet. 3:15-16). Yet Paul knew that, as they would give themselves to maintaining the unity of the Spirit in the bond of peace, the day would come when they would experience the unity of the faith.

A beautiful demonstration of this principle is found in Acts 15. Here many were gathered with various doctrinal viewpoints. Many of the viewpoints were very strong, and yet because they were all committed to one another in the Spirit of God, and because they were submitted to the Word of God, they had the equipment that they needed to resolve their differences. Before that day was over, as they endeavored to maintain the unity of the Spirit in the bond of peace, they all came to the unity of the faith.

The church can only become one as it follows after the one Head, Christ (Eph. 4:13). The foundation of this unity in the church is in its relationship to God. The church is one because its God and Father is one, because its loyalty is to one Lord, because it is indwelled by the one Holy Spirit.

Jesus prayed that the church might be one. If ever anyone prayed according to the will of God, it was Jesus. If anyone's prayer will ever be answered, it will be the prayer of the only begotten Son of God. He prayed that the people of God would be one even as He was one with the Father (John 17:11, 21).

The Father and the Son have a twofold unity. There is the unity of the Spirit. They are one in essence, nature, and divinity. There is also a unity of doctrine (John 7:16; 8:26; 12:49-50), purpose (Matt. 26:39; John 4:34; 5:30; 5:38; 16:10; 17:4), love (John 3:35; 5:20; 15:9-10; 17:23-24, 26), and work (John 4:34; 5:19; 8:29; 14:10-11). God desires this kind of unity in the church as well.

Paul prayed often for the unity of the church. He desired to see unity in many areas. He wanted:

- Unity of mind (Rom. 15:5-6; Phil. 1:27; 2:2; 4:2)
- Unity of fellowship (Rom. 15:7; 1 Cor. 1:10-15; 3:3-8)
- Unity of love (Phil. 2:2)
- Unity of doctrine (Eph. 4:13-14; Gal. 1:8-9; 2 Tim. 1:5-9)
- Unity of witness (Rom. 15:6; Phil. 1:27)
- Unity of Spirit (Eph. 4:3)

If ever the Body of Christ needed to seek unity, it is today, for Christ is coming for a united church.

OTHER LOCAL CHURCHES

When we think about unity, we cannot limit the concept to our own local church. The church that God sees from heaven is much larger than one local assembly in each city. He sees all believers regardless of what label they may have inscribed over their doors.

One of the greatest hindrances for the spread of the Gospel is the division among Christendom. Unfortunately, we spend more time denouncing the sins or errors of one another than we do sharing the Gospel with the lost.

Something has got to change. We must start in our own hearts. What is in our hearts must spread to our local church. What is in our local church will overflow to other churches.

If we are ever going to see any tangible unity, we must change the way we think and talk of other churches and pastors in town. We must begin to pray for them, gather together with them, and strategize together for our cities and towns.

We are all on the same team. We need all players operating at their best. We cannot finish the commission alone. We need every church that names the name of Christ in our area to be a success. If every church were absolutely full to capacity, there would still be so many who have no place prepared for them. We must quit fighting over the same small catch of fish.

UNITY REQUIRES INTENT

Unity does not just happen. If a congregation is going to have unity, it must be worked at. If the church in the city is going to have unity, it will take even more work. Unity is not just the absence of hatred or disagreement. It is an active pursuit. Unity is not just smiling at each other and being cordial to each other when we "bump into" one another. It is actively investing our lives in each other in a strategic way.

It will have to start with the leaders of the local churches. They will have to be the first ones to "walk worthy of their vocation" (Eph. 4:1). Leaders in a community will have to begin to understand their spiritual authority in their region and begin to meet together for prayer, encouragement and strategy against the forces of darkness that would seek to destroy their witness.

This means that we will have to possess the qualities to which Paul makes reference. We will have to have four qualities (Eph. 4:2). First, we will have to possess lowliness. Lowliness is humility that manifests itself in a servant's heart. A servant's heart is one that gets excited about the success of another and is, in fact, willing to sacrifice for that success. It is a humble heart that does not insist on its own way but will set aside its own agenda for a higher cause.

Second, Paul says that we will have to possess gentleness or meekness. Meekness is not defensive and does not have to stand up for its own rights. It is a gentle friendliness that disarms and even quiets the opposition.

Third, Paul says that we will need longsuffering. That means we may have to suffer a long time before we see the fruit of our sacrifice. Long-suffering means being willing to endure offenses and the irritations of others. Longsuffering does not react to every issue for the sake of relationship.

Fourth, Paul says that we must be willing to forbear or bear with one another at times. That means that we must keep on accepting people even when they bother us. We cannot let the little things that annoy us stifle our expression of love for people or we will never achieve unity.

As I write this chapter, I have just returned from a funeral service for a pastor who died of cancer. He was a pastor for over twenty years in a small rural community of under twenty thousand people. He never really had a large work. Most of those who attended his local assembly were related in some way. You could wonder about this man's success. There is some talk of closing the doors of the church upon his death.

However, at his funeral it became very clear to me that this man had much fruit that extended beyond the twenty-five. The funeral was held in one of the largest auditoriums in the town. Hundreds of people were in attendance including nearly every pastor in the town. Four of the pastors from other churches had formed a quartet especially to sing at the funeral. Another local pastor preached the message.

As it turned out, this man had spent over fifteen years trying to get the pastors and churches together. He had "bugged them" until they responded, and as a result ten churches gathered together regularly on a Sunday to unite their congregations for "Roundup" Sunday. There was a unity among the churches that is so rare, but, in this case, that unity was a powerful testimony to the whole region.

This man did not pastor a local church, he pastored a town, and I believe that his labor will pay off in a major way as those pastors continue to walk together as the elders of that community. What a powerful witness!

PASTORS GETTING IT TOGETHER

Relationships among pastors in the same city are extremely difficult to form and maintain. The main reason is that Satan understands how important these relationships are and, therefore, he works extra hard to undermine any effort that might lead to unity.

Satan is a deceiver. His goal in this area is to deceive us into believing a lie. If we believe the lie, it will affect our actions. He wants us to believe that we really do not need other pastors. We will do just fine without them. He wants us to further believe that it is not worth the investment of time, money and sacrifice, to see these relationships grow and develop.

If this deception does not work, he whispers other things in our ears that will keep us apart. He magnifies our differences with each other. He fosters an attitude of suspicion. He feeds the competitive side of our nature and pits us one against the other. He does everything that he can to keep us from realizing that we are on the same team.

Sometimes our hindrances have nothing to do with Satan at all. Sometimes it is just our own schedules and our own natural life. We are busy trying to get our fields to produce. That takes all of the energy that we have. How can we possibly add one more thing to our workload?

Perhaps pastors just do not see city unity as a priority. Or maybe they are waiting for someone else to take the initiative. Or maybe they are fearful of rejection. Or maybe they simply do not know how to pull it off. There are always plenty of justifications for the *status quo*. However, at some point we must put the higher goal above our own personal comfort level and move with purpose into our destiny.

PRESSING THROUGH

Therefore, the time has come to ask the Lord for an impartation of His burden in this area. It begins by spending time in prayer and asking God for an impartation of His heart and a strategy that can be used to bring leaders together. It involves spending personal time in prayer for the local pastors and asking the Lord to put key pastors on your heart on which you can begin to focus. Ask the Lord to direct you to pastors who will be the key to unlock the door to others.

Then it is time to step out in faith by inviting a few leaders to gather with you for city prayer. The time should be spent getting to know each other, praying for common needs in the city and praying for the individual needs in the group. Encourage each participant to invite one or two others whom they feel would carry the same spirit of the group.

As you find success in this way, begin to talk about the needs of the city and how you might work together to minister to some of those needs as multiple congregations.

Make city pastors meetings a priority in your schedule. Don't be afraid to get involved socially with pastors and their spouses. Eventually the group will become strong and supportive of each other.

At some point in time you can develop a formal commitment one to another as elders of the city. This would include things like making a commitment to speak only well of one another, a commitment not to receive an unsubstantiated accusation against one another, a commitment to communicate over wandering church members, a commitment to pray regularly for one another, and a commitment to accountability to one another.

As time goes on, you can continue to grow together by sharing your platform with local pastors. You may even bring the congregations together for special joint services (possibly even Communion services). You may adopt certain service projects in the community that will enable the rest of the city to eat of the fruit of the unity that is growing.

Someone once said that we are going to be spending eternity together in heaven, so we might as well get warmed up here on earth.

UNITY IS WORTH FIGHTING FOR

Unity is such an important key both inside the local church and among the rest of the Body of Christ. It is worth working hard to see it become a reality. This means pastors need to work to keep the unity destroyers to a minimum in their own assemblies. And it means that they must become catalysts for unity in their own cities and towns. Unity is worth fighting for!

Chapter Nineteen

SERVANTHOOD

**KEY #17—*If a church is to grow and prosper
from generation to generation, that church must
understand the principle of servanthood and practice
it inside and outside of the church.***

C hrist personally demonstrated what it was to be great in the
Kingdom of God. He modeled a kind of ministry and lifestyle
that was so radical by the world's standards and so powerful by
God's standard that it changed the world. Jesus personally demonstrated the
power of the Kingdom when He humbled Himself, became a human being,
and was willing to become the sacrifice for sin. He demonstrated this power
to His followers at the Last Supper when He took up the towel and washed
the feet of His disciples.

The church of Jesus Christ must have this same spirit upon it. If the
church is going to touch the world, it will touch it with the love and spirit
of service that Christ had. Love is an irresistible force. Love will gain the
church favor with God and man.

Those who lead the church must model this spirit of love and service
first. For this to take place, there must be a re-examination of the concept
of ministry or "the ministry" and a return to the true biblical concept of
greatness.

WRONG CONCEPTS OF MINISTRY

Whenever you talk to people about the subject of "ministry" or the term "full-time ministry," it is easy for people to get weird. Christians enjoy the game of trying to figure out the answer to the question, "What is *my* ministry?" Or, perhaps even more, "What is *your* ministry?"

In this context, the word "ministry" has come to take on a "superspiritual" ring to it. At times, older believers can intimidate the newer believers with the mystery of this spiritual quest to discover the answers.

The truth of the matter is that the word *ministry* as it appears in many translations of the Bible simply means "service." Instead of asking, " What is my 'ministry'?" I should be asking, "What 'service' am I able to render to others that might be a strength and blessing to them?"

Who is the greatest?

Too many believers are jockeying for position and trying to determine who is the greatest in the Kingdom of God. Too many people are looking for positions where they can sit and be served rather than looking for the towel or the apron of humility with which to wash the feet of others.

They are not unlike the twelve disciples of Jesus before the Holy Spirit supernaturally touched them. Early in the experience of the disciples, they were self-motivated, they were jealous of one another, and any other would-be leaders. They were ambitious for power and placement in the Kingdom that Christ would establish.

James and John epitomized this mentality when they came to Jesus and made a "small" request for the "chief" seats in God's glorious Kingdom, at the right hand and the left hand of Jesus (Mark 10:35-45). They wanted to sit on thrones. They wanted to rule. They wanted to sit and be served.

When the other disciples heard of the request that James and John had made, they were very displeased. Not because they felt that the attitude of James and John was poor and needed adjustment, they were upset because James and John got to Jesus first and there were only two such seats.

To rule or to serve

Something in the heart of the rest of the disciples wanted the same thing that James and John had desired. There is something in the heart of every man and woman that wants the same thing as well. We want position, we want power, we want a name for ourselves and we want to sit while others serve us or minister to our wants.

Sometimes this is the way we approach the Lord Jesus Himself. When James and John approached Jesus, they said, "Master, we want you to do for us whatever we ask." It's as if Jesus was their "errand boy" who existed primarily to tend to their wishes and desires. We call Jesus "Master" and then we want Him to do whatever we ask.

The disciples should have been asking, "Master, what do you want us to do? How can we serve and lay our lives down for you as you have been so willing to do for us?"

When Jesus sensed the motivation in the disciples' hearts, He knew it was time for one of His "friendly chats." Jesus knew that if He were to build a church with this group of apostles, He would have to start with the first and the most important thing—the motivation in their hearts.

Ministry equals service

Jesus proceeded to talk to His followers and teach them about true ministry and true greatness. When you are called into the ministry, you are called into a life of service. If you want to be great in the Kingdom of God, you must humble yourself, become like a little child, and become the servant of all.

This was one of the major problems with the Pharisees of Jesus' day. The Pharisees had a lot of knowledge, but they loved the chief seats, they loved titles, and they loved to have people's respect and homage.

We are living in a day when many people are looking for a "pecking order" in the church. Many are not concerned about who can be the lowest or the chief servant. They are concerned about "who is the greatest." What is the ultimate position that I can attain in the church? Who has the highest rank?

Until we pay heed to Jesus' admonition to His disciples, we will not see a restoration of true ministry to the church. Until we can deal effectively with the "desire for the preeminence" in the heart of man, we will not be able to accept the biblical definition of ministry. If we are not careful, we will not want a true biblical definition, because it will not cater to our desire to rule and be great.

The Gentile way

Jesus made it clear that being motivated by a desire for preeminence was the Gentile way. The Gentile way involves hierarchy where people in authority lord it over those under authority. Jesus said that it was not to be that way among His people.

Jesus must be our pattern for all ministries. He has to be the one after which all Christians pattern themselves. Jesus demonstrated His preeminence when He girded Himself with a towel and washed the disciples' feet (John 13:3-5).

Jesus had to leave the earth physically, but He wanted His work and ministry to continue. When He ascended on high, He distributed the ministry that was in Him to human beings. To some He gave His ministry of teaching. To others He gave His ministry of prophecy. And to still others He gave His ministry as an apostle (Eph. 4:8-11). Every member of the Body of Christ has received a portion of Christ's ministry.

THE ISSUE IS THE HEART

When it comes right down to it, ministry is all about a person's heart. If you were to look up the word *heart* in the dictionary, you would find five main definitions. Each one of these five definitions can be applied to the issue of ministry. The heart is defined as follows:

- The *central* organ of the vascular system
  The focus on this definition is the word *central*. What is central in my life? What is central in your life? You see, whatever is central is the thing around which everything else is organized. If my own

personal interests are at the center of my being, my whole life will be organized in such a way as to satisfy those interests. If the love of Christ and His church is central, I will organize my life in such a way as to serve those interests.

- A hollow structure which maintains the circulation of the blood
  The focus of this definition is the word *circulation*. What is it that stirs or motivates you? What keeps you stirred up and moving in a certain direction? Is it the idea of being rich and famous? Is it the thought of having power and influence? Or am I genuinely motivated by the love of Christ that seeks to serve the best interests of others?

- The seat of the affections and emotions
  The focus of this definition is the word *emotions*. What is it that excites you or touches you in the innermost part of your being? Do you get excited about making other people successful? Do you use your authority and influence to push others forward? If you do, you may have the true heart of a servant.

- One's innermost thoughts and feelings
  The focus of this definition is the word *innermost*. In other words, when it comes to ministry, what really matters is not the external things that you say or the outward actions that you portray but the person that you really are deep within when no one is around or there is no one to impress. Someone has once said, "You are no more a Christian than what you are when no one else is around."

- The vital and essential part
  The focus of this definition is the word *vital*. The word *vital* is associated with life. Ministry that comes from the heart produces life in others.

The most important thing that we can cultivate in ministry is a proper heart. The Bible puts a major emphasis on the heart and the condition of the heart. The heart can be a negative factor, or it can be a positive factor. Notice the following heart conditions referred to in the Bible:

NEGATIVE CONDITIONS	*POSITIVE CONDITIONS*
Hard (Mark 6:52)	Tender (2 Kings 22:19)
Obstinate (Deut. 2:30)	Willing (Exod. 35:29)
Proud (Prov. 16:5)	Humble (Ps. 69:32)
Hateful (Lev. 19:17)	Loving (Mark 12:30)
Double (Ps. 12:2)	Single (Jer. 32:39)
Hypocritical (Matt. 15:8)	Integrity (Ps. 78:72)
Foolish (Rom. 1:21)	Wise (Exod. 36:2)
Stony (Ezek. 11:19)	Soft (2 Chron. 34:27)
Withered (Ps. 102:4)	Enlarged (Ps. 119:32
Perverse (Prov. 17:20)	Meek (Matt. 11:29)
Unbelieving (Mark 16:14)	Believing (Acts 8:37)
Restless (Eccl. 2:23)	Free (2 Chron. 29:31)
Uncircumcised (Acts 7:51)	Circumcised (Rom. 2:29)
Rebellious (Jer. 5:23)	Contrite/Broken (Ps. 34:18)
Wicked (Prov. 10:20	Pure (Prov. 22:11)
Erring (Heb. 3:10)	Perfect (Ps. 101:2)
Whorish (Ezek. 6:9)	Faithful (Neh. 9:8)

God wants us to know our own hearts and to prepare our hearts to be the true servants of the Lord.

KNOWING OUR HEARTS

Knowing one's own heart is no small matter. It is so easy for the wrong things to be in it. We are surrounded by a world that is motivated by so many of the things that are rejected by God. We can be motivated by personal ambition. We can be motivated by money. We can be motivated by a desire for power and control.

It is important to understand what we are saying and what we are not saying. We are not saying that there are no leadership positions in the Body of Christ that need to be filled. God places people in leadership to give parental guidance to His church. The real issue is the spirit by which one acquires and functions in that position. It must not come by personal ambition and political maneuvering. It must come by God's choosing, and it must be exercised out of a spirit of service and humility.

Personal Ambition

Those that are motivated by personal ambition have a great fear of failure and a loss of reputation. They judge place and position as greatness. They are like the disciples who want to sit and be served. They want the highest rank. The Bible addresses those who are motivated by personal ambition. They are categorized as those who desire seven things.

1. To be in the limelight (Matt. 6:1,5; 23:5)
2. To build a name for oneself (Gen. 11:4; Phil. 1:15; 2:3-9)
3. To be great in man's eyes (Jer. 45:5; Isa. 14:13-14)
4. To seek glory (Prov. 25:27; 27:2; John 7:18; Jer. 9:23)
5. To be honored of men (Matt. 6:2; John 5:44)
6. To please or impress men (1 Thess. 2:4; Gal. 1:10)
7. To have a following (Acts 20:30)

The Pharisees of Jesus' day were of such a spirit. They loved to be seen by men. In fact the Scriptures indicate that they did "all their works" to be seen by men (Matt. 23:5). They loved the chief seats in the synagogue. They loved the greetings in the marketplace. They loved to be called by special titles that made them feel important.

Contrast this to Jesus who humbled Himself and made Himself of no reputation (Phil. 2:5-8), Jesus who did not separate Himself by titles or regal attire but mingled freely with people of all walks of life whether they were the beggars on the street, a Samaritan woman at a well, or a person of power and influence. Jesus was able to serve them all equally because He had no personal agenda.

Paul had this same spirit as reflected in his statement, "For though I am free from all men, I have made myself a servant to all, that I might win the more" (1 Cor. 9:19).

Money and Power

Leaders can also be motivated by a desire for money or power. Sad to say, these people make decisions solely on the basis of what is in it for them and how it will enhance their life, their ministry goals, and their influence.

The New Testament gives many warnings concerning money and those who lead the people of God (1 Pet. 5:2; John 10:12; 2 Pet. 2:3; 2 Cor. 12:16-19). Those who serve for money are hirelings. Hirelings can be bought. Hirelings run when they see danger approaching so that they can save their own skin. Hirelings make merchandise of the people of God and use the Gospel for personal gain.

Leaders who serve God for money will find themselves making most decisions on the basis of what it will cost and what it will gain them financially rather than on the revealed will and purpose of God. Not every godly decision and direction will net a financial reward to the person in leadership. Jesus was willing to be made poor so that others could be rich.

The New Testament also gives many warnings about the wrong use of power or authority (1 Pet. 5:3; Matt. 20:20-29). Peter clearly instructs that elders and leaders are not to see themselves as "lords over God's heritage." Instead they are to lay their lives down and be an example of what a believer should look like.

PROPER MOTIVES

The proper motives that should stand behind those who serve God are as follows:

- *Glorifying God.* Whatever we do, we should do it to please and glorify the Lord (1 Pet. 4:11).
- *Love.* We are to minister out of the kind of love that is defined in 1 Corinthians 13 that puts others first and is not self-willed. This includes a love for God (Phil. 2:1; 2 Tim. 2:3-4; John

21:15-16), a love for people (1 Thess. 2:8; Phil. 1:7-8), and a love for God's house (1 Chr. 29:3; John 2:17).

- *Fulfilling God's Will.* Inside each of us should be a desire to apprehend the thing for which we were apprehended. Part of a desire to please or serve God is to fulfill His personal commission to us and become all that God has made it possible for us to become in Christ (Eph. 4:1; Phil. 3:11-14).

- *Winning the Lost.* Our motivation should be the same as Christ's to see everyone saved and come to the knowledge of the truth. Our actions should always be tempered by what bearing this activity will have on the salvation of and witness to others (1 Cor. 9:19-23; 10:33; Rom. 10:1).

- *Rewards.* While it may seem selfish to desire a reward, it is basic to our relationship with God to know that He is a rewarder of those who dilgently seek Him (Heb. 11:6,10,28; 2 Chron. 15:7; 1 Cor. 3:8,14). Rewards promised to the faithful include the satisfaction of accomplishment (1 Tim. 4:6), commendation (Matt, 25:21), success (Josh. 1:8), and a crown of victory (1 Pet. 5:4; 2 Tim 4:6-8; 1 Cor. 9:24-27).

- *A Burning Heart.* An understanding of all that God has done for us in Christ should translate into a burning zeal to see the purposes of God established on the earth (Jer. 20:9; Ps. 39:3).

When this kind of heart is in the leadership of the church, it will translate into the character and nature of the local congregation in which the leaders serve. The church will become a vehicle on the earth through which Christ can continue His ministry of service to the world. This kind of Christianity is what the world is waiting to see.

THE MINISTRY OF JESUS

This is the kind of ministry that Jesus had on the earth when He walked the streets of Palestine. His ministry is summarized in Acts 10:38 where it reads, "how God anointed Jesus of Nazareth with the Holy Spirit and with power, who went about doing good and healing all who were oppressed by the devil."

Jesus came with the world in his heart *to seek and to save that which was lost*. He came to put a face on God and to reveal to the world the love of the Father. He came to put a face on God and love the people of the world the way the Father would. He came to serve and to bring light and life to the heart of every man.

Jesus' Method

Jesus' method of showing the love of the Father was to lay his life down for those who had need. He went about looking for ways to serve and to demonstrate God's love for mankind. He didn't pass out tracts, although tracts have a place. He demonstrated what He taught. He relieved human suffering. He loved the world in a very practical and tangible way.

Our Method

The church of Jesus Christ has been given the same commission to seek and save that which is lost. It is something that we all acknowledge, we write about it, we discuss it among ourselves, we teach seminars on it, we pray about it, we sing about it, but we don't really do it!

Yet the last few years in the church have been characterized by a fresh moving of the Holy Spirit among the people of God. Some have referred to it as visitation, renewal, revival, or refreshing.

There is no doubt that the church has needed a breath of fresh air. There is no doubt that we needed renewing. There is no doubt that we needed a fresh relationship with the Spirit of God to ensure that the church that began in the Spirit would not be completed in the flesh.

But what is the purpose of this or any other outpouring of the Spirit? Why has God so graciously and freely given of His Spirit?

HIS PURPOSE

God has a higher purpose than just our personal blessing or renewal. That is important, because unless we are refreshed and renewed, we cannot be used of the Lord to fulfill our purpose and destiny. But the purpose is not us, it is the world.

Jesus was anointed with the Holy Spirit so that he could preach the gospel to the poor, heal the brokenhearted, and minister deliverance to the captives. God anointed Jesus to go about and serve the harvest by doing good.

God wants us to carry on and fulfill the ministry of Jesus. We have the Spirit of the Lord upon us, and we are to channel that divine anointing and energy to be used toward touching the world through acts of love and kindness so that the people of the world can see the Father's heart of love.

WE HAVE LOST OUR WAY

Somehow we have lost our way from the original purpose. We have separated ourselves from the world to such a degree that we have no influence. We have begun to view the world as our enemy, and as such we have lost much of our ability to relate to sinners and those in need of deliverance.

In addition, we have changed the Great Commission to something that no longer resembles the pattern Jesus gave to us. His challenge was to go into the world and bring the light of the Gospel to those held captive by Satan.

Instead we have built fortresses, polished our theology, debated doctrine, perfected our singing and worship, and invited the world to come and join us. This is the Old Testament pattern of evangelism—to invite those outside of the covenant to "Come, behold the works of the Lord."

Jesus' method was just the opposite. I am thankful that He did not just dump a load of tracts on us and invite us to the great cathedral in the sky. No! He came to us when we were not inclined to come to Him. He came to where we were, living among us, showing us the light of God's love. It is a good thing He did. The gap was too great for any of us to get to God. We could never bridge it.

THE GREATEST COMMISSION

The challenge for us today is to pattern ourselves after Jesus, the greatest evangelist of all time. The New Testament Great Commission or command to us is found repeated many times in the Bible. We are to love God with all of our heart, soul, mind and strength, and we are to "love our neighbor as ourselves" (See: Matt. 19:19; 22:34-40; Mark 12:28-34; Luke 10:25-37; Rom. 15:1-2; James 2:8). This is the Royal Law of love.

By and large, most churches have worked extra hard on the first commandment to love God, but we have not done nearly as well on loving our
neighbor, or we have been confused over what it means to love our neighbor. Some have even misinterpreted this command to justify self-love.

Love in God's mind is an active thing, not a passive thing. Love is something that is demonstrated, not just discussed. Jesus "loved His neighbor" by
going about doing good and healing all that were oppressed of the devil.
Jesus answered the question "Who is my neighbor?" with the story of the
"Good" Samaritan. Essentially my neighbor is anyone I find on my pathway
who has a need.

As Christians we seem to have lost this aspect of Christianity. Somehow
we have felt that if we truly serve the lost, somehow we are approving of the
lifestyle of the lost.

But the New Testament is very clear. We are to love our enemies (Luke
6:27-36). We are to feed and bless them (Matt. 5:43-48). We are to do good
to all men. We are to overcome evil with good. We are to let our light shine
(1 Pet. 3:8-12).

What is this light that we are to shine upon those who sit in darkness?
Matthew tells us very specifically. He says, "Let your light so shine before
men, that they may see your good works, and glorify your father which is in
heaven" (Matt. 5:16).

The light is "good works." Like Dorcas, we are to be "full of good works
and charitable deeds" (Acts 9:36). The people of the world will see these
works and be drawn to the Lord.

GOOD WORKS

Perhaps we are too much the products of grace to focus on "good works."
Martin Luther was strong on grace. The battle cry of the Reformation was
sola gratia, sola fidei, and *sola scriptura.*

Luther was reacting in his day to the idea of a man working his way to
heaven by works of righteousness. He did not like the book of James. He
called it the "straw epistle" because of its emphasis on works.

But James was a pastor. He was tired of hearing about how much faith
people had. He wanted to see their "faith" in a more tangible way. He felt

that if people had the faith they claimed to have, there ought to be a visible demonstration of that faith.

Perhaps the world is looking for the same demonstration from the church today. Perhaps they are tired of empty statements concerning God's love, and they are looking for a living demonstration. Maybe they are tired of tracts that say God loves them and has a wonderful plan for their lives, and they would like to see that love in action. Maybe they need to see some "living epistles."

As Christians we must be careful that we love not just in word or in tongue but in deed and in truth (1 John 3:18). We don't want to deceive ourselves that somehow we can love God whom we have not seen and yet hate our brother whom we have seen. John says, "If someone says, 'I love God,' and hates his brother, he is a liar" (1 John 4:20).

Actually, if we understand God's grace properly, we will understand that God's grace has come to us so that we can pass on that which we have received (Eph. 2:8-10).

I would like to share some areas where our thinking needs to be challenged concerning our true emphasis as believers and the power of "doing good" as a Gospel witness. But to do so means attacking some of our sacred cows or wrong ways of thinking that keep us from being the servants that God desires for us to be.

SOME SACRED COWS

A stronghold is any area of thinking that is not consistent with God's thinking that hinders us from fulfilling our responsibilities as a Christian. Strongholds are not necessarily demon forces; they are thought processes within us that can become a barrier to us. Our thought processes can be shaped by the world, by religious traditions, or by our own experience. They may also be shaped by some good but perhaps "unbalanced" preaching. If we are not careful, some of these ways of thinking can become sacred cows that may need to be slain and offered up to God as a "burnt offering."

Let me discuss ten possible sacred cows that all have an element of truth to them, but can be misdirected.

1. Prosperity and Faith for Abundance

God is revealing much in this area to His people in these days. He is challenging us to believe for the impossible and learn how to tap into His abundance for the sake of the call. We see that God wants to bless us, and as we exert our faith, we can tap into God's abundance and experience miracle supply.

This is an important truth, but it is very important that we understand why God wants to do this. 2 Cor. 9:8 helps us to understand that God gives us extra grace, extra supply, and abundance for the purpose of doing "good works." "And God is able to make all grace abound toward you, that you, always having all sufficiency in all things, have an abundance for every good work."

If we are not careful, we can find ourselves praying for abundance so we can increase and get bigger and better. God would feel much better about blessing us if He knew that we would use it to be channels of that blessing to others like He knew regarding Abraham of old (Gen. 12:1-3).

God has a purpose for riches. Those who are rich in this world's goods are to be rich in good works, willing to give and to share with those in need (1 Tim. 6:17-19).

2. Theological Exactness

We have done well in the theological arena, splitting hairs and debating over issues at times of little or no consequence (much like the Pharisees who strained at a gnat and swallowed a camel). The Pharisees were accurate in their teaching, but their life demonstration was weak. This is why Jesus instructed people to listen to what they said but to not follow what they practiced (Matt. 23:1-2).

Unfortunately, all of our great theology has done little to win the world to Christ. I am not saying that our doctrinal exactness is not important. But Paul wrote to Titus to remind him what is more important. He said, "This is faithful saying, and these things I want you to affirm constantly, that those who have believed in God should be careful to **maintain good works**. These things are good and profitable to men. But avoid foolish disputes, genealogies, contentions, and strivings about the law; for they are unprofitable and useless" (Titus 3:8-9).

Paul said to avoid strivings about "the law." The "law" was their scripture. Surely these debates are important. Unfortunately, we can get so into our debates that they consume all of our energy and we never get to the principle commission. We can debate the meaning of this and the meaning of that. I often wonder how much of what we spend so much energy debating would be considered by Paul to be useless.

3. Praise, Worship, and Spiritual Sacrifices

In a previous chapter I discussed the importance of understanding our New Testament role as priests unto God. There, I emphasized the Godward aspect of our priesthood and spent time highlighting the spiritual sacrifices of praise, worship, thanksgiving, and joy. This is very important and a key to building a great local church.

But the writer to the Hebrews gives us a more balanced view of our priesthood. The priest had a Godward ministry—to stand before God as a representative of the people. But the priest was also to come out of the presence of God and represent God to the people.

Spiritual sacrifices have a Godward aspect, but they also have a manward aspect (i.e. our time, our talents, our substance, and our good works). Notice Hebrews 13:15-16, "Therefore by Him let us continually offer the sacrifice of praise to God, that is, the fruit of our lips, giving thanks to His name. [We tend to stop here] But do not forget **to do good** and to share, for with such sacrifices God is well pleased."

We need to work harder on the manward aspect of our priesthood and become just as perfected in this area of doing good as we have in our worship.

4. Church Attendance

Leaders have worked hard to establish in people's minds that if they are going to be good Christians, they need to attend meetings. They are not to miss church or forsake "the assembling of themselves together."

They have at times done this to the extent that our Christianity can be measured by our church attendance alone. If we attend church, we are good Christians. If we fail to attend regularly, we are poor Christians.

In this concept, the only difference between believers and nonbelievers is what they do on Sunday mornings. Leading people to Christ has become synonymous with inviting people to church.

Hebrews 10:25 is a passage that we use to get people to attend services. But when you read this entire passage, you come up with a more balanced picture. Verses 24 and 25 read, "And let us consider one another in order to stir up love and good works, not forsaking the assembling of ourselves together, as is the manner of some."

We have developed a Christianity that needs meetings rather than a Christianity that meets needs. The purpose of our meetings should be to stir us up toward good deeds.

5. True Spirituality

We have tended to judge a person's spirituality by the "Mary model." People that sit at Jesus feet, who pray hours a day, who prophesy in believer meetings, who "speak in tongues more than ye all," and who fall out under the power are deemed more spiritual.

While the "Mary model" is the most important part, there is another aspect of Christianity that "Martha" modeled. It is the model of service and selfless giving. Martha has gotten a rather "bad rap" in most Christian preaching. Our Christianity does not have to be an "either/or" situation. It should be "both/and."

James defined true spirituality or "pure religion" as visiting "orphans and widows in their trouble, and to keep oneself unspotted from the world" (James 1:27).

In Isaiah 58:6-12, God indicates the kind of fast that He has chosen. It is a fast that loosens the bonds of wickedness, undoes heavy burdens, sets the captives free, and feeds the poor.

6. Studying the Bible

We can spend a great deal of time as Christians studying the Bible and getting to know the Word. This is good, but not for the purpose of getting puffed up in relation to our Bible knowledge. The purpose of our study and preparation in the Word is to thoroughly equip us for every good work. Knowledge puffs up, but love edifies.

Notice what Paul says in 2 Timothy 3:16-17, "All Scripture is given by inspiration of God, and is profitable for doctrine, for reproof, for correction, for instruction in righteousness, [Why?] that the man of God may be complete, thoroughly equipped for every good work."

We tend to study to become good preachers and Bible expositors; however, the fruit of our Bible study should be good works.

7. Government Involvement

Our relationship to governments has sometimes been more like the Jews' relationship to the Romans. We have been a difficult people to rule over at best. We have become quite good at criticizing, picketing, boycotting, and attempting to win them over in the ballot box. But how much have we served our governments and helped them meet the needs of our communities?

We have been good at criticizing leaders and those in authority, but have we been willing to serve them? If we will do charitable acts and good deeds, we may find a place of favor with government leaders in society (e.g. volunteering to help with schools, community needs, homelessness, etc.).

Paul admonished Titus, "Remind them to be subject to rulers and authorities, to obey, to be ready for every **good work**"(Titus 3:1). He also addressed the Christians at Rome, "For rulers are not a terror to **good works**, but to evil. Do you want to be unafraid of the authority? Do what is good, and you will have praise from the same" (Rom. 13:3).

We win governments over not by organizing rallies and voting out bad politicians (although there is no harm in that). We win them by doing good. We prove that we are an asset to society and that the world is a better place because we exist. Everyone likes this kind of church.

8. Dressing for Success

Sometimes we focus on outward appearances in the church. We have become good dressers and real fashion conscious. We have gone to the point that at times the unsaved feel uncomfortable around us because they do not have the right clothes to wear.

However, the Bible is more concerned about how we are adorned spiritually. Women were instructed to adorn themselves with "**good works**" (1 Tim. 2:10). When we adorn ourselves with good works, we will look good to the world.

9. Faith and Works

While it is true that believers are saved by faith and grace, they are saved for the purpose of good works (Eph. 2:10) and every believer should be...

- Fruitful in every good work (Col. 1:10)
- Zealous for good works (Titus 2:14)
- Rich in good works (1 Tim. 6:17-19)

Titus 3:14 says, "And let our people also learn to maintain good works, to meet urgent needs, that they may not be unfruitful." Fruitfulness for us has meant winning souls. But that fruit will not come without our ministry of good works.

10. The Anointing

We have tended to put the concept of the "anointing" into a very mystical realm. We have referred to "the anointing" in the context of prophecy and operating spiritual gifts. We talk about "anointed" preaching, "anointed" services and "anointed" prayer meetings.

The anointing in Jesus' life was not limited to prayer, prophecy, and preaching. The anointing was upon Him to break bondages, set captives free, minister to the poor, and to go about doing **good deeds** (Luke 4:18-19).

REPOSITIONING THE CHURCH

We are living in a time where God wants to reposition the church. He wants to position it as servants to the world. He wants the church to lay its life down for the world even as He did.

It starts with the pastors of the churches. Paul admonished Titus as a pastor and leader of God's people to show himself to be "a pattern of good works." From the pastors, it must spread to the heart and spirit of the local church.

If the church is to be fully successful in these days, it must listen and respond to the admonition of Peter, "Beloved, I beg you as sojourners and pilgrims, abstain from fleshly lusts which war against the soul, having your conduct honorable among the Gentiles, that when they speak against you as evildoers, they may, by your good works which they observe, glorify God in the day of visitation" (1 Pet. 2:11-12).

Chapter Twenty

EVANGELISM

KEY #18—*If a church is to grow and prosper from generation to generation, that church must determine to take Christ's commission seriously.*

hrist gave a commission to His disciples during the forty days that He spent with them prior to His ascension into heaven. They were not to begin implementing that commission until the Holy Spirit came upon them, which happened on the Day of Pentecost. That commission was not just for those early disciples. That commission belongs to us as well.

Christ's commission was a multifaceted commission. It involved being witnesses and preaching the Gospel in all the world. It involved making disciples of all nations and nationalities. It involved pastoring the harvest and teaching those who are harvested to live a separated life. It involved releasing people into the nations.

If the church of today is going to fulfill this commission, we must reach out to the lost. We cannot be satisfied with church growth that is dependent upon Christian people moving from one congregation to another. Many churches today revel in the fact that they have become large, and yet statistics show that in the United States the total number of Christians has not changed significantly for many years.

If the church of today is going to fulfill this commission, we are going to have to get serious about evangelism, church planting, and world missions. We are going to have to preach the vision, raise the money, equip our people, and send the laborers into the harvest. The harvest is still ripe. The laborers are still few. The call upon the church is to be God's instrument to extend the Kingdom of God.

THE MISSIONARY HEART OF GOD

The missionary heart of the local church springs from the heart and nature of God Himself. God's nature is missionary or outgoing. The New Testament defines God in four main ways. God is spirit, light, love, and consuming fire. All of these images share something in common. They all support the missionary heart of God.

1. God is **Spirit** (John 4:24). The significance of this is that as Spirit, God is effulgent, pervading, and impossible to contain.
2. God is **Light** (1 John 1:5). The significance of this is that as light, God is ever penetrating, diffusive, and dispelling darkness.
3. God is **Love** (1 John 4:16,18). The significance of this is that as love, God is always reaching out to include more and more as objects of His love.
4. God is **Consuming Fire** (Heb. 12:29). The significance of this is that as consuming fire, God is never satisfied, burns passionately, and always hungers for more.

When God was dwelling alone in eternity past, He was all of these things. Because of this, He could not remain alone. His very nature demanded that He move out of the perfect comfort zone and create. He would have had fewer problems if He would have just left things as they were. His nature of love drove Him forward. You see, having a minimal amount of problems was not His goal.

THE MISSIONARY HEART OF THE CHURCH

The missionary heart of the church springs from the fact that the local church is the instrument of God to fulfill His eternal purpose. The eternal purpose of God involves the following (Gen. 1:26-28):

- A spiritual offspring in the image of God
- Offspring reproducing after the likeness of God
- Offspring who come to a place of maturity and authority
- Offspring who are instrumental in bringing the entire earth under the order or rule of God

In other words, God wants a large family or a company of people in His image, reflecting His character and heart that will grow to maturity and be able to come to a place of sharing in His work. The local church is the instrument that God will use to extend His Kingdom and to accomplish and fulfill His purpose.

God's charge to the first family was to be "fruitful and multiply and fill up the earth." God's vision was not limited to a small little family in a perfect little place. He set man in a garden in Eden with the goal that, as man fulfilled the charge given to Him, the borders of the garden would be extended until the whole earth was filled with the glory of the Lord—until the whole earth reflected God's nature and Kingdom.

God put His blessing on Abraham so that He could reach unto all nations (Gen. 12:1-3). Israel was to be His instrument to mediate God's love to the rest of the world (Exod. 19:5-6). The temple of Solomon was established as a place where the whole world could meet with God (1 Ki. 8:28-30, 41-42, 59-60).

God so loved the world (John 3:16). God's vision was inclusive not exclusive. God desires many sons, not just a few quality ones. God's heart will not be satisfied until every nation, tongue, and tribe is reached with the Gospel of God. The Gospel is for all. God desires that none would perish (2 Pet. 2:9). We know that some will perish, but God's arms of love are desirous of everyone. We want our arms to be as big as God's arms.

The Commission to the Church

The missionary heart of the church finds its impetus in the commission given to it by Jesus Himself. The commission that Jesus gave to the church reflects God's eternal purpose and includes the following elements:

- Preaching the Gospel to **every creature** and **every nation** under heaven (Mark 13:10; 16:15; Luke 24:47)
- Witnessing of Christ to **the ends** of the earth (Acts 1:8)
- Baptizing **all** those who respond to the Gospel (Matt. 28:19)
- Making disciples out of **all** those who are converted (Matt. 28:19)
- Bringing healing and deliverance to **all** those in such need (Mark 16:15-18)
- Teaching the converted a lifestyle of obedience to **all** of God's commands (Matt. 28:20)

The Condition of Mankind

The missionary heart of the church is further fueled by the condition of mankind apart from Christ. Apart from Christ all people are sinners and are under the sentence of death (Rom. 5:12). Apart from Christ all people are children of wrath (Eph. 2:3). Apart from Christ all people are alienated from the life of God (Eph. 4:18). Apart from Christ even upright, moral, and decent people are lost and need to be saved (Rom. 3:23; John 3:3; Acts 11:13-14). Apart from Christ all people are destined for eternal damnation (Rev. 20:10-15).

The Message We Bear

The missionary heart of the church is inspired by the message that it bears. That message is called the Gospel of Jesus Christ, and it has been entrusted to the church. It is the most important charge that could be given to man. It is absolutely essential that all people hear the Gospel because:

- Jesus is the **only way** of salvation (John 14:6; Acts 4:12; 1 Cor. 8:4).
- The message of the Gospel is the power of God unto salvation (Rom. 1:16).

- The message of the Gospel is a message of reconciliation (2 Cor. 5:18-19).
- The message of the Gospel opens the door to abundant life (John 10:10).

Angels are not going to accomplish this mission. This message has been entrusted to the church. The church is God's instrument on the earth to extend His Kingdom through the preaching of the Gospel. The missionary heart of the church must be activated by the realization that the commission of Christ will only be fulfilled **by the church in the church age.** Notice the following:

- God does His work through His church (Matt. 16:18; 2 Cor. 5:9-21), not angels (1 Pet. 1:12).
- The message of the Gospel must find its voice in God's people (Rom. 10:14-15).
- The church must reach the world prior to the Second Coming of Christ, because after that there will be no more opportunity (2 Thess. 1:3-12; 1 Thess. 4:13-18).
- If the church does not do it, it will not get done (Eph. 3:8-13).

The Church Is to Be Self-Propagating

The missionary heart of the church should be motivated by being a mature expression of the local church. Every mature local church should be autonomous; that is, self-governing, self-supporting, and self-propagating.

- Every mature local church should be **self-governing;** that is, it contains within itself the power to make all final decisions regarding the vision and function of the local assembly.
- Every mature local church should be **self-supporting;** that is, it has the ability within itself to fund the vision and the functions of the local assembly.
- Every mature local church should be **self-propagating;** that is, it has the ability to reproduce itself in spiritual offspring and perpetuate itself into the next generation.

The local church propagates in several ways. It propagates by:

- Reaching **individual souls** through aggressive evangelism in its local community.
- Raising up and equipping **leaders** to carry responsibility and vision.
- Extending the Kingdom of God in their nation by **planting** other reproducing local churches.
- Touching **the nations** of the world through their own or cooperative efforts with other local churches to plant and strengthen churches and their leaders worldwide.

Every mature local church should take seriously the commission of God given to mankind (Gen. 1:26-28) and of Christ given to the church (Matt. 28:18-20).

THE EARLY APOSTLES

The apostles in the New Testament understood the challenge. They were motivated by the love of God, they were partakers of His nature, and as such, they reflected His heart. They were totally caught up in the purposes of God. This was not a sideline to them. It was the purpose for which they existed.

The apostles were fully persuaded that God had indeed acted in history. They knew that Christ had died for all mankind (Acts 2:39; 10:34-35; 15:13-18; 1 John 2:2; 4:14). They knew that apart from Christ all would be lost, both Jews and Gentiles. The love of Christ constrained them or compelled them and kept pushing them forward (2 Cor. 5:14).

THE APOSTLE PAUL

The apostle Paul was also a man with God's perspective. He recognized that every church was surrounded by multitudes without God and without hope (Phil. 2:12-16). He commended local churches for their efforts in evangelizing their communities and beyond their borders (Rom. 1:8; 1 Thess. 1:8). He encouraged the churches to abound in the work of the Lord (1 Cor. 15:58).

For Paul the supreme mission was to reach the lost (1 Cor. 1:17). Therefore, he did not dwell on the achievements of the past but continually pressed forward using whatever means he could to spread the Word (1 Cor. 9:22).

TODAY'S CHURCH

The church of today must have the same heart. We must be willing to get out of our comfort zone to see the harvest come in. The reason the local church exists is to be God's instrument to fulfill His purpose.

The local church is people, not an institution, not an organization. It is us. The individual members of the local church are going to have to do this—not angels, not the government, not our rich uncle, not some mass crusade, not TV or radio ministries, not some other parachurch organization, and not the Holy Spirit. We do not simply pray for the harvest to come in. We are to pray for laborers to go into the harvest.

Unfortunately, the church of today is woefully unprepared to be the reaping instrument that God is looking for in this day. The net of the church is broken and is in serious need of mending.

One of the greatest hindrances to receiving the harvest today is the spirit and attitude of the believers themselves. Just as in the early church there was a struggle for those who had been in the way for a long time (the Jews) to receive the new harvest that God was bringing in (the Gentiles), the church-going people of today can resist the harvest by their very attitude.

Jesus found the same to be true with His own disciples. Jesus came preaching a Kingdom message that was inclusive of all. It did not matter what their backgrounds were or what their customs were—Jesus' gospel was for everyone.

Some wonder why Jesus, who was such an open and powerful ministry, did not have more followers at the end of His earthly ministry. Was it because there was something wrong with His message? Was it because Jesus' message was so hard that it repelled the masses? Was there something wrong with Jesus' demonstration of love? No! A thousand times, NO!

The problem was not with Jesus. The crowds loved Jesus. Jesus was like a human magnet to the hurting, wounded, and bruised. Jesus' attitude of openness was inclusive, and multitudes were drawn to Him.

The problem was not with Jesus. The problem was with the disciples. The attitude of the disciples effectively neutralized the love and compassion of Jesus. The love of Jesus drew people, but the negative, divisive, bigoted, narrow, and exclusive spirit of the disciples ran those same people off.

We are living in a day when God is sending forth messengers to preach the true Gospel of the Kingdom, which is beckoning men to come. The harvest is getting very ripe, and it is time for the church to arise and reap. But is the church a ready harvesting instrument? Is the church going to be able to rise to the occasion? Or will we be like the disciples who neutralized what Jesus was trying to do?

THE ATTITUDE OF THE DISCIPLES

The attitude that was evidenced in the early life of the apostles is the same attitude that we struggle with in the church today. Fortunately, the apostles had a supernatural encounter with the Holy Spirit that transformed them into ready harvesters for the Lord. Their early attitudes can serve as a warning to us not to have the same attitudes. Notice these ten instances in the life of the pre-Pentecost disciples and see if they are not a challenge to the church today.

1. In Matthew 14:13-16 (see also Mark 6:36 and Luke 9:12), the people who had been following Jesus and listening to His messages were hungry and in need. What was the response of the disciples? They told Jesus to "send them away." The disciples were a referral service. They didn't want to deal with people with real problems; they only wanted to work with the people who were whole. Jesus said to the disciples, "You give them something to eat."

2. In Matthew 15:21-28, Jesus was testing the faith of a Gentile woman who was pleading with Him to help her demon-possessed daughter. In reality, the attitude of the disciples was being tested. Rather than taking up this woman's cause, the disciples revealed the prejudice in their own hearts and told Jesus again to "Send her away," or as the Knox translation says, "Rid us of her!" The

disciples were not interested in dealing with the demon possessed. They were not interested in people who were non-Jews.

3. In Matthew 17:14-21 (see also Mark 9), the disciples are trying
   to cast a demon out of a boy. Their ministry is at stake here.
   When they fail miserably, Jesus saves the day and ministers to
   the boy. The disciples ask Jesus why they could not cast out the
   devil. Jesus let them know that to minister in this way requires a
   life of prayer and fasting. Were the disciples interested enough in
   the lost and demonized of this world to give up a meal or two
   for them? Not at this time. The harvest will not be truly
   touched with the arm of the flesh. It will take the power of the
   Spirit working through the surrendered life. It will not be
   touched with a spirit of complacency, but with hearts of passion
   for the lost.

4. In Mark 10:13-16 (see also Matt. 19:13-15; Luke 9:37-42;
   18:15-17), the disciples fail another test. Here they seem to have
   a low regard for small children. They seem to think that bringing adults to the Lord is more important than bringing children.
   Perhaps the reason for this is that they were interested in sitting
   on thrones, and children are not of the voting age necessary to
   put them on these thrones. They were not interested in ministering to people who could not give them a lot in return.

5. In Mark 10:35-45 (see also Matt. 20:20-28; Mark 9:33-34; Luke
   9:46-48), the disciples were arguing about their favorite subject,
   who would be greatest and who would get the chief seats. They
   were not concerned about serving; they were only interested in
   ruling. They were not interested in humble service; they wanted
   to sit and be served. As long as they had this attitude, they
   would not be able to minister to the ones that God would send
   to them.

6. In Mark 14:3-9 (see also Matt. 26:6-13), the disciples got real
   nervous when a woman who was known to be a harlot inter-
   rupted their meeting and made a huge scene in their nice little
   gathering. People do not always respond to the Lord in pre-

dictable ways. They are not used to our forms and our "sacred cows." The disciples cared more about their comfort and forms than they did about the soul of this poor woman.

7. In Luke 9:49-56, the disciples evidently believed that they were the only show in town. They were the only true church and everything had to come to and through them. If others were trying to reach people, the disciples must work to stop them. They had a sectarian spirit that kept them from cooperating with other reapers for the sake of the harvest. The disciples had the attitude that "if they are not for us, they are against us." Jesus reverses this and says, "If they are not against us, they are for us." One church or one group of churches will never reap the harvest. We need each other, desperately.

8. In Luke 19:1-7, Jesus was criticized for associating with sinners. In fact, over and over again this charge was leveled against Him (Luke 7:36). I'm sure that Jesus would say, "How can you reach sinners if you never interact with them?" So often our teaching on being separate from the world system has helped us to isolate ourselves from the people of the world. Jesus was a friend of sinners. Not a friend of their sin, but He was a person who was always relatable to them and approachable by them.

9. In John 4:9 and 27, the disciples demonstrate prejudice and a spirit of favoritism. They didn't like the Samaritans, and they were not afraid to say so. In addition, they didn't care much about women. In fact, they were quite shocked that Jesus did not share their opinions in this matter. The disciples thought that their Gospel was for one race or one gender of people. Prejudice is an enemy of the harvest.

10. In John 12:1-8, the disciples were again shocked at the unusual behavior of a woman who had been touched by the ministry of Jesus. They seemed to be more concerned about money than about people. They valued possessions more than the harvest. They somehow forgot that people are the most important thing in the world. They are the only things in the world that are

eternal and as such will spend eternity in heaven or hell based on their relationship to Jesus.

These were the followers of Jesus. These were those who were going to be commissioned to build the church and preach the Gospel to the world. But they were not ready harvesters. Their attitudes kept the harvest away.

When you read the book of Acts, it is clear that God did a real work in each one of the lives of the disciples of Jesus. In the book of Acts, these men were willing to lay down their resources and their very lives for the harvest.

God wants to do the same thing in the church today. He wants to change our hearts. He wants to make us into ready harvesters. He wants to impart to us the Spirit of Jesus that is filled with love and compassion for the lost.

PROPER ATTITUDES OF A READY HARVESTER

If we're willing to learn from those early disciples, we can identify our own attitudes that keep us from fulfilling the charge that God has put before us. We can cultivate these ten attitudes:

1. *Love the sinner the way God does* (John 3:16). God does not expect us to love sin, but, at the same time, He wants us to love the sinner. When we love the sinner, it does not mean that we condone their sin. Loving the sinner does not mean that we participate with them in their sin. However, if we are going to win the lost, we must love the lost as Jesus loves the lost.

2. *Adjust priorities, putting people ahead of possessions.* As Christians, we must denounce the spirit of materialism and the god of money. We must realize that all of the resources that God has given to us are not given to us for our pleasure alone. We must not feel that keeping our nice things nice is our only priority in life. We must be willing to get our new carpets dirty with the muddy shoes of the unsaved.

3. *Ask God for His heart of compassion.* We are not just interested in a feeling of pity. We want God to give us a heart of compassion that will motivate us to get personally involved in meeting the

needs of others. We can't just "send them away." We have got to allow ourselves to be equipped to meet the needs of those that God sends to us (James 1:27; 1 John 3:17).

4. *Maintain a servant spirit.* No matter how long we have been Christians, we must never outgrow our servant spirit. We must continue to seek for ways to serve, not ways to be served. We must not be seeking to rule or to be recognized, but we should only be thinking of how to get the job done.

5. *Become a feeder of new converts.* Every Christian should be able to disciple a new convert. The elders and church leaders can only minister to so many. Don't always be sending people away to be fed. You feed them. Learn how to do it. Put some time and effort into it.

6. *Deal with your personal prejudice and favoritism.* In Christ there is neither male nor female, slave or free, Jew or Gentile, rich or poor, black, red, yellow, or white. All are precious in His sight! James tells us that we cannot be a people of faith giving glory to God when there is prejudice in our midst.

7. *Be patient with new converts.* It takes a while for them to learn the language, to learn our forms, for the hemlines to go down, for all the changes to take place. Accept them as they are and let the Holy Spirit deal with them. Certainly we need to address sinful areas, but let's make sure we know the difference between sin and a simple violation of our traditions, forms, and unique Christian culture.

8. *Get a vision for children and young people.* Most people who get saved do so before the age of twenty. The youth of today are the church of tomorrow. Determine never to minimize the conversion of a child who has the potential of living a full life for the Lord. Children can be so moldable and are full of such potential in God.

9. *Encourage all harvesting.* It doesn't matter if the harvesting is attached to your name. It doesn't matter if we do not fully agree on each and every point. The other churches in town are not against us. They are on the same side!

10. *Get serious about the harvest.* Pray, fast, intercede, get radical! We can't be complacent about the harvest when we understand the destiny of those who do not know Christ.

WE CAN DO IT!

The good news is that we can do it! There is hope for the church. With the help of God we will be able to follow the example of Jesus and be willing to become uncomfortable (laying down our lives) so that others can have life. For this to happen, we must ask God for an adjustment in our hearts so that our hearts are as big as His heart and as full of compassion as His heart. We must ask God for an enlargement of our vision that includes our entire community and beyond. We must ask God for a spirit of generosity that sees resources as tools to touch the world.

Chapter Twenty-One

MAINTAINING FIRST LOVE

Key #19—*If a church is to grow and prosper from generation to generation, that church must determine to maintain a first-love experience among its membership.*

J esus came to the church of Ephesus in the book of Revelation with words of commendation and words of challenge (Rev. 2:1-7). He commended them for their love for the Word and their pure doctrine that had exposed heresy and false apostolic ministries. He commended them for their tireless activity when it came to a zeal for good works. But He also challenged them concerning their personal relationship to Him.

It is so easy to become church experts and doctrinal critics and yet miss the Lord of the church or the Man of the Book. We can lose sight of what it is all about. God created man for relationship. He wants a relationship with us more than anything else.

As we seek to honor Him in building a church that is technically correct in every way, we must remember not to lose Him in the busyness of it all. Mary and Joseph lost track of Jesus in the midst of religious activity. Everything that they were doing was religious in nature, but at some point they realized that Jesus was not in the midst of them (Luke 2:43-45). When they discovered their loss, they had to go back and find out where they left Him.

Jesus warned us that in the end times there would be a growing cold of people's passion (Matt. 24:12). This is one of those trends or tendencies that we must resist. We always want to have the attitude of David when he said, "As the deer pants for the water brooks, so pants my soul for you, O God" (Ps. 42:1). We want to be those who fulfill the first and greatest commandment to love the Lord our God with all of our heart, soul, mind and strength (Mark 12:30).

LOSS OF FIRST LOVE

First-love relationship with the Lord is like so many other things in our lives. You don't have to consciously choose to lose it. All you have to do is to neglect to cultivate it, and all of a sudden you wake up one day and find it gone. It is so parallel to the marriage relationship. If you do not consciously invest in it, you can wake up one day and realize, "I don't love him or her anymore!"

A number of years ago Bill Gothard published a pamphlet that addressed the issue of first love in our lives. He gave twelve evidences that we have departed from a first-love relationship. They are as follows:

1. When my delight in the Lord is no longer as great as my delight in someone else, I have lost my first love (Mark 12:30).

2. When my soul does not long for times of rich fellowship in God's Word or in prayer, I have lost my first love (Mark 12:30; Ps. 42:1).

3. When my thoughts during leisure moments do not reflect upon the Lord, I have lost my first love (Mark 12:30; Ps. 10:4).

4. When I claim to be "only human" and easily give in to those things I know displease the Lord, I have lost my first love (Mark 12:30; John 14:15; 15:10).

5. When I do not willingly and cheerfully give to God's work or to the needs of others, I have lost my first love (1 John 3:17).

6. When I cease to treat every Christian brother or sister as I would the Lord, I have lost my first love (Matt. 25:40; John 13:34).

7. When I view the commands of Christ as restrictions to my happiness rather than expressions of His love, I have lost my first love (John 14:21).

8. When I inwardly strive for the acclaim of this world rather than the approval of the Lord, I have lost my first love (1 John 2:15; John 15:19).

9. When I fail to make Christ or His words known because I fear rejection, I have lost my first love (John 15:20).

10. When I refuse to give up an activity I know is offending a weaker brother, I have lost my first love (Rom. 14:15).

11. When I become complacent to sinful conditions around me, I have lost my first love (Matt. 24:12).

12. When I am unable to forgive another for offending me, I have lost my first love (1 John 4:20).

These are the symptoms of a loss of a first-love relationship with the Lord. These symptoms can occur in the life of an individual or in the life of a local church. Sometimes we can get so busy working for the Lord that we miss or don't actually have time to cultivate our relationship with Him. We lose our intimacy with the Lord.

I recall a saying I heard once. It went like this, "Don't get so busy making a living that you forget to make a life." We can get so busy doing the things that make our lives work, that we forget what life is really all about. We were first and foremost created for a relationship with our Maker.

These same things can happen in marriage relationships, and they can happen in local churches. The key is that we recognize our tendencies, and we recognize the symptoms of the problem when it occurs. When we do that, then we can pull ourselves back to center.

REMEMBER AND REPENT

When Jesus ministered a word of correction to the church at Ephesus, He did not just point out their problem, but He also gave them a solution to their problem. He said that if they were going to return to a first-love relationship, they would need to "remember; …repent and do as they once did" (Rev. 2:5, NEB). The Phillips translation says, "Repent and live as you lived at first."

Sometimes the longer we have been Christians or the longer we have been married, the harder it is for us to remember what first love was really like. If we have been serving the Lord for most of our lives or we have been married for over thirty years, it has been a long time since actual first love was experienced.

In the mid-seventies, I was in Ireland with a team of young adults. I was married at the time, but most of the others on the team were not. We were going to be there for over a month and a half. Three of the guys on the team were going to be married within thirty days of our return. Even though I had been married for over five years, I got a real refresher course in first-love relationship.

In observing the lives of these three engaged men during that forty-five-day trip, I was able to put the admonitions of the Lord into practical terms. I was able to remember what one did when one has a first-love relationship.

DO AS YOU ONCE DID

Jesus said, I want you to remember, repent and do as you once did. It is when you do the things that you did at the first that your love relationship is fostered. Here are the ten things that I observed as marks of first-love relationship that apply either to the Lord or to any other object of your affection (e.g. spouse).

1. *Once we thought and talked about the Lord (or our spouses) all the time.*
   When we first became Christians, we could not stop talking about the Lord. For many of us it was almost obnoxious. Much like a guy who goes on and on about his girlfriend. The Lord was the subject of every sentence and the topic of every conversation. Unfortunately, as time goes on, we can almost be embarrassed to name the name of Christ in certain settings.

2. *Once we tried to please the Lord (or our spouses) at all times.*
   When we first became Christians, we were so concerned that we not offend the Lord in any way. We were careful and guarded in our actions and were sensitive to the voice of the Holy Spirit. Unfortunately, as time goes on, it is easy to become callous to the voice of the Holy Spirit and begin to return to activities and conversations that we know are less than pleasing to the Lord.

3. *Once we shared our most intimate thoughts, desires and feelings with the Lord (or our spouses).*

When we first became Christians, we were so childlike and open about our innermost thoughts and feeling before the Lord. Personal confession was easy. Intimate fellowship was the order of the day. We discussed everything with the Lord. Unfortunately, as time goes on, we often close up and become secretive and very surface in our relationship.

4. *Once we included the Lord (or our spouses) in all of our plans, present and future.*

When we first became Christians, we would not think of not discussing all of our plans, present and future, with the Lord. We couldn't imagine a future without the Lord. It was not uncommon to hear someone say we will do this or that "if the Lord wills." Unfortunately, as time goes on, the Lord can become less and less a factor in the decisions that we make. People will make major changes in their lives without even consulting the Lord in prayer for His direction.

5. *Once we talked to the Lord (or our spouses) as much as possible.*

When we first became Christians, it was easy to skip our lunch and go to the car to read our Bible and pray. It was easy to get up in the morning to pray. We would talk to the Lord before we went to sleep in our beds. We would turn off the radio in our cars and pray while we drove from place to place. Unfortunately, for many people, times have changed. Most Christians do not maintain a regular daily prayer life with the Lord. They come to the Lord when they are in trouble, but there is no consistent day-by-day communication with Him.

6. *Once we befriended the Lord (or our spouses), speaking only good of Him.*

When we first became Christians, we were defenders of the faith. Just let someone try saying something negative about the Lord. We would stick up for the Lord whenever His name was taken in vain. Unfortunately, when first love grows cold, we can find ourselves bringing railing accusation against the Lord if things do not go exactly the way we think they should go. Sometimes others may even need to remind us of our relationship to the Lord.

7. *Once we loved to be in the presence of the Lord (or our spouses) continually.*

When we first became Christians, it was an absolute delight to be in His presence and to gather together with other believers. We would look for any meeting that we could find where we could meet with the Lord and be fed from His Word. Unfortunately, as time goes by, we may get to the place that we look for any excuse not to attend worship services and prayer meetings.

8. *Once we loved to praise the Lord (or our spouses) for even the smallest things.*

When we first became Christians, we acknowledged the Lord in everything. We learned the principle of "in everything give thanks." We would thank the Lord for the sunshine, and we would thank the Lord for the rain. We would "praise Him in the morning, praise Him in the noontime, and praise Him when the sun goes down." Unfortunately, as time goes on, it is easy to lose our perspective and become "spiritual crybabies." We can lose our appreciation for all of the little things that God has given to us.

9. *Once we put the Lord (or our spouses) first in all things.*

When we first became Christians, the Lord was number one in our lives. Many of us (myself included) came in under teaching that emphasized the Lordship of Jesus in every area of our lives. Lordship meant that Jesus was the ruler of all, His Kingdom was supreme, and everything else in our lives was a distant second or third. Unfortunately, as time goes by, we can go back to some of the old gods of materialism and recreation where God struggles to find a place in our lives.

10. *Once we were very sensitive to the feelings of the Lord (or our spouses).*

When we first became Christians, we were almost hypersensitive to the voice of the Lord. When you love someone, you do not want to do anything to offend him or her in any way. Therefore, you are always taking spiritual readings to make sure that the person you love is not offended by anything you have done. At the same time, you listen for clues in the way they speak to you to pick up on moods, feelings, and desires. We know the Lord has feelings and the Holy Spirit can be grieved. After a while we can begin to take that person's or the Lord's affection for granted and we can lose that sensitivity and willingly offend.

This is a picture of first love. It is so important that we follow the advice of Jesus to keep that relationship fresh. This applies to every believer. It applies to every spouse in the marriage relationship. And it equally applies to every local church.

FOSTERING FIRST-LOVE RELATIONSHIP

So how does a church foster the first-love relationship? How does it return to the things that were done at the first? Here are some of the things that will foster first love in the local church:

- Keeping Jesus at the center of every activity (children, youth, adult)
- Preaching Christ and Him crucified
- Singing love songs to Jesus and making sure that He is exalted
- Focusing on being a God-pleasing church above a man-pleasing church
- Making prayer and communion with God a priority
- Scheduling regular times of fasting for personal and corporate direction
- Highlighting testimonies of salvation and personal encounters with the Lord
- Making the experience of the presence of God in our gatherings a priority
- Teaching and modeling communion with God especially among leaders

- Equipping every member with the ability to share Christ with the lost
- Reminding the people to keep first things first (Ps. 27:4)

Jesus needs to be at the center of our worship, preaching, and outreach. He needs to be the topic of our conversation both inside and outside of the local church. This begins with the leaders and flows from there to the rest of the people.

THE RESULT

Jesus made it very clear to the church at Ephesus that if they cultivated the first-love relationship, there would be great reward. He indicated that they would once again have access to the tree of life. You see, Jesus is the tree of life. If our churches are going to have life, the members of those churches must be eating of the tree of life.

When you are eating of the tree of life in your relationship to Him, several things happen. First of all, the love relationship becomes progressive. That is, the relationship grows and become "sweeter as the days go by." In essence we will "keep falling in love with Him, over and over, and over and over again."

The second fruit of a first-love relationship is that the habits and interests of the one you love become your habits and interests. There is an exchange that takes place. When we wait upon the Lord and seek to please Him, we become more and more like Him. Our hearts become more reflective of His heart.

The ultimate reward for maintaining the first-love relationship is that the two become one. This is not something that just happens overnight, but it is the fruit of a commitment to maintain first love and to continue to do as we once did for a lifetime.

As we build the church alongside of the Lord, let us pay careful attention to the principles that build the house, but let us never forget to exalt, treasure, and enjoy the Man of the house, the Lord Jesus Christ!

The LORD has been mindful of us;
He will bless us;
He will bless the house of Israel;
He will bless the house of Aaron.
He will bless those who fear the LORD,
Both small and great.
May the LORD give you increase more and more,
You and your children.
May you be blessed by the LORD,
Who made heaven and earth.
Psalm 115:12-15

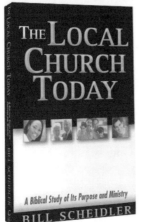
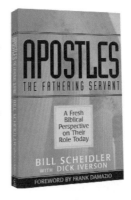

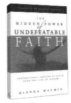

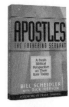